W9-BCC-543

BETHANY
COLLEGE
LIBRARY

DISCHARGED

427.974 SM75F

Smoky mountain voices

GAYLORD S

SMOKY MOUNTAIN VOICES

SMOKY MOUNTAIN VOICES

A Lexicon of
Southern Appalachian Speech
Based on the Research of
HORACE KEPHART

HAROLD F. FARWELL, Jr.,
& J. KARL NICHOLAS
Editors

THE UNIVERSITY PRESS OF KENTUCKY

Copyright © 1993 by The University Press of Kentucky

Scholarly publisher for the Commonwealth,
serving Bellarmine College, Berea College, Centre
College of Kentucky, Eastern Kentucky University,
The Filson Club, Georgetown College, Kentucky
Historical Society, Kentucky State University,
Morehead State University, Murray State University,
Northern Kentucky University, Transylvania University,
University of Kentucky, University of Louisville,
and Western Kentucky University.

Editorial and Sales Offices: Lexington, Kentucky 40508-4008

Library of Congress Cataloging-in-Publication Data

Farwell, Harold F., 1934-
    Smoky mountain voices : a lexicon of southern Appalachian speech
based on the research of Horace Kephart / Harold Farwell, Jr. and J.
Karl Nicholas, editors.
        p.   cm.
    Includes bibliographical references.
    ISBN 0-8131-1823-9 :
    1. English language—Dialects—Appalachian Region, Southern—
Glossaries, vocabularies, etc.   2. English language—Dialects—
Great Smoky Mountains (N.C. and Tenn.)—Glossaries, vocabularies,
etc.   3. Appalachian Region, Southern—Popular culture—
Dictionaries.   4. Great Smoky Mountains (N.C. and Tenn.)—Popular
culture—Dictionaries.   5. English language—Spoken English—Great
Smoky Mountains (N.C. and Tenn.)   6. English language—Spoken
English—Appalachian Region, Southern.   7. Americanisms—Great Smoky
Mountains (N.C. and Tenn.)   8. Americanisms—Appalachian Region,
Southern.   9. Figures of speech.   I. Kephart, Horace, 1862-1931.
II. Nicholas, J. Karl (James Karl), 1939-   .   III. Title.
PE2970.A6F37   1993
427'.974—dc20   93-19156

This book is printed on recycled acid-free paper meeting
the requirements of the American National Standard
for Permanence of Paper for Printed Library Materials.

♾

Contents

BETHANY COLLEGE LIBRARY

Acknowledgments

We wish to acknowledge, first of all, the gracious financial assistance furnished by the Fred A. Moss Charity Trust, which provided a $2,000 grant toward the completion of this project.

Secondly, we must thank our graduate students who made the initial search for words and definitions in the journals, correspondence, and Kephart's published material on language. Our thanks go to Clover McLeod, Sarah Moore, Pam Stalley, and Beverly Van Hook. Special thanks are owed to Beverly, who not only assisted in copying but also led us to two erstwhile lumbermen from Macon County, North Carolina—Lowell and Eugene Monteith—who provided valuable information concerning undefined logging terms. Their names appear parenthetically in the text.

Also supplying definitions were our friends and some new acquaintances—all long-time residents of western North Carolina: Irene Hart, Carl Lambert, Dan Pittillo, Harry Rice, Rex and Weaver Taylor, Pelham Thomas, and Carrie Witherbee, whose names accompany several entries. Special thanks are due George Frizzell of the Special Collections Department of Hunter Library at Western Carolina University. George not only made the Kephart materials very accessible to us but contributed his own special knowledge as a native of the Smokies. Another person most helpful to us was George Ellison, who allowed us to use an early version of his biographical sketch of Kephart. Angelique Galskis is also due our heartiest thanks for careful work on the manuscript and helpful commentary based on her experience with the dialect she remembered from growing up in southern Illinois.

We are especially grateful to Michael Montgomery of the University of South Carolina, who read an early version of this work and provided us with encouragement and helpful suggestions. He then carefully read the completed manuscript and once again shared his expertise with us. Our book has profited much from his wise commentary.

More difficult to thank are those friends and acquaintances of Kephart's in and around Hazel Creek, whose names populate the pages of his journals and even figure in *Our Southern Highlanders.* Names like Bob [Barnett], "Bob's mother," and his wife, Mrs. B. or M.B. [Mistress Barnett] occur time and again, and we have included them parenthetically. We have treated in a similar fashion the following less frequently mentioned personages: Granville and Lily Calhoun, Mrs. Cooper, Mollie and Dave Davis, Nancy and Columbus ("Lum") Gunter, Matt Hyde and Mrs. H[yde], "Old Pete" or Pete Laney, Bill Morris, Becky Pilkey, Walt Procter, "Old Man" Stiles, Mrs. John Thomas, John Walker's wife, Jim Wallace, Bawley Joe Welch, and Adam and John Wilson. All these names appear either on Kephart's personally drawn maps of the Hazel Creek area (MS 80-24.2, folder 25), or in pencil lists of names from Hazel Creek and neighboring communities. We suspect that quotations ascribed to "Louis" may refer to Louis Hampton; those to Aunt Nance and Uncle Mark may refer to the Cooks. All these are names also listed on the maps, but we are totally at a loss to identify Dred, R.S.F., C.A.S., Ingram, Ledford, Parks, Whaley, and Ben Henry—though most of these names are common enough in the area. Like "Schuler," identified as from neighboring Dillsboro, North Carolina, some of these may have been from nearby communities, or may even refer to obscure printed sources.

Introduction

The purpose of this book is to bring to light a unique collection of data on the speech of the Southern Appalachians. It focuses on the special words used by the people who lived in or near the Great Smoky Mountains of North Carolina in the years immediately before the National Park was formed—roughly the first third of the twentieth century. This collection, made by Horace Kephart, was clearly a labor of love as well as one of scholarship.

Kephart had been a librarian before he came to live in the Smokies on Hazel Creek, and he remained a collector all his life. The data he assembled on language is especially significant because it records so large a sample of mountain speech in its "classical" form—that is, in the period of its last isolated flowering before it came under the influences of radio, the Sears catalogue, television, paved roads, and tourists, those "outlanders" or "foreigners" who came from outside the mountains. The people whose speech Kephart recorded included the generation born just before or during the Civil War, those reared during Reconstruction, and those who would usher in our own century. These were the last people to escape the enormous pressure to make their dialect conform to that of other Americans—to say, for example, "y'all" rather than "y'uns," "groceries" rather than "victuals," "bust" instead of "flander," or "next to" instead of "fernenst."

Kephart's notes on mountain dialect are unusually full, especially in the sheer number of words he recorded in his journals. Equally important to us today, though perhaps not regarded as very scholarly by Kephart himself, were the numerous quotations (phrases, sentences, even brief dialogues) he sprinkled through his book, *Our Southern Highlanders,* and recorded in the journals. We have elected to present the data in the form of a word list, a miniature dictionary of Appalachian mountain dialect, to make it useful and accessible. But in order to furnish contexts for the token words, we have accompanied the definitions, wherever possible, with one or several of the quotations Kephart recorded. We cannot overemphasize the value of these illustrative quotations. Not only do they make the word list more comprehensible, but they—as much as the words themselves—supply the scholar, as well as the casual reader, with delightful echoes of Smoky Mountain voices.

About Kephart

Today Horace Kephart is perhaps best known as the author of *Our Southern Highlanders* and as one of the prime movers in the creation of the Great Smoky Mountains National Park. But facts about his life are difficult to discover. He was a loner, given to reclusive ways and bouts with the bottle. He sought the wilderness as a curative for his depression, but if the Carolina mountains restored him and won his allegiance, they did not make him an open or expansive person. He was never famous. He was merely a well-educated professional who headed south in 1904 in the throes of a mid-life crisis, looking for peace of mind. For the next three years he lived on Hazel Creek near Bryson City, North Carolina.

After arriving in the mountains, he worked no more as a librarian; rather, he supported himself by his writing, particularly his numerous articles for camping and outdoor periodicals. But his early library training had enabled him to do painstaking research very well—whether that meant collecting data about camping or woodscraft or about peculiar expressions and dialect patterns. Perhaps it was the librarian's disposition that drove him to collect things, almost as a compulsion. For collect things he did—maps, recipes, wood lore, camping paraphernalia, boy scout manuals, Indian relics, tall tales, botanical information. Very little escaped his scrutiny, and much survived him.

With the meticulousness of the trained cataloguer, he entered scraps of information into his journals, a practice he apparently continued until his death. The journals consist of clippings from and comments upon his readings. They include drafts of articles which eventually found their way into print. They also contain list upon list of words, most not defined.

It is clear that from the time of his arrival in North Carolina Kephart had determined to be a careful observer and a precise recorder of the dialect of the mountaineers. In *Our Southern Highlander*, he tells us that he always carried a notebook in his shirt pocket to record bits of information. "It has been my habit to jot down, on the spot, every dialectal word or variant or idiom that I hear, along with the phrase or sentence in which it occurred; for I never trust memory in such matters" (281).

Exactly what combination of experiences served to produce this amateur linguist and dialectologist is not clear. Kephart had received no formal training in linguistics; he was, nonetheless, more than adequately prepared for his avocation. He was both well-traveled and well-educated when he came to the mountains.

Born in East Salem, Pennsylvania, in 1862, he went westward with his family five years later to the Iowa frontier settlement of Jefferson, about fifty miles from Des Moines, where he lived the next eight years. He spent another year at Cedar Rapids, where his father taught at Western College. In 1876, the Kepharts returned to Pennsylvania, where the young Horace enrolled at the age of fourteen in Lebanon Valley College, focusing his chief attentions on languages—Greek, Latin, and French. In 1879, he was graduated from Lebanon Valley and traveled north to complete a year of studies at Boston University. It was there that his interests turned to librarianship. His next five years were spent in Ithaca, New York, working for Willard Fiske at the Cornell University Library. He spent six months during the winter of 1885-1886 in Florence assisting Fiske with a collection of Petrarch manuscripts, and there he learned a passable Italian.

While assistant librarian at Yale the following year, he became interested in the Finnish national epic, the *Kalevala*, and purposed to translate it. He prepared himself for the project by learning Swedish so that he could use the only texts then available for studying Finnish. Just how far this translation project proceeded is not known, but Kephart did report in 1887 that he had completed the translation of a French article on Finnish phonetics as well as the Swedish "Fritheof's Saga." Obviously Kephart's linguistic background was extensive.

Kephart's early travels—from Pennsylvania to Iowa and back, and then to major universities in New England—coupled with his ever-growing interest in languages helped to tune and refine his ear to the differences in the shifting dialects he could not help encountering, both in his everyday activities and in his studies.

Kephart's tenure at Yale Library ended in 1890, when he accepted the job of head librarian at the St. Louis Mercantile Library. He dedicated himself over the next dozen years to increasing the collection, particularly the holdings dealing with the westward expansion. At this time he contemplated a career in writing and proposed to investigate thoroughly the increasing collection of frontier works that had come to dominate his life. A nervous breakdown in 1903, however, forced him to leave the library—and his family—to seek solace and restoration in the only locale that he had found at all therapeutic during the two troubled years leading up to his crisis—the wilderness and its solitude.

Kephart had made numerous trips to the Ozarks during his years in St. Louis. Now he found in the Smokies the peace he needed for recovery. The first three years he spent on Hazel Creek brought a return to health and an all-consuming enthusiasm for mountain life and customs. As George Ellison speculates, it is as though Kephart found in Appalachia the kind of eighteenth-century frontier existence that had so fascinated him during the years leading up to his breakdown.

Determined to write of his experiences among the mountaineers, Kephart was reluctant to start until he had cross-checked the initial impressions he had collected in his first three years at Hazel Creek against a broader background of the southern mountains. To this end he left Hazel Creek in late 1907 and traveled extensively through the Appalachian range—eastern Kentucky, eastern Tennessee, northern Georgia and Alabama—comparing the lives and folkways of the natives he encountered there with those he had become familiar with in the Smokies. His journals bear testimony to his interests noted in these travels, but especially to his concern for dialects.

In 1910, Kephart returned to North Carolina and took up permanent residency in Bryson City, although he regularly spent his summers camping at the head of Deep Creek in the Smokies. He published *Our Southern Highlanders* in 1913 and his "Word List from the Mountains of Western North Carolina" in 1917. Until his death in an automobile accident in April 1931, Kephart lived frugally but comfortably on the returns from his writing, enjoying the mountains he loved. His last major undertaking was his advocacy for a national park in his beloved mountains— a dream he did not live to see fulfilled but whose realization he was assured of before his death.

The Kephart Dialect Materials

The only material Kephart published relating directly to the Appalachian dialect was one chapter, "The Mountain Dialect," in *Our Southern Highlanders* and an article in *Dialect Notes* (1917), a sampling entitled "A Word-List From the Mountains of Western North Carolina." The latter consisted of some four hundred words and expressions that, like the information in his book, emphasize the most novel qualities of the language rather than what was typical. In that, as in focusing specifically on archaic words in the dialect, he was following the fashion of his time and the practices of his informants, whose word lists he incorporated verbatim. Like other students of dialect, Kephart believed that the chief value of mountain speech lay in its preservation of old forms that were not to be found in other English dialects—not even in England itself.

Today we understand that every dialect preserves something old just as it introduces novelties. While the presence of archaisms in mountain speech is interesting, it is hardly the only special feature. Nevertheless, it was precisely that antiquarian quest for "Elizabethan" English that prompted Kephart to begin his collecting, and for that we are grateful. From the data he accumulated we have been able to construct a much fuller and truer description of the mountain dialect, one which goes beyond depicting its quaintness.

As one might suspect of an inveterate collector like Kephart, his published material represents only the tip of an iceberg. The

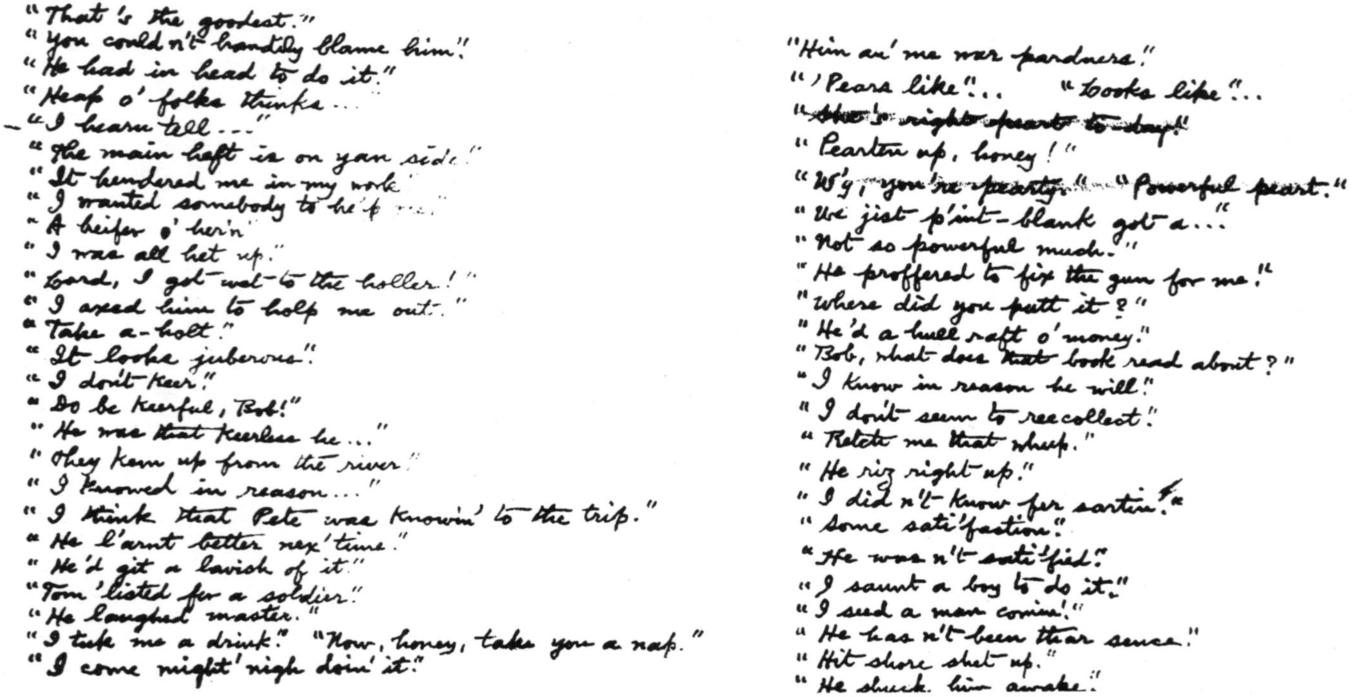

"That's the goodest."
"You couldn't handily blame him."
"He had in head to do it."
"Heap o' folks thinks ..."
"I hearn tell ..."
"The main haft is on yan side."
"It hendered me in my work"
"I wanted somebody to he'p ..."
"A heifer o' hern"
"I was all het up."
"Lord, I got wet to the holler!"
"I axed him to holp me out."
"Take a-holt."
"It looks juberous."
"I don't keer."
"Do be keerful, Bob!"
"He was ~~that~~ keerless he ..."
"They kem up from the river."
"I knowed in reason ..."
"I think that Pete was knowin' to the trip."
"He l'arnt better nex' time."
"He'd git a lavish of it."
"Tom 'listed fer a soldier."
"He laughed master."
"I tuk me a drink." "Now, honey, take you a nap."
"I come might' nigh doin' it."

"Him an' me war pardners."
"'Pears like" ... "Looks like" ...
~~"She's right peart to-day."~~
"Pearten up, honey!"
"Wy, ~~you're pearty.~~" "Powerful peart."
"We jist p'int-blank got a ..."
"Not so powerful much."
"He proffered to fix the gun for me."
"Where did you putt it?"
"He'd a hull raft o' money."
"Bob, what does ~~that~~ book read about?"
"I know in reason he will."
"I don't seem to reecollect."
"Retch me that whup."
"He riz right up."
"I didn't know fer sartin."
"Some sati'faction."
"He wasn't sati'fied."
"I saunt a boy to do it."
"I seed a man comin'."
"He hasn't been thar since."
"Hit shore shet up."
"He shuck him awake."

A portion of a page from one of Kephart's journals.

journals contain considerable material that never saw publication. Clearly, he used some of the journal entries in his published work, but others were ignored or collected later. Exactly when items were entered is almost never clear because dates are rare. Much is jumbled together, and in general the journals, a collection to which he added constantly and at random, seem more like scrapbooks than conventional literary journals. A list of words may appear in two or three varieties of ink. Nor can we even be sure which of the journal entries represent Kephart's own research since he included information, sometimes whole lists, sent to him by friends or readers.

One such friend and contributor was William Bird, a young instructor at Western Carolina College in Cullowhee, North Carolina, about twenty-five miles from Kephart's Bryson City home. Bird was later to become dean of the college and eventually its president, and it was through his advocacy that the Kephart papers came to be housed in the Western Carolina University Archives, where they have been kept since 1973. The collection contains over two hundred books, twenty-seven journals, and over thirty boxes of papers. Copies were recently made of Kephart's papers housed at the Pack Memorial Library in Asheville, so all Kephart's memorabilia are now accessible at Hunter Library in Cullowhee.

Of all this material, which included some pretty funky camping gear at one point, that which seems of incontestable value now is the record of speech he heard among his neighbors in Bryson City and up Hazel Creek, that is, in the immediate vicinity of the Smoky Mountains. "I have myself taken down from the lips of Carolina mountaineers some eight hundred dialectal or obsolete words," he asserted in his book (356), and the American Dialect Society dignified this claim by publishing his note in its journal. In fact, his claim seems modest, as the number of words in the following list testifies. His minuscule hand crowded the pages of his journals with lexical items from such specialized fields as medicine, botany, hunting, and logging.

The list of logging terms, which consists of over fifty items, is particularly instructive, since it reveals another facet of Kephart's penchant for collecting. Kephart drew the terms from several

books that treat timber harvesting in New England and Canada
(see Fraser, Hubbard, and Springer in the accompanying bibli-
ography), but he was quite selective in his choice of items. We
suspect that his selection was guided by his acquaintance with
lumbering practices in the Smokies—that he listed only those
terms that had the ring of familiarity.

Our Method

In preparing this compilation of Kephart's Appalachian dialect
terms, our method has been to remain as faithful to Kephart's
aims as possible, while extending and amplifying the collected
data that saw publication during his lifetime.

To be sure, the word list includes all the published linguistic
fossils that were the inspiration for Kephart's collecting activities
and that were published during his lifetime, but we have also
been able to add many others that he was too reserved to include
except in the privacy of his journals—terms like "ambeer," a
variant pronunciation of "amber," a metaphor for tobacco juice;
"hells," impassable rhododendron thickets; or "flood," a verb
meaning to menstruate.

Second, we have added a host of neologisms—new words or
sayings created by Appalachian mountaineers: coinages like
"long sweetening" (molasses) as opposed to "short sweetening"
(brown sugar); delightful euphemisms like "tooth brush" for
snuff stick; or expressions like "lengthen the apron strings" to
describe pregnancy. The fact that these were obviously not Elizabethan survivals rendered such terms less interesting and hence
unfit for publication in the early part of this century, but Kephart
dutifully preserved them—and many more.

Third, we have added terms reflecting the speech patterns of
the Smokies but whose currency was not limited to that region,
such as the logging terms mentioned earlier, or the names for
plants and animals: "maypops" or "apricots" for the fruits of the
passion flower, "catamount" for mountain lion, or "tomtit" for
the Carolina chickadee. Kephart perhaps hesitated to offer for
publication terms he knew were not exclusively Appalachian.
But he understood that a dialect is more than just what is unique.

Writing to Mary Hunter (July 31, 1926), he suggested, "Of course only a few of the words on my list [in *Dialect Notes*] are peculiar to the N.C. mountains. No dialect is made up of unique expressions. It is an ensemble that marks off one dialect from another." His position seems correct to us, so we have included many terms which we feel may have been characteristic of mountain speech, but may not have been localisms—words limited to the mountains. We have attempted, whenever possible, to determine the dialectal spread or boundaries associated with the tokens we have listed. To determine these boundaries, we have consulted such sources as the *Dictionary of American Regional English*, the *Dictionary of American English*, the *Dictionary of Americanisms*, and Hans Kurath's *Word Geography of the Eastern United States* in an attempt to assess whether the words or expressions appearing in our list were limited strictly to Southern Appalachia or whether they were to be found also in Southern, Midland, or other regional speech. Our bracketed commentary reveals these attempts.

Except for what appears in brackets, all the information in the word list is from Kephart's work. The portions not in quotation marks appear to be Kephart's own words. Quotation marks surround material from informants that Kephart quoted or represent quotes borrowed from other sources. At times we have quoted Kephart's source itself for clarification, although he had cited only a page number. Where a quotation was found in two or more sources without substantial change, we have cited the sources within one set of parentheses, thus: (A;B 12). Occasionally Kephart used brackets, and in these instances we have marked them with his initial [-K.] to avoid confusion.

Finally, we have included dialect usages never intentionally collected by Kephart but which emerge from the quotations appearing in his published works, correspondence, or journals—for instance, the use of "as" as a relative pronoun in "you wunt find ary critter *as* has a good word to say about the revenue."

It is this last category of dialect terms—the chance encounters taken from the quotations—that has proved to be the most fruitful for our research. It was our intention to supply the terms in Kephart's lists with as many illustrative quotations as we could. What we did not anticipate was that these quotations would yield an accidental abundance of terms that were not archaic, exotic, or atypical. What we encountered, rather, was the typical, the unremarkable—but the very bedrock of Appalachian speech.

Some Cautionary Comments

As our earlier discussion demonstrates, the real benefit to be derived from Kephart's determination to find local or obsolete words is not simply in the numbers of such items but in their reliability as accurate reflectors of the speech of ordinary mountain people. We believe the data he collected to be generally good, but in making this assessment we must issue some warnings. Items Kephart recorded as he heard may in some cases have been totally individualistic speech patterns—matters of idiolect rather than dialect. One wonders, for example, whether the expression "Goodman" for God, identified as a "child's term" in the published word list, might not be explicitly that—one child's term. He lists "cockyolly bird" as a child's word in the journals with an accompanying quotation, but again his methods do not make clear whether he heard this once or often. Similarly, we have no way of knowing how extensively some words appearing in the lists were used: "ingons" for onions, "luzzeries" for luxuries, or "midder-man" for a middle man. Kephart's method was to collect material under topics (often with illustrative quotations), then to extract key terms from those pages and reorganize the terms under a variety of headings. We have assumed that although the terms may have come from a variety of sources—published fiction, specialized reports (like the forestry reports), and his next-door neighbors—his listing of a word (often many times) itself suggests that he considered the term a part of the Southern Appalachian dialect. However, often we had nothing but lists with no clues as to their sources or meanings! His lists fill almost all of volume two of the journals, for example, and, though wonderfully rich, they also lead to insoluble puzzles.

But we have no reason to suspect Kephart's ear or to question his integrity as a reporter. The quotations, especially, suggest he had a keen ear for the cadences, the inflections, and even the omissions of mountain speech. If not a poet himself, he had something like a poet's ear for language. He loved the striking metaphor, the unusual comparison, and especially the comic thrust of the dialect he recorded. His one effort to pull all his random notes together in the chapter on dialect in his book focuses, as we might expect, on the quaint vocabulary. He considers pronunciation only briefly, the unusual grammar hardly at all, even ignoring the frequent use of the double modal, like "might could" so common in mountain speech. Yet, despite these limitations in the scope of his discussion, he is accurate and often shows clear insight. He recognized, for example, that the speech of the mountains was similar to that of "Pennsylvania and the West," anticipating the findings of later scholars such as Kurath, who would classify this dialect as a third major dialect of American English, neither Northern nor Southern, but "Midlands."

In the opening paragraphs of that chapter on mountain dialect, Kephart tells a very revealing story of a mountaineer who is offended by the effort of author John Fox to represent the local dialect through unusual spelling. "Why that feller don't know how to spell!" the man exclaims. Kephart's efforts to explain the use of "phonetic" spelling to represent dialect does nothing to assuage the mountaineer, who responds astutely: "You educated folks don't spell your own words the way you say them." Tru enuff!

And this is the final warning. Kephart's use of this anecdote is cautionary, a reminder to all his readers that it is all too easy to be condescending about someone else's dialect. Kephart himself rarely is. His story is a wonderful illustration of his sensitivity to the social implications of dialect study, to what today would be called its sociolinguistic aspects. It is precisely that sort of sensitivity that enabled him to collect so fully and to record so accurately the words which follow.

A Lexicon of
Southern Appalachian Speech

Note: For publication facts, see Bibliographic Note, pages 187-191.

KEPHART'S WORKS
A "Word List"
B *Our Southern Highlanders*
C correspondence
D logging and hunting lists
J journals

SECONDARY SOURCES
OED   *Oxford English Dictionary*
DA   *Dictionary of Americanisms*
DAE   *Dictionary of American English*
DARE   *Dictionary of American Regional English*

A

a: [1. *prep.*, variant of *on.*] "Sis blouses her waist a-purpose to carry a pistol" (B 356). "the cattle all huddled up a-top each other" (B 78). "with the dogs a-top o' him" (B 101). [Chiefly S., DARE] [2. *prep.*, variant of *in.*] "seed sign a-plenty and it's spang fraish" (B 93). [3. *progressive marker* ⟨ OE an-.] "He'd been a-goin' with 'at gal for a year" (C 3). "I ain't a-gwine to" (J 2:589). [Throughout U.S., esp. in Midl., SW; less frequently S., NEng; chiefly among less educated and rural speakers, DARE] [4. contracted *have/has.*] "I'd a-bruk some bones" (B 306). "I'd jest nachelly a-shot him" (J 2:589, 642). "If I'd a-been thoughted enough" (B 359). [S.App., also MO, TN, DARE] [5. grace syllable.] "Pringle's a-been horse-throwed down the cliff" (B 299). "I gotta me a deck of cyards" (J 2:589). "Come a-Wednesday" (J 2:629). [S.App.; DARE contains first two citations, but mistakenly uses the first as an example of contracted have/has.]

acknowledge: [*n.* knowledge.] "to the best of my acknowledge" (J 2:639). [Also Gullah, DARE.]

acrost: [*prep.*, variant of *across*] (B 351). "There wasn't no walk-log acrost the creek" (J 1:322f). [Throughout U.S., DARE]

adopt: *v.t.* to contract. "He *adopted* a rheumatiz" (A; J 2:476; B 296). (J 2:605) [S.App., DARE]

afeared: [*adj.*, variant of *afraid.*] When the mountain boy challenges his mate: "I dar ye—I ain't afeared!" his verb and participle [sic] are of the same ancient and sterling rank, . . . we trace [them] as far as the time of Layamon (B 362). (J 2:489, 597, 642; 14:80; C 1, 2) [Formerly widespread, now chiefly S., S.Midl., DARE]

afore: [1. *conj.* before; listed in Fox as archaic (J 2:489).] Contemporary with the *Canterbury Tales* (B 362). "Jest afore it got quite fernent me, I shot" (J 4:749). (B 170) [2. *prep.*] "If this wind'll only cease afore mornin'" (B 77). [3. *adv.*] "Seems to me like I heered that name afore" (J 4:725). (J 2:642) [Formerly widespread, now chiefly S., Midl., DARE]

agg up: *v. phr.* to egg on. "Both sides *agged it up*" (A).

agin: [1. *conj.*,] variant of *against*, by the time. "*Agin* he wakes up." Also W.Res., Ill., N.Eng., Ky. (A; C 2). "*Agin* I git thar" (J 10:83). [Chiefly S., S.Midl., DARE; fairly common in S., but regularly used in S.Midl., Kurath] [2. *prep.* before, in anticipation of.] "*agin* Christmas" (C 2). [Chiefly Midl., DARE] [3. *prep.* in opposition to.] "till a horse couldn't stand up agin it" (B 77). [Now chiefly S., Midl., DARE]

ahind: [prep., adv., probably variant of *behind*.] (J 2:603). [Chiefly Midl., old fashioned, DARE]

aidge: [n.,] variant of *edge*. Also N.Eng., Ky., W.Res., Ill. "Smoke come in and cripsed up the aidges of the leaves" (A).

ails: [*v.* to be afflicted, ill.] "Whut you reckon ails me?" (B 299). Sick John Cable ("who's allers ailin', to hear him tell") (J 10:643).

aim: *v.i.* to plan, to calculate. "I *aimed* to go to town." "How do you *aim* for me to get it?" Also W.Res., Ill., S.Car., Ky., Mass., N.Dak., Ariz. (A; J 2:429). "The woman's aimin' to go to meetin'" (B 371). Obsolete (J 2:605). (C 2) [S., S.Midl., DARE]

ain't: [*v.* have not.] "I ain't got none" (B 32). [Among items listed as "aversions," K noted:] Oysters. "I ain't no bugeater" [with the additional comment:] probably thought them snails (J 2:421). "That gal Imey ain't got a spoonful of sense" (M.B.) (J 2:637).

air: [1. *adv.*, variant of *here*.] "What brings ye up this air way-off branch" (J 4:793). [2. *v.*, variant of *are*.] "Run, Kit, back to the Medderses an' ax what air they" (J 4:738). [The same quote ends "ax who *is* he!" in B 276; a similar quote was recorded from McG[owan] in J 2:611:] "Run home and ax what air they." [Also:] "We air that!" (J 2:611). [Formerly widespread, now chiefly S., S.Midl., DARE]

allers: [*adv.*, variant of *always*.] "I allers did hold it was a mighty triflin' sort o' man'd let either his dog or his woman starve" (She [M.B.?] (J 2:642). "A bear allers dies flat on his back, onless he's trapped" (B 102). "Old Man Proctor allers *will* have a good, big fire, and, by George, hit was just like pullin' teeth to come away from it" (J 4:735). (J 2:603)

all-fired: [*adj.*,, *intensifier:* real.] "Guess I run her half a mile through all-fired thickets" (B 91). [Widespread, DARE]

all-overs: *n. pl.* nervousness. "Every time I go to studyin' about it I git the *all-overs.*" [Joel Chandler Harris wrote of *The Vicar of*

Wakefield: "It touches me more deeply, it gives me the 'all-overs' more severely than all others." The word here means 'thrills.' (C.A.S.)—K] Also Mass. (A). [The first quote is identified "(M.B.)" in J 2:476.] (J 2:601) [Chiefly S., S.Midl., DARE]

almanick: [*n.*,] variant of *almanac*. Also N.Eng., Ky., W.Res., Ill. (A). "Bob, git the almanick and see when that feller'll full up" (J 2:423; B 326). [Also spelled **almanic** in J 2:642p, J 6; DARE lists this pronunciation as chiefly NEng, S.Midl.]

ambear or **ambeer:** [*n.* amber, a metaphor for tobacco juice.] "Hit *doesn't* look nice to see a woman cuddin' this home-made tobacco, that's strong enough to kill a snake, and squirtin' ambeer around everywhere" (J 2:438). (J 2:605, 642) [Chiefly S., S.Midl., DARE]

ambry: [*n.* a cupboard, locker, or pantry ⟨ L. *armarium,* a chest for arms.] "He keeps his liquor and pistols locked up in the ambry" (J 23:53). [A learned or bookish word whose occurrence in common speech K deemed peculiar.]

angelico or **jellico:** [1. *n. Ligusticum acetaefolium.*] "the strong-scented roots of which are eagerly sought and eaten by boys and hogs" (Gray). Bartram says, "aromatic carminative root, tastes much like that of ginseng, though more of the taste and scent of anise-seed." In high estimation with Indians and Whites (J 1:67). [2. adj.] "smell as strong as an old angelico sow" (J 1:67, 2:439).

annesseptic: [*n.*, variant of *anaesthesia.*] "He come out from under the annesseptic" (J 2:639). [An obvious malapropism. K's journal does not reveal whether this was a single occurrence or whether the term achieved widespread currency.]

antic: *adj.* clownish, grotesque, ludicrous. "He's as *antic* as a jaybird when he takes the notion" (A). [K quotes Fox to suggest the word has "English dialect authority" in J 2:489.] (J 2:605, 642; J 6) [Chiefly S.Midl., DARE]

antigadlin': *adv. slantdicular* [i.e., slanted.] (A). out of plumb or out of square (B 368-69). [S.App., DARE; also **antigodlin'**]

anywhars: [*adv.*, variant of *anywhere.*] "The law wunt let us have liquor shipped to us from anywhars in the State" (B 122).

any ways (soon): [*adv.* very.] "Not any ways soon, I don't reckon" (J 2:611). [Now chiefly S., S.Midl., DARE]

Appalachy: [*n.*, variant of *Appalachia*] (J 18:7).

apricots: [*n.* fruit of the passion flower, *Passiflora incarnata,*] also "maypops" (J 26:23). (J 1:71) [Chiefly S.Midl., DARE]

apt: [*adj.* likely.] "As apt as any way" (J 2:641).

Arbuckle's coffee: [*n.* a brand of coffee popular throughout S. and SW. Still remembered by those of an older generation as the standard in coffee beans, it lingers in folklore: in Mississippi there is an old saying, "He couldn't tell sheep shit from Arbuckle's coffee." The reference in J 2:419 is followed by a comment that suggests the method of brewing the coffee in the mountains was much like that described by cowboys:] Few mountaineers use sugar, and none cream. Grounds never cleaned from pot until accumulation is so great that they must be. Coffee bitter from long boiling, almost invariably very weak.

argify: [*v.* to argue] (J 2:603). [S., S.Midl, DARE]

arm-strong-machine: [*n. phr.*] hand-mill [comic] (B 365). [DARE also applies this term to other tools such as scythes, sickles, and saws.]

arn: [1. *v.,*] variant of *earn.* Also Ill., N.H. (A). [2. *n.,*] variant of *iron* (A). "His shootin'-arn" (J 2:401). (B 352) [3. *v.* to iron (clothes).] "I had to *arn* all day" (Schoolgirl C.S.N.S. 5 July 1926) (C 11).

arrer: [*n.,* variant of *arrow.*] "I shot a great big cockyolly bird once't with my bow and arrer" (J 4:56). [S.Midl., DARE]

arter: [1. *v.,* variant of *ought to.*] "It arter be drug" (McGowan) (J 2:339). [2. *prep.,* variant of *after.*] The same man at different times may say . . . *atter* and *arter* or *after.* (B 353). [NEng., S., DARE; see also **atter.**]

ary: [*adj.* any, ever a.] "Let ary thing go wrong in the fam'ly— fever, or snake bite, or somethin'—and we can't git a doctor up hyar less'n three days" (B 121). "'I ain't goin' to spend *ary* nother nickel' (9 Aug. 1926. Horse-shoeing shop.)" (C 11). "My dogs can foller ary trail" (B 81). (J 2:603) [Esp. S., Midl., DARE; also **ar:**] "'There's not ar dishrag. They're all in here boilin''' (Bonnie Morgan, cook. 29 July, 1926)" (C 11). (J 2:605)

as: [*rel. pron.* that, which.] "You can search these mountains through with a fine-tooth comb and you wunt find ary critter as has a good word to say for the revenue" (B 170). [Formerly widespread, now chiefly Midl., S., DARE]

as how: [*adv.* how.] "I ain't sayin' as how" (J 2:642w).
ast: [*v.*, variant of *asked*.] "if anybody ast him what he was a-doin'" (J 2:441). [Chiefly S., Midl., DARE]
'at: [*pron.*, variant of *that*.] "He'd been a-goin' with 'at gal for a year" (C 3).
atter, atterwards: [*prep.*, *adv.*, respectively,] variants of *after*, *afterwards*. Also Ill., N.Eng. (A). "chased off atter a wildcat" (B 90). "He ain't no bigger than a bar of soap atter a hard day's washin'" (J 1:272). "a good spell atterward" (B 370). (C 2) [NEng, S., DARE; see also **arter**.]
atwixt or **atween:** [*prep.* between; atwixt is listed as an "archaic form" in J 2:597;] contemporary with the *Canterbury Tales* (B 362). "They had a grudge atwixt them" (J 4:853). "Right sensibly atween the shoulders I've got a pain" (B 299). "Keep yer tongue atween yer teeth" (J 10:84). [Also TN, NY, IN, KY, DARE]
aujience: [*n.*, variant of *audience*.] "If they's ary man in this aujience that don't agree with me, that's his lookout and not mine" (J 4:779).
awar: [*adj.*, variant of *aware*; listed as an "archaic form" J 2:597] contemporary with the *Canterbury Tales* (B 362). "I have heard illiterates say awar" (J 2:599). [S.App., DARE]
away: [*adv.* far.] " 'They're gettin' *away out of here* fast' (School had just closed). 9 July 1926" (C 11). [Also AR, GA, TX, KY, DARE]
awmost: [*adv.*,] variant of *almost*. Also W.Res., S.Car. General in careless pronunciation (A). (C 2)
ax or **axe:** [*v.*, variants of *ask*.] "Run, Kit, down to the Mederses, and ax who is he!" [Note also the variant ordering of the indirect question.] (B 276; cf. J 4:738). "We're poor; but we don't ax no favors" (B 119). Ax for ask and kag for keg were the primitive and legitimate forms, which we can trace as far as the time of Layamon (B 362). "I axed him to holp me out" (J 2:641). "Axe the woman gin you can git a bite" (J 4:723). (C 3) [Chiefly S., Midl., DARE; see also **ast**.]

B

Babtis': [*n.*] variant of *Baptist*. N.Eng., Ky., W.Res., Kan. (A). "She holds to the Babtis' and him to the Methodis'" (J 4:775). (B 352; C 2)

babtize: [*v.t.*] variant of *baptize*. N.Eng., Ky., W.Res., Kan. (A).

back: [1.] *v.t.* to address; from the days before envelopes. "*Back* this letter for me." Also Ill., Kan., Neb., Ky. (A). "I want you to back it to mistress" (J 1:322). [2. *adv.* previously, prior, in the phrase, "this three year back," i.e. "for the last three years"] "It was that old buck that everybody's shot at, and missed, this three year back" (B 91).

back door trots: [*n. phr.* diarrhea—in the days when the outhouse was out the back door.] (J 2:475). [Widespread, DARE]

back-house: [*n.* outhouse, privy.] "What you think Adam'd do if he was to come here and find everything lookin' like a backhouse?" / "I reckon he'd go to takin' his galluses down" (J 4:763). [Also TN, DARE; along with *privy* widespread throughout E.U.S., Kurath.]

backings: *n. pl.* liquor produced by continuing distillation after whiskey is made. Also Ky. (A). [S.Midl., DARE]

backsliding: [*pres. part.* falling into sin after having made some sort of Christian commitment] (J 4:777).

bacon: *v.t.* to make bacon of. "Reckon I'll haffter kill that hog and *bacon* it up" (A; J 2:443). (J 2:601) [Also MA, VA, MS, DARE]

bad blood: [*n. phr.* antagonism, hatred; K notes that after a conviction for murder] there was "bad blood" between the Bakers and the Whites (B 404).

bad off: *adj. phr.* ill. "The old man was right *bad off*." General (A; J 2:475). "She's here—but she's bad-off" (C 2). (J 2:642w) [Esp. S., S.Midl., DARE]

bait: [1.] *n.* a full meal. "I et me a *bait* o' ramps, and tasted them for a week *afterwards*." Also S.Car. (A). [Note, however, in his book K qualifies this:] "I et me a bait" literally means a mere snack, but jocosely it may admit a hearty meal (B 367). [Chiefly S., S.Midl., DARE] [2. *n.*] provisions [specifically for the loggers' camp or carried on special rafts, called "wanguns"] (Springer 170) (D 1).

baker's eggs: [*n.*] "straight evaporated whole eggs as it comes from the shell [not just yolks]" (C 8).

bakin'-powders: [*n.* baking powder;] always used as plural noun. "How many bakin'-powders has you got?" (B 371). [Chiefly App. DARE]

bald: [*n.* a natural meadow perched on the top or in the high saddles of the mountains.] The best pasturage is high up in the mountains, where there are "balds" covered with succulent wild grass that resembles Kentucky blue-grass (B 42). The "balds" furnish rich summer pasturage. Cattle are usually driven to the mountains about April 1st and are brought back in November. Some remain all winter (J 2:361). (B 76) [S.Midl., esp. S.App., DARE]

ballet: [*n.*,] variant of *ballad* (A). Other songs followed . . . mere snatches from "ballets" composed, mainly, by the mountaineers themselves (B 82). [Also VA, KY, Ozarks, PA Mts., DARE]

ball-hooter: [*n.*] log-roller (B 269). [Logger's term. " A ball-hooter is a man who peels the bark off a tree which has been cut on a mountain. The man turns the tree and peels the bark off of it so it will slide down the mountain on its own" (L. Monteith); "Indians at Hennessee Sawmill in Jackson Co., N.C., use this term today" (B. Van Hook); cf. **ball-hooting crew**, the crew used to roll logs downhill] (D 1). A foreign term introduced by lumbermen (J 2:607). ["Foreign" may mean from outside the mountains; [also NEng., GLakes, DARE]

band: [*n.* a large collection of timber gathered together for movement downriver; loggers' term] "cribs [of timber] . . . are again bound together . . . into 'drams' or 'bands,' sometimes called, each dram containing about twenty-five cribs; these drams again bound together make up a 'raft' " (Fraser 340) (D 1). [See also **crib, dram, raft**.]

banded up: [1.] *part. phr.* bandaged. "I was *banded up* for about three weeks" (A; J 2:475 is the source, but adds more conventionally: "It took about half a sheet tore up for one time bandagin'.") [2. *v.*] to bandage a wound (J 2:597). [Listed under "ailments" in J 2:642s.]

banjer: n. banjo. Also Ky. (A). "My goodness! if we didn't have a hog-killin' old time that night—two banjers and a fiddle" (M.B.) (J 4:761). "Hells banjer!" (B 169). Banjer Branch (Madison, N.C.) (J 26:84). Quill Rose's old mule [named] "Banjer Picker" (J 2:649).

bar: n., v., variant of *bear* (A). (C 1, 2)

bark: [v.t. to bump, to bruise.] "So's I wouldn't bark my shins" (B 102). [OED lists usage from 1850, but DARE suggests earlier association with scalping.]

barker: [n.] "the man who hews the bark from that part of the log that is to drag along the snow, and assists the teamster in loading. The other end rests on the sled and is drawn by horses or oxen. The barker is fourth in the loggers' chain of command" (Springer 92) (D 1).

barking exercises: [n. phr. a display of religious enthusiasm] Men and women at the camp-meetings fell victims to "the jerks," "barking exercises" (B 344). [Chiefly S.Midl., DARE]

barrow: n. [usually a castrated pig.] a male pig (C 1).

bassoon: [v. to make a noise like a bassoon.] "I have heard that thing whined and bassooned next door till I wanted to get up and lick the the whole darned settlement" (J 4:775).

bat: [v. to wink or blink.] "[He] bat fast his eyes" (J 2:641) [Widespread, DARE]

batch: [v.i. to] "live in a house temporarily and under primitive or crude conditions" [as a bachelor might] "I batched in that house for more'n a month" (C 3). [DARE suggests that the term could also apply to a man and woman living together out of wedlock, although that reading seems unlikely here.]

battern: n., [variant of *batten*: "In a loom, the movable frame that presses into place the threads of a woof" (Webster's Third).] In weaving the arm that knocks in the thread (A). [W.NC, DARE]

battle: v.t. to bat with a wooden battle [i.e., to wash clothes by beating them with a wooden beetle.] "She was *battlin'* clo'se." Also Nova Scotia (A). "To battle clothes with a paddle" (C 2). [Chiefly S., DARE]

battlin' block: [n. a block of wood] on which the family wash is hammered with a beetle ("battlin' stick") if the woman has no washboard, which very often is the case (B 320).

battlin' stick: [*n.* a beetle.] In washing clothes they were beaten with a piece of wood, called either a battlin' stick or battlin' block (J 2:417).

bead: *n.* in moonshine whiskey, iridescent bubbles that form when the liquor is shaken up. Also Ky. (A). [The moonshiner's] testing is done entirely by the "bead" of the liquor, the little iridescent bubbles that rise when the vial is tilted. When a mountain man is shown any brand of whiskey, whether a regular distillery product or not, he invariably tilts the bottle and levels it again, before tasting; if the bead rises and is persistent, well and good; if not, he is prepared to condemn the liquor at once (B 135-36). The first distillate is pure alcohol, which is too strong to give a "bead" (J 3:951.23). [Also GA, MS, KY, DARE]

bealin': *vbl. n.* suppurating. "It went to *bealin'*." Also S.Car. (A). [Chiefly App., DARE]

bear grass: [*n.* a liliaceous plant having edible bulbs; probably *Yucca filamentosa.*] "as greens, also eaten raw by children (Miles 17) (J 2:433). [S., W., DARE]

bearing-she or **barren-she:** [*n.* a pregnant female.] "A bearing she?" [Is she pregnant?] (J 4:749). [Used in place names:] Barren-she Mt. (Nicholas, W.Va.) Barren-she C[ree]k. (Pike, Ky.; McDowell, W.Va.) (J 26:84). (J 2:599) [Cf. K's own phrasing:] killing bearing females as well as legitimate game (B 69).

bear sign: [*n.* bear scat, scratchings, or tracks.] "Le's saunter around this laurel and see if we find any bear sign" (J 4:749).

bear wallow: [*n.* a depression, like a "sink," in which bears roll about.] Bear-wallow Bald (Swain, N.C.) (J 26:76).

beast, beest, beasties: [*n.* horse.] beest (J 2:361). Critter and beast are usually restricted to horse and mule (B 369). The ancient syllabic plural is preserved in beasties (horses), nesties, posties, trousies (these are not diminutives) (B 359). (J 2:489) [Chiefly S.Midl. DARE; see also **critter**]

beat: [1. *v.* to avoid payment. In the question, "Who's got to beat?" (J 2:649; B 371) it appears to mean "Who is it we have to avoid paying?"; cf. DAE.] [2. *v.* to excel, to top] "I slep' last night to beat a hen a' peckin'" (M.B.) (J 2:625).

beatenest: [*adj. superlative:* most extraordinary. After] a blizzard [in which] seventeen cattle climbed upon each other for warmth and froze to death in a solid hecatomb, a herdsman . . . assured me that "that was the beatenest snowstorm ever I seen" (B 72; J 1:37). "Well, I wish't I may never! (if you ain't the beatenest . . .)" (J 2:613). [Chiefly S., S.Midl., DARE]

beat (one's) time: [*v. phr.* to] "get the best of (one) in a courtship rivalry." "He'd been a-goin' with that gal for years, and then that other feller come along and beat his time" (C 3).

beat time: [*v.*] "to kill or waste time on a job." "He can beat time the best I ever saw" (C 3). [DARE also lists "beat in time" with the same meaning. Chiefly Midl.]

bed it: *v. phr.* to lie abed. "I ain't goin' to *bed it* no longer." (A; B 356; J 2:641). [There are other entries: "entertainment: bed it" (J 2:642p; J 6).] [W.NC, S.App., DARE]

bed: [*n.* a patch or small field, especially tobacco.] (J 2:642). [Also KY, SC, DARE]

bed-cords: [*n.* the rope cords used to hold up the mattress.] "Traces are made of hickory or paw paw, as also are bed-cords" (Allen, "Cumberland") (J 2:455).

beef: [*n.* a single bovine.] Bob, opening a can of corned beef, said, "When we butchered a beef, we used to throw away the guts" (J 2:421). [DARE attributes to Pl. States, TX; see also **beeves**]

bee-gum: [*n.* bee-hive; made from a hollow log, often but not necessarily of the gum tree:] hives made of cuts from hollow logs (B 224). [Used comically, in the advice that if tooth-jumpin' does not work,] "You might as well stick your head in a bee-gum and fergit it" (J 2:470). [Chiefly S., S.Midl., DARE]

bee-'lasses: [*n.*] (honey) Bob smacks his lips, "Bee-lasses!" (J 2:421).

been: *p*[*ast*] *p*[*art.* finished.] "Set down and eat you some supper." / "No, I've *been*" (A; J 2:621; cf. B 372). [Listed under "dialectal idioms":] been (to supper) (J 2:611).

beer: *n.* still beer: among moonshiners. Also Ky. (A). When done, the sugar of what is now "sour mash" has been converted into carbonic acid and alcohol. The resulting liquid is technically called the "wash," but blockaders call it "beer." It is intoxicating, of course, but "sour enough to make a pig squeal" (B 134). [Chiefly S.App., DARE]

beeves: [*n.* cattle.] Very few of them kill beeves, as they do not relish the meat (J 2:405). [See also **beef**]

bell-tail: *n.* rattlesnake (A; J 2:601).

belong: 1. *v.i.* to be due. "The train don't *belong* to come till 12:15." 2. [*v.*] to intend. "I *belong* to go to town tomorrow." Also Ky. (A). (C 2) [S., S.Midl., DARE]

bemean: *v.t.* to abuse, [to] shame by chiding. "She *bemeaned* him." Also Kan., Ky. (A). "She was allers bemeaning him" (J 4:855). [Listed under "unusual terms" (J 2:599).]

benasty: *v.t.* to befoul, [to] besmear. "The little feller tumbled down and *benastied* himself to beat the devil" (A; B 357 reads "Little Jimmy"). (J 2:601, 642) [S.Midl., DARE]

bench-legged: [*adj.* in current usage, "bow-legged with feet turned in" (Rex Taylor).] "A bench-legged feist" (J 2:371). [Also VA, DARE]

bereft: [*adj.* mad, bereft of senses.] "Are ye plumb bereft?" (J 4:853). [Also S.GA, N.FL, DARE]

bettern: [*v.* shouldn't, coined from the adverb.] "We better git some wood, bettern we?" (B 357).

betwixt: [*prep.*] "between. The interesting thing about this good old word is that it is rarely ever heard here except among the most illiterate" (C 3). [Chiefly S., S.Midl., DARE]

bid: [*v.t.* to ask, to pray, to command.] "I bid him not to do it" (J 4:853).

biddable: [*adj.* obedient.] "He was the most biddable boy I ever saw" (J 2:639). "That blind mare is the most biddable thing I ever saw" (J 2:642). [Chiefly S., S.Midl., DARE]

big: *v.t.* to get with child. "Doc Orr *bigged* Sis' Posey." Also S.Car. (A). "Doc Orr bigged Sis Posey one time, but old Mis' Posey and Jim knocked it sky-high with red-pepper tea" (J 4:841). [S., S.Midl., DARE]

biggity: [*adj.* snobbish, uppity.] "He's biggity and upheaded, and I'm glad to be shet o' him" (J 23:77). [S., S.Midl. DARE; see also **brigaty**]

Big Ike: [*n.phr.* used adverbially, superior, boldly; as in the expression, "to act Big Ike."] "furriners actin' Big Ike" (J 10:83). "He tried to act Big Ike and sass her back" (Miles) (J 2:637, 10:82). [S., S.Midl., DARE]

big meetin' time: [*n. phr.* period of camp meeting or revival.] The season for camp-meetings is from mid-August to October. . . . (I say this with no disrespect: "big-meetin' time" is a gala week, . . . as much secular as spiritual to the . . . people) (B 343). [S. S.Midl., DARE]

big sticks: [*n. phr.* comic understatement; the traditional phrase was "The Great Forest."] The forest that surrounds us (B 205). [NEng, GLakes, DARE; cf. **sticks**]

bile: [1. *v.t.* to boil.] "I biled that beef a day and a night, and then couldn't stick a fork into the grain" (J 2:428) [S.Midl., NEng, DARE]. [2. *past part.*] "the government is ary thing but a president in a biled shirt who commands two-three judges and a gang of revenue officers" (B 210). [3.] *vbl. n.* crowd. "The hull kit an' *bilin'* of 'em." Also Ill., Neb., NEng., Ky. (A) [S., S.Midl., NEng, DARE] [4. *n.* feud—a metaphorically appropriate mispronunciation of broil] "this man was 'in the bilin' '" [the feud] (B 310). [5. *n.* a boil; a skin infection; listed under "skin diseases" (J 2:477).]

biler: [*n.* boiler, usually the pot to boil food in; listed with cooking terms] (J 2:429).

bilin' pieces: [*n. phr.* cuts of meat so tough they were boiled.] All parts except the cheap "bilin' pieces" were sold (B 43). All cuts [were] the same price except "bilin' pieces" (J 2:443). The flesh of wild mt. cattle is lean, tough, stringy, and has a peculiarly watery flavor, rather than juicy. Unpalatable broiled, fried, or roasted. Boiled too. (J 2:428).

biscuit bread: [*n. phr.* shortening bread, biscuits.] (J 2:592). (B 360) [Chiefly S.Midl., DARE]

bitty: [*adj.*] short for "bit of a." "A leetle *bitty* feller." Also Ill., S.Car. (A). "little bitty dogs" (B 94). "There ain't nary bitty sense in it" (J 2:641).

blackgyard: [1. *n.*] variant of *blackguard.* Also Ky. (A) [Midl., DARE] [2. *v.t.* to call names, to vituperate] "They was a-blackgyardin' one another" (J 4:853). [S.Midl., DARE]

black pine: [*n.*] pitch pine (*Pinus taeda*). [Pitch pine is usually *Pinus rigida*; Dan Pittillo suggests the only *taeda* near the park was introduced near Fontana Dam after the dam was completed, and in current local usage "black" = *rigida*.]

blade fodder: [*n.*] tops of corn stalks. Also Ky. (A). Blades or leaves of corn, dried and used for cattle feed (J 2:361, 599). [Chiefly S.Midl., DARE]

blame, blamed: [*adj.*, euphemisms for damn/damned.] "All these here glass winders is blame foolishness to *me*" (B 305). "What makes you so blamed contentious?" (B 75). [See also **darn**]

blather: [*n.* nonsense, idle talk.] "Don't give me none o' yer blather" (J 4:853, 10:83). [Listed in Fox as "English dialect" (J 2:489).] (J 2:391, 599)

bleat up: [*v. phr.*] to call or decoy a deer by bleating like the fawn. To "bleat up" a deer (Lewis and Clark 1052, note) (D 2). [Obs., DA]

blind house: [*n.*] the "blind" or windowless one-room cabin (J 2:371). In "blind" houses the doors are left open all day even in winter, to serve as windows, and part of a side or end log is cut out to admit light elsewhere (J 2:373). [K traces origins to:] Irish hovels, Norwegian saeters, the "black houses" of the Hebrides (B 322).

blindshootin': [*vbl.n.* in feuds, shooting from ambush, i.e., from a blind] (J 2:597). A real mountain feud . . . is marked by suave treachery . . . "blind-shooting," and general heartlessness and brutality (B 421).

blind tiger: [*n. phr.* a speakeasy.] There was information that Lafonte was running a blind tiger (B 175).

blinky: *n.* milk slightly soured. Also Kan., Neb., Mo. (A). "To be slightly sour" (C 2). [Although K indicates this is a noun in his word list, it also appears as an adjective in "blinky milk." (J 2:429).]

blobber-lipped: [*adj.* thick-lipped.] (J 1:27). [Also KY, DARE]

block: *v.i.* blockade. "He's *blockin'* over in Hell's Holler" (A).

blockade: 1. *n.* moonshine whiskey; also the manufacture of it (A). "If I'd age my blockade it would bring a fancy price" (B 137). 2. *v.i.* to make moonshine whiskey (A). "Blockadin' is the hardest work a man ever done. And hit's wearin' on a feller's narves" (B 140). four brothers who were blockadin' near his father's house (B 175). "Sorter shamed to tell . . . In jail . . . we was up fer blockadin'" (J 4:725). [S.Midl., DARE]

blockader: [*n*. a person who distills liquor illegally.] Here an illicit distiller is called a blockader, his business is blockading, and the product is blockade liquor (B 126). [Also Alleghenies, DA]

Blockader's Glory: [*n*. comic name for Sugarlands, the area in the Great Smokies which was once the haven of moonshiners and is now the location of the National Park Headquarters—*sic transit gloria mundi*.] For many a year it had been known on our side of the mountains as Blockaders' Glory, which is the same as saying Moonshiner's Paradise (B 213).

blockade liquor: [*n*. moonshine, corn liquor.] The product is blockade liquor (B 126).

block house: *n*. a "block house" is one of logs hewn square [the traditional S.App. log cabin] (J 2:373). [DAE supports this definition; DARE suggests a housed raised off the ground as in a fortification, something different.]

blood purifiers: [*n. pl.* herbal medicines.] "The small tubers of the roots [of Dutchman's Breeches or Turkey Corn are] known as 'blood purifiers' " (Asheville *Citizen,* 22 Jan. 1928) (J 2:480).

bloody Breathitt: [*n. phr.,* the county in E. Ky. that was the scene of family feuds] The outbreak of another feud in "bloody Breathitt" (B 12).

bloody flux: [*n*. dysentery; listed among "ordinary diseases" (J 2:469).] [Obs., DA]

blossom-bushes: [*n*.] garden flowers (A). flowers (J 2:359, 597). (J 6) [Also NEng, DARE]

blossoms: *n. pl.* flowers; also called *purties.* Also N.Eng. (A).

blouse: [*v*. to gather loosely about the waist, as a blouse.] "Sis blouses her waist a-purpose to carry a pistol" (B 356). (J 2:601) [Always prounounced with the -z sound, DARE]

blow: [*n*. a storm.] "Durn this blow, anyhow! No bear'll cross the mountain sich a night as this" (B 79).

blowed: [*v.,* variant of *blew.*] A weak preterite supplants the proper strong one (B 358).

blow down: [*n*. an area in which all the trees have blown down or over, sometimes even leaving enough of the root system intact so the trees can live—a special benefit to loggers. E. Monteith remembers seeing a big "windfall" in Graham County in 1936, which he thinks must have been the result of a tornado, that uprooted acres of trees. He suggests that this was more common in hemlock forests since hemlocks do not have tap roots.] (D 1) windfall (Hayward xvii, 146). "Then break my own back kerryin' meal through the blow downs and laurel" (J 26:63). [Also NH, ME, MS, KY, NW, DARE]

board: *n.* a riven clapboard or shingle; others are called *sawed boards*. Also Ky. (A). "Riven shingles" (C 2). [S., S.Midl., DARE]

boardin'-place: [*n. phr.* a residence offering rooms and board.] "An' then fer boardin'-place—well, there warn't much choice. There was one house, with one room" (B 468).

boar's nest: [*n. phr.*] "shanty on a raft [loggers' term]—any batchelor's [sic] shanty" (D 1). [Esp. W. DARE]

bobcat: [*n.*] wildcat [*Lynx rufus*] (J 26:56). [DAE lists American origin, but citations suggest widespread usage.]

bobtailed: [*adj.* stubby-tailed.] "He's as hard to steer as a bobtailed calf" (J 10:82).

bodaciously: [*adv.*] bodily or entirely. "I'm bodaciously ruint" (seriously injured). "Sim greened him out bodaciously" (to green out or sap is to outwit in trade) (B 368). "I got a good one on him—greened him out bodaciously" (J 2:459, 10:82). "I'm bodaciously tired out" (B 107). [Chiefly S., S.Midl., DARE]

bodily: [*adv.* physically.] "A good dog is the only livin' thing'll stay with a man till it bodily starves to death." [For his wife's acidic rejoinder see **allers**] (J 2:642).

body lice: [*n.* lice primarily feeding on the body as distinguished from the extremities, especially the sucking louse (*Pediculus humanus humanus*). These differ from head lice; see K's list of insect pests:] "Chinches," "body-lice," and "head-lice" (J 2:435). "Body-lice is easier to get shet of than head-lice" (J 2:438).

bogus: [*adj.* counterfeit.] "It's a fair mimic of silver but it's bogus and good fer nothin' " (J 10:83). [It is interesting that this quotation obviously refers to a counterfeit coin. This concrete use, as opposed to the more usual metaphorical extension, was the earliest one. Cf. DA, DAE]

bone: [*v.*] "to dun, to ask in a challenging manner. 'I boned him for some money he's been owin' me for a long time' " (C 3). [Widespread, DARE]

bones atter pickels: [*n. phr.* a skinny, poor thing, comic metaphor.] "She's just bones atter pickles" [if pickles are the appetizer, she is not much of an entree] (J 2:475).

bonny: [*adj.* beautiful; listed among "Optimistic Names":] Bonny (Morgan, Ky.) (J 26:83).

booger: [*n.*] demon, ghost, goblin; still current as adj. in the phrase "booger movies," i.e., horror movies. Listed as "Not peculiar to mts., but unknown to the Standard" in (J 2:603.] "I wish t' the booger'd git him." (M.B.) (J 2:689).(J 4:779) [S., S.Midl., DARE]

boogerman: [*n.*] the devil (C 1) (J 2:689). [A young girl on seeing her first Negro cried:] "My goddamighty, Mam, thar's the boogerman—I done seed him!" (B 24). [Chiefly S., S.Midl., DARE]

book: *n.* magazines or pamphlets (A). Mountaineers and valley people alike call a magazine or a pamphlet a "book" (J 2:399). A magazine is always called a "book" in this region, as, I think, throughout the South (B 318).

book-keep: *v.i.* to act as bookkeeper. "He *book-kept* for the camp" (A). "My boy Jesse book-kept" (B 356).

book larnin': [*v. phr.* an education, especially secular.] The mountain clergy, as a general rule, are hostile to "book larnin,'" for "there ain't no Holy Ghost in it" (B 345).

books: [*n.* book time, time to read.] "'It is books' (School is in session)" (C 2). [Chiefly S., S.Midl., DARE]

boom: [*v.t.* to confine logs in the main channel of a river; loggers' term.] "The first business of the drive [when the rivers are swollen in the spring] is to collect all these scattered timbers, and 'boom' them into the main channel of the river, that is, confine them there by long half-square logs called 'boom timber,' fastened at the ends by 'boom chains.' These will sometimes line the true banks of the river for miles at a stretch and effectively prevent any waywardly inclined timber from straggling into the adjoining submerged regions" (Fraser 281) (D 1). [See **drowned lands**]

boomer: *n.* the red squirrel [*Tamiasciuvus hudsoniscus*] (A). Out of a tree overhead hopped a mountain "boomer" (red squirrel), and down he came, eyed me, and stopped (B 87). (J 2:601, 26:56) [See **mountain boomer**]

borned: [*past part.*, variant of *born*; listed under:] corrupt form of the verb (B 358). "Borned in the kentry and ain't never been out o' hit" (B 429).

borry: [1. *v.*,] variant of *borrow*, to lend. "Will you borry me some sugar?" Also Ill., Ky. (A; J 4:731). "They had the book, and they borried it to us to read" (B 235). [2. *v.* to borrow:] "Did ye come to borry fire coals? That's the common word with us when a body 'pears to be in a hurry" (Louis) (J 4:723). [The question is expanded in B 324:] that you're in sich a hurry you can't chat?"

boundary: *n.* a farm, a fenced-in field, a large, unfenced estate, such as a tract of timber land (A). "landed property" (J 6). (J 2:605) [Midl., DARE]

box house: [*n.*] a board shanty (J 2:373). [S.Midl., esp. Ozarks, DARE]

bracer: [*n.* an alcoholic drink.] "He's so homely, he has to take a bracer afore he can look hisself in the glass" (J 10:82). [Also GA, MO, DARE]

brad: *v.t.* to fasten with brads. "He had no way of *braddin'* it." Also N.Eng. (A). (J 2:601)

brags: [*n.* boasts, bragging.] "Well, he can make his brags about how he done me up, but . . ." (J 10:82). "He made his brags" (J 2:642). "They could make their brags about it . . . of how they done him up" (MacG[owan]) (J 2:611). [DARE cites usage only in ME, MN, WI]

brake: [*v.* to slow down.] The sled . . . "brakes" automatically in going downhill (B 42).

branch: [*n.* a small stream; in the mountains a spring leads to a fork or branch, thence to a creek or a river; "brook" is not used.] "What brings ye up this air way-off branch?" (J 4:793). [Note that K's northern dialect is revealed in his "Preface" to B:] should you step aside at the first brook crossing, turn "up the branch," and follow the rough by-road (B 7). [Chiefly S., S.Midl., DARE; exclusively in W.VA, NC, Kurath]

branch-water: [*n.* stream water.] "Stingy? Him! He won't drink the branch-water till there's a flood" (J 10:82). [S., S.Midl., DARE]

branch water people: [*n. phr.* those living up in the branches, i.e., higher in the mountains.] We went among the Cherokees and among the white "branch water people" (B 196-7). We still shall find dire poverty the rule rather than the exception among the multitude of "branch-water people" (B 323).

brash, braysh, bresh: [1. *n.,*] variants of *brush.* Also Ky. (A). [**brash** is listed as English dialect retention in Fox (J 2:489); also listed in J 2:603, 642o.] braysh (B 352). "take to the bresh [to ambush someone]" (J 3:899). Both . . . were shot dead "from the bresh" (B 405). [2. *n.* cuttings from trees] "Brash 'eap" (J 2:340). [S.Midl., DARE]

brass knucks: [*n. phr.* (usually "knuckles") "linked metal rings or a metal bar with holes for the fingers," used in fighting (Webster NW).] Many of the young men carry home-made billies or "brass knucks" (B 416). [Sole citation in DA is taken from F.A. Sondley's *Asheville and Buncombe County,* 1922.]

bread: [1.] *n.* corn bread. Biscuit[s] are called biscuit bread (A). [2.] *v.t.* to provide with daily bread. "He's got enough corn to *bread* his family all winter." Also Kan., Ky. (A). (J 1:262)

break the Sabbath: [*v.phr.* to fail to observe Sunday as a day of rest; in what follows it serves as comic exaggeration.] "Them fellers ain't tradin' enough up there to break the Sabbath" (Jim Wallace) (J 2:461). Sometimes a man is "churched" for breaking the Sabbath (B 346).

breakfust, brekfust: [*n.,* variants of *breakfast.*] "Brek-k-k-fust!" . . . / "Where's that brekfust you're yellin' about?" (B 83). [Perhaps this is simply an instance of eye dialect, but we suspect otherwise, since K was keenly aware of the condescending effect of such visual tricks. We suspect his spelling is an attempt to capture what he perceived to be a departure from standard pronunciation, with the vowel of the first syllable slightly lower than standard and that of the second syllable slightly lower and more centralized /brɛkᵀf⁻ˡʌst/].

breast: [*v.t.* to walk abreast.] "I had enough men to breast that mountain about ten steps apart, and we just combed it" (J 23:8l).

breath: *n.* a moment. "I'll be there in just a *breath.*" Also Me., N.H. (A; J 2:641, 642w). (J 2:605)

breathe: "*v.t.* to speak. 'Don't breathe that to anyone' " (C 1).

breechless: [*adj.* without trousers.] Matt ruefully surveyed his almost denuded legs . . . "Boys, I'm nigh breechless!" (B 92).

[DARE, citing *North Carolina Folklore* (1952), suggests "hen-pecked," clearly not the meaning here.]

breed: [1.] *v.i.* to experience the nausea and abnormal appetite of pregnancy. [17th century survival. R.S.F.—K] Also Me. (A).

breedin' also **a-breedin':** [entries under these forms suggest the term may have meant or implied something more general, such as childbearing, or possibly the discomforts and pain of childbearing:] "She's a-breedin'." Some of the women have no attendance [in childbirth] at all, not even the assistance of another woman (J 2:469). [Also VA, MS, ME, DARE]

brethering: [*n.* brethren, brothers.] "My brethering, you'll find my tex' somers in the Bible " (J 4:779). [Also KY, DARE]

brickle: *adj.* brittle. Also Kan., Nova Scotia (A). (B 352) [S., Midl., DARE]

brigaty: *adj.* foppish; also overbearing, stuck up. "Doctor Adams is *brigaty* among women." [Also] Ky. Also **brickaty,** and (in negro lingo) **biggety** (A; J 2:637). "You'uns won't be so feisty and brigaty atter this, will ye!" [Feisty and brigaty] "mean nigh about the same thing, only there's a differ. When I say that Doc Jones thar is brigaty among women-folks, hit means that he's stuck on hisself and wants to show off. . . . feisty means when a feller's allers wigglin' about, wantin' ever'body to see him, like a kid when the preacher comes" (B 94). (J 2:642; J 6; C 2) [Chiefly S.App., DARE]

bright: *n.* polish. "The *bright* sorter wore off." Also N. Eng. (A; J 2:40l reads "bright's"). [Listed under "quaint idioms" in J 2:605.]

brile: [*v.*, variant of *broil*.] (B 352).

brogans: *n. pl.* coarse shoes. [In La. **bro-anz**—K] Ill., N.Eng., Ky., N.Y. (A).

brogue: [1.] *v.i.* to go afoot. "Where are you a-goin'?"—"Jes' *broguin'* about" (A; J 4:734). In every settlement there is some-body who makes a pleasure of gathering and spreading news. Such a one . . . had [many ways] of announcing his mission by indirection. Here is the list: "I'm jes' broguin' about." / "Yes, I'm jest cooterin' around." [The list continues, adding san-terin', prodjectin', traffickin', spuddin', shacklin', and loaf-erin'.] And yet one hears that our mountaineers have a limited vocabulary! (B 276-77). [The same list with minor differences appears in J 4:734.] [2 *v.t.* to walk] "I brogued it" (C 1). [Chiefly App., DARE]

brought on: *adj.* [*phr.* store bought] imported. "This here *brought on* meat ain't noways as good as home-made meat." Also Ia., Ky. (A; J 2:428). (J 2:601) [Chiefly S.Midl., DARE; see also **fotch on**]

bruk: [*v.t.*, variant of *broke.*] "He bruk his laig" (J 2:475). "He threw a full fruit jar out o' the cyar." / "How do you know it was full?" / "Because it just bruk; it didn't flander" (J 2:639). "Well, when Moses got mad he bruk all the commandments at one crack" (J 10:74). "I fired a shoot as she riz in the air, but only bruk her wing" (B 91). (B 358)

brung: [*v.*, variant of *brought.*] A strong preterite with dialectal change of the vowel (B 358). "What brung ye up this air way-off branch?" (J 4:737).

brute: [*n.* bull.] Usually restricted . . . to a bovine. A bull or boar is not to be mentioned as such in mixed company, but male-brute and male-hog are used as euphemisms (B 369). [S.Midl., occasionally NE, DARE; see also **beast, critter**]

bubby: [*n.* Carolina allspice (*Calycanthus floridus*)] "sweet shrub." "I want some bubbies" (C 2). [S.App., DARE]

bubby bush: [*n.*] burning bush (*Euonymus americanus*) [Possibly a very local usuage but elsewhere in this area bubby bush is not often heard and bubby is *Calycanthus* (Dan Pittillo).] (A). (J 1:71)

buck vine: [*n.* listed among local plants, but undefined] (J 1:67).

budget: *n.* parcel, luggage. "Have you got your *budget* made up?" (A). Some highland usages that sound odd to us are really no more than the original and literal meanings, as budget for bag or parcel (B 370). [Chiefly App., DARE]

bug: *v.t.* to kill bugs on. "Jim's out *buggin'* taters." General (A). (C 2)

bullbat: [*n.*] nighthawk [*Chordeiles minor*] (J 26:54). [S.Atl, Gulf States, SW, scattered S.Midl., DARE]

bull-tongue: [*n.* the common plow, the single-bladed plow.] The common plow was a "bull-tongue" (B 37). "An implement [used to plow] hardly more than a sharpened stick with a metal rim. Often drawn by an ox or a half-yoke. But one may see women ploughing with two oxen" (Allen, "Cumberland") (J 2:338). For the rough work of cultivating the hillsides a single steer hitched to the "bull-tongue" was better adapted (B 42). [S.Midl., DARE]

bumblings: *n. pl.* whiskey (A). [More narrowly defined in B as adulterated whiskey:] all of the moonshine whiskey used to be pure . . . but every blockader knows how to adulterate, and when one of them does stoop to such tricks he will stop at no halfway measures. Some add washing lye . . . then prime this abominable fluid with pepper, ginger, tobacco, or anything else that will make it sting. . . . Such decoctions are known [as] . . . "pop-skull," "bust head," "bumblings" (B 137). [The following suggests the term may have been used generically, as in A—just for whiskey, unless Mistress Barnett was flippant or malicious:] "I'm goin' to send your folks some o' them big red apples, and Andy a pint o' bumblins" (M.B.) (J 4:729). [S. App., DARE]

bumbly: *adj.* buzzing. "Hit makes a *bumbly* noise in a feller's head" (A; B 137). [Cf. **bumblings**]

burning bush: [*n.* Indian Arrow-wood. (*Euonymous americanus*). At present this term refers to *E. alatus*, the species that turns bright red in the fall. Flowers] June. Dark Purple. (J 26:29).

buryin': [*vbl. n.* a funeral. "I went to the buryin'" (J 2:483).

buryin' ground: [*n.* cemetery.] "But I disremember which buryin' ground they-all planted ye in" (B 78). [Widespread, DARE]

bushwack: [*v.t.* to ambush.] "The blockaders bushwacked them . . . and shot my deputy through the brain with a squirrel rifle" (B 173). As for bushwacking, "Hit's as fa'r for one as 'tis for t'other. You can't fight a man fa'r and squar who'll shoot you in the back. A pore man can't fight money in the courts" (B 421). [Widespread, DARE]

busted: [*past part.* of *v.*, broken.] "You'll spy, to-morrow, whar several trees has been wind-throwed and busted to kindlin'" (B 77).

bust head: [*n.* adulterated blockade whiskey.] (B 137). [See also **bumblings**]

by: *prep.* after. "An hour by sun"; i.e. past sunrise. Also S.Car., Ky. (A; J 2:629). " 'by sunrise' (after)" (C 2) [S., S.Midl., DARE]

by gobblies: [*euphemistic exclamation* by God!; marked (HK) so it may be K's own expression.] (J 2: 613).

by godlings: [*euphemistic exclamation* by God!] Quill Rose "told me once that all good red-liquor was aged, and that if I'd age my blockade it would bring a fancy price. Well, sir, I tried it; I kept some for three months—and, by godlings, *it ain't so*" (B 137).

by jinks: [*euphemistic exclamation;* "probably an alteration of jynx (wryneck); from the use of wrynecks in witchcraft; something that brings bad luck (Webster's Third).] "By jinks, it was cold!" (B 86).

by Ned: [*exclamation:* Ned refers to Satan.] "By Ned, they just rid sapplin's, gittin' out o' thar!" (J 2:367).

by sun: [*prep.* after sunrise.] "An hour by sun." (an hour after sunrise) (J 2:629).

C

cabbage: [*n.*] always used as plural: "I'll have a few more of them cabbage" (B 371). [Also FL, GA, Ozarks, DARE]

cag: [*n.*] variant of *keg*. Also Ill. Ia., Kan., N.Eng., Ky., N.Y., (A). The primitive and legitimate form . . . which we trace as far as the time of Layamon (B 362). [See also **kag**]

cage the bird: [*v. phr.* a square dance step in which one dancer from a foursome is encircled by the others.] "First couple cage the bird with three arms around" (Haney 52) (B 338; J 4:761 also quotes Fox and M.B.). [W. DARE]

caigy: *adj.* full of sexual desire. Also Ill., Kan. In N.Eng. applied to a high-spirited horse (A). Since the Appalachian people have a marked Scotch-Irish strain, we would expect their speech to show a strong Scotch influence. So far as vocabulary is concerned, there is really little of it. A few words, caigy (cadgy), coggled, fernent, gin for if, needcessity, trollop, almost exhaust the list of distinct Scotticisms (B 354). (J 9:843) [Chiefly S.Midl., DARE]

cain't: [*v.*, variant of *can't*.] "Durn you, Bill Cope [a hunchback], you're so cussed crooked a man cain't lay cluss enough to you to keep warm" (B 103). "a plumb cur, of course, cain't foller a cold track—he just runs by sight" (B 80).

calf love: [*n.* immature infatuation] "Love sick! Calf love, Puppy love! Oh sugar, oh honey, oh 'lasses candy" (J 23:63).

call: [1. *n.* reason, cause.] "He had no call to do it" (J 4:853). "We-uns hain't no call to be ashamed" (B 119; K here substitutes "call" for "necessity," which is found in the same quote in J 2:641). [S.App., DARE] [2.] *v.t.* to mention. "Ain't you never heard Tommy *call* my name?" Also N.Eng. (A). Call [is used] for name or mention or occasion (B 370). "To mention" (C 2).

camboose: [*n.* the common cooking area or the large rectangular, open-pit fireplace located in the center of the shanty which the loggers shared; Fraser (24) has a drawing; he says it was "used in baking" (44).] "Smoke is the pest of the shantyman's domicile. It requires very considerable mechanical ingenuity, and practical experience, so to construct the camboose and the opening in the roof immediately above it, with its log chimney of few or many feet in height, that the smoke may escape freely and fully. . . . Notwithstanding the smoke and ashes and cinders of the *camboose*" (Fraser 23-24, 53) (D 1). [N.Atl, DARE]

cane: *n.* sorghum. Also Kan., Ky. (A). (C 2)

cant dog: [*n.* cant hook.] "A tool similar to a peavy, [which is 'a heavy wooden lever with a pointed metal tip and a hinged hook near the end: used by lumbermen in handling logs' (Webster NW)], but lacking the spike; used [with pries and handspikes] to turn square logs on a carriage [or to roll logs into water so they can float downstream.] Not used today" (E. and L. Monteith). "All hands are in the water . . . lifting with heavy pries, hand spikes, and cant dogs to roll those massive sticks [logs] into the brook channel" (Springer 156) (D 1). [Chiefly NEng, DARE]

capias: [*n.* a writ issued by a court ordering an arrest; variant of *copias*, Latin for subpoena.] "The devil with a capias!" (J 2:642). [See also **onpias**]

cap shooter: [1.] *n.* a gun with percussion lock. [2.] **cap shooting:** *adj.* "Sure as a *cap-shootin'* gun" (A).

captain: n. one who excels. "He's a *captain* on the floor to dance." "He's a *captain* to tell a tale." Also Kan., Ky. (A; J 4:761). "He's a captain of a farmer" (C 2). (J 2:642)

care to: [*v. phr.;* specifically, in the expression "I don't care to (+ verb)," what is implied is "I don't mind," or since this is a kind of understatement, "I'd be glad to."] " 'I don't care if I do.' (I will gladly)" (C 2). " 'I don't care.' [i.e., 'I don't mind if I do']— in answer to an invitation to go somewhere or do something" (C 1). [Chiefly Midl., DARE]

carry: *v.t.* to accompany, to escort. "He *carried* her to church." Also Ill., S.Car. (A). "I aim to carry her to church" (C 2). When a mountain swain "carries his gal to meetin' " he is not performing so great an athletic feat as was reported by Benjamin Franklin, who said, "My father carried his wife and three children to New England" (from Pennnsylvania) (B 370). [K is being ironic; Franklin's dialectal use of "carry" is like that of the mountains.] [S., S.Midl., DARE; common in DL, MD, VA, NC, SC, Kurath]

carryin's on: [*v. phr.,* or more precisely, a nominalization; impropriety] "I won't have such carryin's on in my house" (Bob) (J 4:737).

case: [*n.* "a person peculiar or remarkable in some way" (DAE); K probably intended some such meaning because the term is listed under:] "personal description—character" (J 2:642p).

Castellites: [*n.* an unidentified religious sect; possibly an erroneous allusion to the Campbellites.] (B 344-45).

catamount: [*n.* apparently used indiscriminately for both the cougar or panther (*Felis concolor*), and the bobcat or lynx (*Lynx canadensis*); K assumes that his informants meant only the latter (perhaps because the panther was being extirpated from the area of the Smokies), but they may not have. The term may have been retained as part of the active vocabulary of speakers of K's acquaintance by being applied to any wildcat, even as it was dropped among those speakers who never saw a panther.] Once in a blue moon a lynx is killed in the highest zone of the Smokies. . . . Our native hunters never heard the word lynx, but call the animal a "catamount" (B 99). [Chiefly S., S.Mid., N.E., DARE]

catawampus: *adv.* Mixed up; all awry. Also Ill., Kan., N.Eng., Ky. (A). "You got that all catawampus" (J 2:641). (J 2:601) [Chiefly S., S.Midl., DARE]

catridge: [*n.*, variant of *cartridge.*] "Git me some thirty-eight special catridges" (J 23:83).

catty-cornered: [*adv.*] "diagonally. 'He went kinder catty-cornered across the field'" (C 3). [Chiefly S., S.Midl., DARE]

cavil: [*v.* to quibble; listed (J 2:599) with "unexpected use of literary terms"; K suggests that this word is part of the App. mountaineer's active vocabulary, while it is merely part of the passive or reading vocabulary for mainstream speakers.] "They stood thar and caviled about it" (B 361).

cavort: [*v.i.* to romp, prance, frolic.] "But who ever seen luxury cavortin' around in these Smoky Mountains?" (B 121). [S.Midl., now widespread, DARE]

chair-bottoming: [*vbl. n.* caning chairs.] "Chair-bottoming is easy settin'-down work" (J 2:457).

chance: *n.* that which the occasion offers. "A poor *chance* of a place to spend the night." "Now you see the *chance* [at table— K], help yourself" (A; J 4:753). [Also **chancet, chanct**] "They sot awhile and then Pruitt pinched the other feller and says, 'Le's go out and give them a chancet to clean up'" (J 2:439). "Your chanct is ruined" (B 85). [NEng, VA, S.App., DARE]

chaps: [*n.* children.] (J 1:298; C 1). [Chiefly S., S.Midl., DARE]

char: [*n.* ashes.] For tooth ache—burn writing paper on a plate, throw away the char, apply the brown oily residue to the cavity of tooth (J 2:470).

chaw: [*n.* a chew, a plug.] "Gimme a chaw o' terbacker." / "I don't carry none, fer I'm tryin' to quit" (Ben Henry) (J 4:731).

chawin': [*pres. part.* of *v.* to chew.] "They'll run right in on the varmint, snappin' and chawin' and worryin' him till he gits so mad you can hear his tushes pop half a mile" (B 81).

checkerbacker: *n.* downy woodpecker [*Dendrocopus pubescens*] (A). (J 1:73) [W.NC, DARE]

cheer: [*n.*,] variant of *chair.* Also Ill., S.Car., N.Eng., Ky. (A). "Yeou cayn't help a-havin' bad thoughts come inter yer head, but yeou hain't no necessity [K edited in "call"] fer ter set 'em a cheer" (Frost 314) (J 2:641). "Set you a cheer" (J 4:723). "When she [a pregnant woman] sot down on a cheer, her knees hardly showed " (J 1:288). (C 2)

chimbley or **chimley:** [*n.*,] variant[s] of *chimney.* Also W.Res., Ill.,

Kan., N.Eng., Ky. (A). (C1) "You can set by the fire and spit out through the chimbley" (B 323).

chinch: *n.* bed-bug. [*Cimex lectularius,* not the chinch bug (*Blissus leucopterus*) since "chinch" is consistently listed with "vermin" (J 1:75, 2:642).] Also La., Ill., Ky. (A). [Chiefly S., S.Midl., DARE]

chinch weed: [*n.* aromatic herb.] "Smells like bedbugs" (J 1:67). [In one of K's seasonal lists of plants he records:] Sept. 28. Chinch weed. Leaves turning to claret and maroon. A rather handsome foliage plant with disagreeable odor (J 1:69).

chip in: [*v.* to contribute.] So three men, let us say, will "chip in" five or ten dollars apiece, and purchase a second-hand still (B 128). [A metaphor based on poker; DA cites various colloquial uses.]

chisel down: [1.] *v. phr.* [to] beat down. "I *chiseled him down* right smart on the coffee business" (A; J 2:459). [2. *v. phr.*] "to bring down to earth" (C 2). (J 2:642s) [Related to "chisel," meaning "to cheat"; W. DAE]

chist: *n.,* variant of *chest.* Also Ill., N.Eng., Ky. (A). "I've got a hurtin' in my chist" (J 2:475). "Give her some easin' powder for that hurtin' in her chist" (B 299). "a thumpin'-chist" [a box] (B 136). (C 2)

chitten wood: [*n. phr.,* variant of *chittam wood* or *chittinwood*; DARE suggests several types according to locales; probably the one K would have encountered is the smoke tree, *Cotinus obovatus.*] (J 1:71).

choppers: [*n. pl.* the men in a logging crew who] "select, fell, and cut the logs" (Springer 92, 94) (D 1). [Listed under "cutting crew":] 1 chopper (J 2:642y).

chuck: [*n.* a cut of meat, usually from the neck and/or shoulder.] [He] drew out a chuck of salt pork, and began slicing it with his jackknife (B 75).

chunk: [*n.* a solidly built or heavy-set person.] "He arrested Tom Hayward, a chunk of a boy, that was scared most fitified and never resisted more'n a mouse" (B 170). [Also KY, DARE]

chup: [*n.*] Acadian flycatcher [*Empidonax virescens*]; bird found in thickets (J 26:54).

church: *v.t.* to expel from a congregation (A; J 4:775). Sometimes a man is "churched" for breaking the Sabbath (B 346). "They churched Pitt for tale-bearin'" (B 356). [Chiefly S.Midl., DARE]

church house: *n.* the church building itself. Also Kan. (A). (J
2:601; 4:775) [Chiefly S., S.Midl., DARE]

chute: [n. a narrow funnel in rapids on the river.] "Jams" [occur
frequently at spots] "commonly called 'chutes,' . . . generally
narrow, crooked, and precipitous descents of the river, forming, consequently, foaming and turbulent rapids, and frequently terminating in most dangerous eddies and
whirlpools" (Fraser 302). "Chutes" [are scenes] "of fearful mu-
tilation and loss of life" (Fraser 312) (D 1). [Widespread—in
Chicago's old amusement park, Riverview, an early version of
the "flume" water rides was called "Shoot the Chutes."]

cinniment or **cinnyment:** [*n.*, variant of *cinnamon.*] "His cinniment and vennyline" (J 10:82). [J 2:241 reads:] Pete's "cinnyment and vennyline" [i.e. vanilla].

citizen: *n.* a native: as distinguished from *furriner.* Also Ky. (A).
"I alus heerd he was a good citizen" (C 2). (J 2:642, J 6)

civet cat: [*n.*] little striped skunk (J 26:56). [In the fur trade it is the
little spotted skunk (*Spilogale putorius*) rather than the common
or striped skunk (*Mephitis mephitis*) which is known as civet cat;
see Palmer.]

clar: [1. *adj.* certain.] "I ain't right clar in my mind as to B.M. raelly
ownin' that property" (J 18:29). [2. *v.i.* to become clear, especially to be free of cloudiness.] "So, when it blows like this,
they [the bears] stay at home and suck their paws till the
weather clars" (B 79). [3. *v.t.* to remove, to make clear.] "Thar,
I've cl'ared me a patch and grubbed hit out" (B 36). [4. *adv.* all
the way, completely.] "He slammed clar out on the floor" (J
2:164). "We followed him clar over to the Spencer Place" (B
106). [DARE lists all four uses and labels them S. and S.Midl.]

clever: *adj.* accommodating; good-hearted. Also Ill., Neb., Ky.
(A; C 2). Clever [means] obliging (B 370). [Formerly NEng, now
S., S.Midl., DARE]

cleverly: *adv.* fully. "He wasn't *cleverly* grown—just a slick-faced
boy" (A; J 1:298). [Also TN, CT, DARE]

clift: *n.* [variant of] cliff. Also Ill., N.Eng., Ky. (A). "Pringle's a-been
horse throwed down the clift" (B 299). (C 2; J 2:642) [Also **rock clift**;
listed among pleonasms, B 360] "I fell over a rock clift" (B 106).

clim: [*v.*, variant of *climbed.*] "The bear clim a tree" (B 106). (B 358)
[Other forms include:] **"clem(b)** climbed. 'He clem(b) a tree' "

(C 3), **clomb** from Fox's list of Chaucer terms (J 2:489), and **clum** (C 1; J: 2:489.]

climb down: [*v.i.* to descend.] Hour after hour they "climb down" (B 139).

close: [*adj.* near or dear.] "His wife is very *close* to my wife. They are good friends." (W.E. B[ird], Head, English Dept. C.S.N.S. [Cullowhee State Normal School]) 3 July 1926 (C 11).

clo'se: [*n.*, variant of *clothes*.] "She was *battlin'* clo'se" (A).

clus or **cluss:** [*adv.*, variants of *close*.] (B 352). "A man cain't lay cluss enough to you" (B 103).

coal: *n.* charcoal. —**fire coal**, a glowing ember (A). "Bring a coal to light his pipe" (C 2). [DAE suggests that the plural *coals* is more frequently used to refer to embers or charcoal.]

cock-a-hoop: [*adj.* intoxicated.] "And him all cock-a-hoop with the Doctor's liquor" (J 23:70).

cock-loft: [*n.* a loft.] "Sometimes a cock-loft over the living room is used as a bunk room" (J 2:375). [Old fashioned, DARE]

cock-lord: [*n.* a name like "cock-o-the-rock"; rooster-like.] "All right, Mr. Uppity Cock-Lord, I've got your number" (J 18:27).

cockyolly bird: [*n.* a child's word, reference uncertain.] "I shot a great big cockyolly bird once't with my bow and arrer" (said by a child) (J 4:56).

coggled up: *p*[*art*]. *phr.* rickety; wobbly. "That's the most *coggled up* far [fire—K] I ever seed" (A). "This is the wust coggled-up fire I ever seed, to fry by" (B 75). [K suggests that the term is a Scotticism (B 354).]

coil: [*n.*] The word coil is variously pronounced quile, querl, or quorl (B 352). [See also those spellings.]

cold bite: [*n.* a cold supper.] [She] said she could give us "a cold bite." And she did not even warm the coffee (B 226).

cold slice: [*n.* term listed under "cooking" but not explained; it is followed by a quote (which may be related) that suggests our "leftovers":] "When one arises from such a table he is fit for any crime" (J 2:421).

collogued: [*v.* to tell secrets;] archaic form (J 2:597). "They all set in and collogued together" (J 3:1001). [Another instance of a learned or literary word which seems to have been part of the App. mountaineer's active vocabulary. S.Midl., DARE]

come: [1. *v. preterite,* variant of *came.*] "Hit come into her head to
. . ." [i.e., she considered] (J 2:641). [2. *v.* to begin] "Hit might
come a shower tonight" (J 1:38). "Hit comes on to rain" (J 2:611).
[Cf. **come it, come on.**]

come back by: [*v. phr.* to call again.] (J 2:642).

come clear: [*v. phr.* to confess.] He will come clear in court (B 267).

come grass, come June: [i.e. as of next spring, next June, etc.]
"You remember the big storm three year ago, *come grass,* when
the cattle all huddled up" (B 78; J 2:629). The hillsmen say "a
year come June" (B 370; J 2:629). "Come a-Wednesday" (J
2:629).

come it: [1. *idiomatic* for "it happened," "it came to pass."] "How
come it was this: he done me dirt" (B 371). [2. *v.* to bear, to
stand] "I love strong coffee, but when I get on the down-go
I cain't hardly come it" (A).

come on: [*v. phr.* begin/begun; listed under "dialectal idioms."
"Hit comes on to rain" (MacG[owan]) (J 1:38; 2:611). "I had it in
head to plow to-day, but hit's come on to rain" (B 371).

come, widdy widdy: [call for ducks and geese] (J 2:371).

common: [1.] *adj.* ordinarily, as in the phrase **in a common way.**
"*In a common way* he's generally in here by the five of a
mornin'" (A). [2. *adj.* usual, ordinary] "How's the mast this
year?" / "Better 'n common" (J 2:361). "Howdy Tom, How's
your folks?" / "'Bout as common. How are you." / "I'm not
much" (J 10:83).

company: [*n.*] a boarder is called "company" (J 4:719). [Also ME,
NH, DARE]

confidence: *v.t.* to place confidence in. "I don't *confidence* them
dogs much" (A; B 356). "I don't confidence much in him" (C 2).
"That larned me that you needn't to confidence a mule" (Parks)
(J 10:84). [Chiefly S.Midl., DARE]

conk or **konkus:** [*n.*] "There is a cancerous disease peculiar to the
pine tree, to which the lumbermen give the name 'conk' or
'konkus'" (Springer 99) (D 1). "The conk or bracket seen on
affected trees is the fruiting organ" (Forest Service 15).

conkesy or **conchy:** [*adj.*] "wood decayed by a fungus growth" [is
called "conchy"] (Springer 99) (D 2). [See also **doated, doted,**
or **dozed wood.**]

consarn: [*v.*, variant of *concern;* listed with **fixin'** under "words with many meanings," none of which are given in J 2:605.] "You're a mighty busy somebody about things that don't consarn ye" (MacGowan 45) (J 2:605).

considerably: *adv.* for the most part. "My parents were *considerably* Scotch." Also Ky. (A). [Cf. "My foreparents war principally Scotch" (B 429).]

constancy: [*n.*, listed but not defined under "coinages" in J 2:601; DARE notes this term in the adverbial phrase "as a constancy," meaning habitually, and gives the following quote: "I can't do it as a constancy."]

contentious: [*adj.* quarrelsome.] "What makes you so blamed contentious?" (B 75). [Listed under "Traits, disposition" in J 2:642.] (J 6) [Another instance of a learned or literary word in the active vocabulary of the App. mountaineer.]

contrary: [1. *adj., adv.* unfavorable/ unfavorably.] "When the wind blows 'contrary' the house is filled with smoke, and cooking is difficult if not impossible" (J 2:373; cf. B 323). [2. *v.* to upset] "I didn't do nary thing to contrary her" (B 357). [Chiefly S.Midl., DARE]

co-oborate: [*v.* to corroborate.] "Co-oborate the testimony" (J 2:639).

cookee: [*n.*] "cook's assistant," (Springer 172). "From 'cook's mate' to 'hewer' was from the bottom to the top of the chain of men [in a lumber camp]" (Fraser 27) (D 1). The cookee banged his poker on a piece of iron swung from a string to call all hands to dinner (B 232). [Widespread, loggers' term, also listed under "camp crew":] Cook, 2 Cookees (J 2:642y).

cookery crib: [*n.* a portable galley; logs are bound together into cribs or rafts and floated down river; that which carries the provisions for the men is the cookery crib.] "If you can manage to get on the 'cookery crib,' which carries all the provisions and cooking utensils, then you may consider yourself quite safe, as it is constructed with all the skill and care that the most experienced raftsmen can bestow" (Fraser 341) (D 1).

cooking: [*v.* to distill/ distilling.] Here many a dismal hour of night is passed when there is nothing to do but to wait on the "cooking" (B 131).

'coon or **coon:** [1. *n.* raccoon (*Procyon lotor*).] " 'coon skins" (B 33). [2.] *v.t.* to steal. "I had to *coon* an ace of hearts" (A; J 4:755). [Also IL, KY, DARE] [3.] *v.i.* to creep like a coon, clinging close. "I *cooned* acrost on a log." Also Ill., KY. (A; C 1). [S., S.Midl., DARE]

cooter: [1. *n.*] a box-tortoise (B 277). Cooter C[ree]k. (J 26:76). [2. *v.* moving like a turtle, lazying around] The noun is turned into a verb with an ease characteristic of the mountaineers. . . . "I'm jest cooterin' around" (B 277; J 4:734). "Sam orter be cooterin' around some'ers" (J 4:722). (J 2:597) [Chiefly S.App., DARE; DARE believes the verb is a Scotticism and therefore unrelated to the noun, but it certainly seems a metaphoric extension in the use above; cf. **brogue**]

coot up: *v. phr.* to revive. "After the rope broke they *cooted him up* and hung him sure enough next time" (A).

corkus: *n.*, variant of *caucus*. Also W.Res., Kan., N.Eng. (A). (B 351)

corncracker: [*n.*] a mill "no larger than a hackney coach. Stones grind a bushel of corn a day, and are left to themselves" (Ziegler) (J 2:453). (J 1:10)

corndodger: [*n.* "a cake of corn bread often shaped by hand and fried on a griddle, baked in an oven, etc. . . . served with cabbage or greens" (Webster's Third).] "Upon accepting an invitation to dine, the water was turned upon the wheel of the mill close by, and fresh meal was soon served in the shape of a hot corndodger" (Carrington) (J 2:453). [Chiefly S., S.Midl., DARE]

corner men: [*n.* men who notch the logs and fit them into place to make a square corner in building cabins or other log structures; cf. DA.] The mountain home of to-day is the log cabin of the American pioneer . . . a pen that can be erected by four "corner men" in one day and is finished by the owner at his leisure (B 314).

corners: [*n. pl.* in square dancing, the dancer who is not one's partner but next to one, at the corner of the square.] "Eight hands up and go to the left; half and back; corners turn; partners sash-i-ate" (Haney) (B 337).

corner-tree: [*n.* a tree used as a boundary marker in surveying.]

He and a preacher had marked a false corner-tree which fig-
ured in an important land suit. On cross examination he was
asked: . . . "Do you consider it consistent with his profession
as a minister of the Gospel to forge corner-trees?" "Aw Sir,"
replied the witness, "religion ain't got nothin' to do with corner-trees!" (B 346-47). [The quote is attributed to Adam Wilson
in J 4:829.]

cornfeed: *v.t.* to feed (hogs) with corn (A). Dilly Welch has good
meat; she "gentles" pigs; "corn-feeds them" (J 2:366). (J 6) (C 2)

corn in the milk: [*adj. phr.* fresh or soft, juicy corn.] "When corn is
in the milk, bake thin pone in 15 minutes. Later when corn is
half hard, add a little soda and bake 20 minutes" (J 2:403).

corn juice: [*n.* corn liquor, white lightnin'.] "Corn *juice* is about all
we can tote around over the country and git cash money for" (B
123). [Also TN, W., DARE]

corn pone: [*n.* corn bread baked in a small, oval loaf.] Corn pone,
usually mixed up with nothing but meal, salt, and water,
though sometimes with sour milk; baked in Dutch oven, or in a
cast iron spider (J 2:419).

corp: *n.*, variant of *corpse*. Also S.Car. (A).

co't: [*n.*, variant of *court;* holding court = courting.] "When yo're
a-holdin co't and sech-like maybe you'll want to shet the do'
sometimes—" (J 2:376). [Michael Montgomery notes that this
is a "very odd citation for a mt. speaker." K has a number of
other examples of r-lessness; perhaps the result of hearing
Coastal Southern from someone who moved into the area. He
acknowledges the rarity of "Do'," "Yo'," etc. (B 355)]

cotch or **cotched:** [*v.*, variants of *caught*] "I cotch hell from the
woman" (J 4:855). "I cotch a rabbit" (J 4:749). "She cotched him
by the ye'r [ear]" (J 1). cotch (in all tenses) or cotched (B 358).

counterpin or **countirpin:** *n.*, variant[s] of *counterpane* [a bed-
spread]. Also Ky. (A). "countirpin" (C 2). (J 2:399) [Chiefly S.,
S.Midl., DARE]

county site: [*n.*] county seat (A; C 2). "I'd haffter walk nineteen
miles out to the railroad, pay seventy cents the round trip to the
county-site" (B 396). [Chiefly S.App., DARE]

coupling: [1.] *n.* joint of the sternum. "Chop through the *coupling*
of that bear." [Not as in Oxf. E.D.—K] (A). [2.*n.* "the part of the

body that joins the forequarters to the hindquarters" (Webster's Third).] "That hoss is short in the coupling" (J 2:361).

couplin' pole: [*n. phr.* the pole joining a team of horses.] "That road's so crooked a horse steps over the couplin' pole" [i.e., he must turn at right angles, at least—but this is comic hyperbole] (J 1:322).

courting: *pres. part.* attending court; litigating. "Bill, are they *courtin'* up there yit?" Also Kan. (A).

court week: [*n. phr.* the week in which court is in session.] During "court week" . . . when the hotels at the county-seat are overcrowded with countrymen (B 293). "Court-week" draws bigger crowds than a circus (B 393).

cove: [*n.* a shut-in, small valley] (J 2:338). "Laney wouldn't stay in Cades Cove as long as lightning'd lay on a limb" (J 2:429).

cove farm: [*n.*] a farm "in the cove or hollow at the mouth of a 'branch'" (Vincent, "Retarded," 3) (J 2:338).

coverlid: [*n.*] "counterpane (Mrs. Victor Brown, Aug. 5, 1926)" (C 11).

cow-brute: [*n.* a bull] Brute [is restricted] to a bovine (B 369). Pleonasms are abundant . . . cow-brute (B 360). (J 2:361) [See also **brute**.]

cowcumber: [*n.*, variant of *cucumber*] "Mrs. Keller quoting her grandmother. July 22, 1926" (C 11).

cow slobber: [*n.* spiderwort.] Laney says that in Missouri the plant called cow-slobber (*Tradescantia virginica*, also *T. rosea*) is used for this purpose [i.e. snake bite] (J 2:473).

crabs: [*n.* body lice, *Pediculus humanus humanus.*] "When you got lice in your balls, you got crabs; when they git in your eyebrows, they got you" (J 2:435).

crack o' day: [*n.* dawn] (J 2:629). [Cf. **peep o' day**]

crap: [*n.*, variant of *crop*] "I can raise me two or three severe craps" (B 36). "I can't make a crap on no sich land" (J 2:342). (J 2:348)

crawley: [*n.*] coral berry (*Symphoricarpos s.*) (J 26:35).

creel: *v.t.* to wrench. "I *creeled* my knee (neck, back)" (A).

c'reen: *v.i.* to bend the body to one side. "I noticed a catch in my back ever' time I c'reened" (A).

creosut: [*n.* variant of *creosote.*] For tooth ache—burn writing paper on a plate, throw away the char, apply the brown oily residue to cavity of tooth. "It's the creosut does the work" (Bob) (J 2:470).

crep: [*v.* variant of *crept.*] "I crep up on him" (J 4:749).

crib: [*n.* a log raft; loggers' term.] "The timber 'sticks' are bound together . . . into 'cribs' . . . these cribs are again bound together, though in a manner easily to be unloosed, into 'drams,' or 'bands,' . . . containing about twenty-five cribs; these drams again bound together make up a 'raft'" (Fraser 340) (D 1).

crips: *v.t.* to crisp. "Smoke come in and *cripsed* up the aidges of the leaves." In N.H., Mass., also **crips, cripsy,** *adj.* (A).

critter: [*n.* variant of *creature;* almost any animal life, even insects; K suggests that "Critter and beast are usually restricted to horse and mule" (B 369), and in J 6 the term is listed under "livestock," but his own quotations do not always reflect this distinction.] "ridin' critter"—a horse (J 2:361). Blooded cattle thrive in the valleys, but the backwoodsman does not want "critters that haffter be gentled and hand-fed" (B 43). "you can search these mountains through with a fine-tooth comb and you wunt find ary critter as has a good word to say for the revenue" (B 170). [In another passage an illiterate minister attacks "them acorn-fed critters (i.e., comfortable Christians) that has gone New Light over in Cope's Cove" (B 341); see also **beast**]

crockery: [*n.* earthenware pots, dishes.] "I can't afford that [a rumpus] where there's two hundred dollars' worth of crockery lyin' handy" (B 233). [Widespread, DARE]

crooks: [*n.* bent or curved wood.] The runners [of sleds] are usually made of natural sourwood crooks, this timber being chosen because it wears very smooth and does not fur up nor splinter (B 42).

crope: [*preterite* of *creep;* Fox lists as a Chaucer word, J 2:489.]

cross-spelling: [*n.* misspelling.] (J 4:767, 2:601).

cross-vine: [*n.*] tendrilled Trumpet-flower (*Begonia crucigera*) (J 2:615). [Flowers] Apr. June. Orange and yellow. Used for "tea" (J 26:15).

cryke: [*n.,* variant of *creek;* it is not clear what difference in pronunciation, if any, is implied; another "Chaucer word" from Fox, J 2:489.]

cuckold: *v.t.* In the usual literary sense [i.e. to commit adultery with another man's wife is to "cuckold" him.] (A). [Listed under "literary terms" in J 2:599.] I had supposed the words cuckold and moon-calf had none but literary usage in America, but we often hear them in the mountains, cuckold being employed both as a verb and a noun (B 361). (J 4:843)

cucumber: [*n.* cucumber magnolia (*Magnolia acuminata*).] "Lumbermen now pay 40¢ a thousand for cutting soft woods, such as poplar, cucumber, and ash; 50¢ to 60¢ for hard woods (J 2:463). [Flowers] May-June. Greenish yellow (J 26:22).

cud: [1.] *n.* quid. Also N.Eng., W.Res., Ill. (A). "Have a cud of baccy ma'am" (C 2). [2.] *v.t.* to chew (A). "Hit *doesn't* look nice to see a woman cuddin' this home-made tobacco, that's strong enough to kill a snake, and squirtin' ambeer around everywhere" (J 2:438).

cull: [*n.* bad timber; loggers' term. "A log which is thrown away as scrap because it is not of useful quality. Still in use" (L. Monteith)] "rotten, twisted piece [of timber] that is hardly worth taking to market" (Fraser 302) (D 1).

cur: [*n.* usually a dog of mixed but indeterminate breed, but K has one man speak of a "plumb cur" and adds, "a cur ain't got no dew-claws" as if a specific mongrel type were involved (B 80-81).] "The Plott curs are the best [bear dogs]: that is, half hound, half cur—though what we-uns calls the cur, in this case, raelly [sic] comes from a big furrin dog that I don't rightly know the breed of. . . . talk as you please about a streak o' the cur spilin' a dog; but I know it ain't so—not for bear fightin' in these mountains" (B 80).

curiosity or **cur'osity:** *n.* object exciting curiosity. "He was a plumb *curiosity*." Also N.Eng., W.Res., La., Ill., Ky. (A; J 2:637 reads "cur'osity").

curoner: *n.*, variant of *coroner* (A).

cuss: [1. *n.* a slang expression, roughly equal to "critter," a person or another creature; the tone may vary from anger to grudging admiration:] "You onry cuss!" (J 10:82). "But he's a foxy cuss" [said of a deer] (B 91). [2. *v.t.* cuss = curse; cussed = accursed]

One house . . . will be so small that "you cain't cuss a cat in it 'thout gittin' ha'r in yer teeth" (B 323). "Durn you, Bill Cope, [a hunchback] you're so cussed crooked a man cain't lay cluss enough to you to keep warm" (B 103).

cuss fight: [*n.* a verbal battle; a swearing contest] "Him and Sam fell out and had a cuss fight" (J 4:853). "By that time the land will be so poor hit wouldn't raise a cuss-fight" (B 36). [S., S.Midl., DARE]

cut: [*v.t.* to hurt, to cut down to size, as in contemporary slang] "It cut him to the gizzard" (J 4:785).

cut a pigeon-wing: [*v. phr.* to perform a dance step, the pigeon wing.] He cut a pigeon-wing, twirled around with an imaginary banjo, and sang (B 81).

cut nail: [*n.* a nail with a square tip; in "tooth-jumpin'":] "You take a cut nail (not one o' those round wire nails) and place its squar p'int agin the ridge of the tooth, jest under the edge of the gum. Then jump the tooth out with a hammer" (B 301).

cut shines: [*v. phr.* to play tricks, monkeyshines; to misbehave] "If you cut any shines, you're goin' home in a pine box" (J 23:80).

cut up: [*v. phr.*] "misbehave. 'He kept a cuttin' up in church'" (C 3).

cut up copper: *v. phr.* to destroy a still [made of copper]. "Last winter there came a revenue in here and *cut up* a lot of *copper* on Jones' Creek" (A). (C 2)

cyar: [*n.*, variant of car, automobile] "He threw a full fruit jar out o' the cyar" (J 2:639).

cyards: [*n.*, variant of *cards*] "I gotta me a deck of cyards" (J 2:589; B 351). (J 4:755)

cyarn: *n.*, [variant of] *carrion* (A).

cymblin or **cymling:** [*n.* "a summer squash having scalloped edges" (Webster's Third); listed under "crops" in J 2:642q.; "Swing the Cymblin" is a "play-party" social game (B 338).] [S., S.Midl., DARE]

D

d′: short for *don't.* "I d′know." General (A).

dad-burned: [*past part.* euphemism for *damned.*] "Then the dad-burned gun wouldn't stand roostered [cocked-K]; the feather-spring had jumped out o' place" (B 101). [DAE lists this term as a lower form of colloquialism and provides an example from the TN mts; S.Midl., DARE; cf. **darned**]

daddy: [*n.* father; it isn't clear why K records this under "Relationships" with "Foreparents" (J 2:642p), but Irene Hart and Weaver Taylor report that for their grandparents (roughly the generation of the 1860s or 1870s) "Maw" and "Paw" were common, that in rural areas north of Asheville at the beginning of this century "Pap" or "Pop" might have been preferred, and that "dad" was "the fancy word" and "daddy" might have been rare when K was collecting. Another list in J 1:298, including "Paw," "Pappy," "Dad" with the note "Bob calls his father 'Billy,'" tends to confirm the novelty of "daddy"; DARE lists the term as widespread but somewhat more frequent in S., S.Midl.]

danger: *adj.* dangerous. "That's a powerful *danger* axe" (A). (J 2:642) [W.NC, S.Midl., DARE]

dar: [*v.t.,* variant of *dare.*] When the mountain boy challanges his mate: "I dar ye—I ain't afeared!" his verb [i.e. dar] and participle are [traceable to] . . . the time of Layamon (B 362). [Also AL, MS, DARE]

darned: [*past part.,* euphemism for *damned.*] " . . . I wanted to get up and lick the whole darned settlement" (J 4:775). [Widespread, DAE]

dauncy: *adj.* fastidious; squeamish [cf. **daunch,** Oxf. E.D.-K]. In Ky., in the sense "dizzy" (A). [Listed in section on eating and cooking with quotes:] "I ain't dauncy." "She's mincy about eatin'" (J 2:429). A remarkable word, common in the Smokies, is dauncy, defined for me as "mincy about eating," which is to say fastidious, over-nice. Dauncy probably is a variant of daunch, of which the Oxford *New English Dictionary* [i.e., OED] cites but one example, from the *Townley Mysteries* of *circa* 1460 (B 363). [DAE provides four citations dating from 1864 but defines the word as "frail, sickly, not robust," a definition consistent with the four contexts appearing there but unsuited to the ones cited above. DARE lists both meanings and locates the former in S.Midl. and the latter in the N.Midl.]

dawtie: [*adj.* small; listed as a "diminutive" with "bitty": J 2:591.]

dead'nin': *n.* a clearing made by girdling the trees. Also Ky. (A). Practiced not only because it is the easiest and speediest way of clearing, but also because it prevents such trees as chestnut, buckeye, and basswood from sprouting from the stump. See 1905 Forestry Service Bulletin 33:20 (J 2:340) "Many of these steep mountain fields are abandoned before the girdled trees fall to ground." (See Wilson in 1901 Report) (J 2:344). (C 2; listed J 2:340, 603, J 6) [DAE provides an illustrative sentence from Morley's *Carolina Mountains* (1913) as well as seven others dating from 1791. Chiefly S.Midl., DARE]

dead water: [*n. phr.* old stale water.] Water that has stood overnight is "dead water," hardly fit to wash one's face in (B 306). [Cf. DAE, which refers to "water in which no current is perceptible."]

declar: [*v.*, variant of *declare*, rhyming with *are* rather than *air*] "I declar I nigh sultered" (J 2:475).

deedies: [*n. pl.* young offspring of chicken; listed under "poultry" in J 2:371, and as a "coinage" in J 2:601; Carrie Witherbee informs us that "when the old mother hen hatched out baby chicks," her mother would call the chicks "deedies"; listed as S. in both DA and DAE; S., S.Midl., DARE.]

deestric': [*n.* variant of *district*.] "She got, I reckon, about the toughest deestric' in the ceounty, which is sayin' a good deal" (B 468).

den: [*v.i.* to make a den, to hibernate.] "the Tennessee side of the mountain is powerful steep and laurely, so't man nor dog cain't git over it in lots o' places; that's whar the bears den" (B 79). [DA and DAE list this meaning and add "den up." Esp. S., S.Midl., DARE]

denote: [*v.* to be a sign of, to indicate] "Them clouds denote rain" (B 361). "That sky denotes snow" (J 1:38). [An example of a learned word in general use.]

desert: [*past. part.*] short for *deserted.* "A very *desert*-lookin' place" (A). [Listed under "Quaint idioms" and "Obsolete" in J 2:605.] (C 2)

devilmaint: *n.,* Variant of *devilment* (A; C 2). [Chiefly S., S.Midl., DARE]

devillin'or dev'lin': [*vbl. n.* being naughty, bedeviling.] "Bob [who is playing solitaire and refusing to help his wife], now, quit yer dev'lin'" (J 1:296). devillin' (J 2:605) [Chiefly S., S.Midl., DARE]

devil's shoestring: [*n.*] cat gut, goat's rue (*Cracca virginiana*). [Flowers] June-July. Yellowish-purple. Tough stringy roots (J 26:30). [DARE states that the use of this term to refer to goat's rue or its roots is chiefly S. or S.Midl.; in NC it refers to the hobble bush.]

dew-claw: [1. *n.* the functionless toe on the inner side of a dog's leg.] "A cur ain't got no dew-claws—them dogs has" (B 81). [2. *adj.* having dew-claws.] "Mebbe you-uns don't know that a dew-clawed dog is snake proof" (B 8l). [DARE finds nothing exceptional about the use of the term with respect to dogs but cites several instances in which the term refers to parts of the human anatomy.]

dew pizen: [*n.*] presumably the poison of some weed, which dissolved in dew, enters the blood through a scratch or abrasion. . . . "Dew pizen comes like a risin', and laws-a-marcy how it does hurt!" (B 303; a fuller report attributed to M.B. appears in J 2:471.] (J 2:597) [Also KS, DA; S.Midl., esp. S.App., DARE]

dib: [*n.* bit.] A tablespoonful [of liquor], in company, was his limit. Stomach so weak it could not stand more at a time. Just "a little dib," you know, now and then, to tone it up (B 200). [Cf. **dip.**]

differ: [1. *n.* difference. "Hit don't make no *differ.*" Slang [K's label] (A; B 357; J 2:641). "They mean nigh about the same thing, only there's a differ" (B 94). "What differ does it make how come it? (J 2:642). [Chiefly S., S.Midl., DARE] [2. **differ of a** appears to be a variant of "different" and to function adjectivally, as in:] "In a *differ* of a place" (A; J 2:642w). differ of (J 2:601) [3.] *v.i.* to make a difference. "It didn't *differ* what that cow [weighed] (A). "Hit don't differ" (C 2). [Also TN, DAE; S.App., DARE]

dilitary: *adj.* [variant of] *dilatory.* Also Ill., Kan. (A). "She's so dilitary!" (B 361). "He was the damndest dilitariest about it!" (J 2:637). [Another learned word, mispronounced but apparently in common use; S.App., DARE]

dingy: [*adj.* dark, threatening.] "The elements looks a little dingy; I think hit's goin' ter rain" (J 10:83).

dip: [*n.* small amount, pinch.] "Give me a dip o' your snuff" (J 4:733). [Cf. **dib**]

dirt, in the phrase **"done me dirt"**: [*n.* harm, wrong—especially with respect to one's reputation] "How come it was this: he done me dirt" (B 371; J 10:83). [DAE refers to this expression as slang of American origin and suggests a wide distribution, as does DARE.]

disablest: *superl.* antonym of *ablest.* "We're all strong enough to work, except Johnson; he's the *disablest* one of the family (A). (J 2:60l)

discarn or discern: *v.t.* to perceive. "He was blind, but he could *discern* when the sun was shinin'" (A). "discarn. To perceive." (Cox) (C 2). [Bird regularized Cox's spelling when he copied his list in C 3; perhaps K followed Bird in A, rather than his earlier informant, Cox, and *discarn* is more accurate; at any rate, this is another instance of a learned or literary word in the mountaineer's active vocabulary.]

disconfit: *v.t.* to inconvenience. "I hope it has not *disconfit* you very bad" (A; J 4:741; B 368). To disfurnish or discon*fit* means to incommode (B 368). "Don't let it disconfit you" (C 2). (J 2:601) [Cf. **discomfit,** a learned word mispronounced but in general spoken use. Chiefly S.App., DARE]

disencourage: *v.t.* to discourage (A). (C 2; J 2:603) [Chiefly S.Midl., DARE]

disfarnish or disfurnish: *v.t.* to deprive (oneself). "Don't *disfurnish* yourself" (A; J 4:741, 10:83). To disfurnish or or discon*fit* means to incommode (B 368). "disfarnish. To deprive" (C 2). (J 2:603) [S., S.Midl., DARE]

disgust: *v.t.* to have a distaste for. "I *disgust* bad likker" (A; B 356). [DARE lists this as a relic form found in S.App., Ozarks.]

disremember: [*v.t.* to forget.] "I mind about that time, Doc; but I disremember which buryin' ground they-all planted ye in" (B 78). (J 2:603) [Scattered, but chiefly S., S.Midl., DARE]

dittany: [*n.* mint used as herbal tea.] stone mint (*Cunila origanoides*). [Flowers] Aug.-Sept. Purple-pink. Very aromatic, used for "tea" (J 26:39). On being told that "store tea" cost a dollar a pound, the mountaineer responded that] he preferred dittany or sassafras or goldenrod (B 98). "There's no tea you buy in the stores that's better than this table-tea" (Mrs. B[arnett]) (J 2:433). Recommended for snakebite by resident physician at Tate's Springs, Tenn. (Ingram) (J 2:481).

div: [1.] *pret.* of *dive.* Hurried. "I *div* right out and hired me a cook." [Also] Ky. (A). (C 2) [2. variant as above of "*dove*," used conventionally:] "The bear div down into a sink-hole with the dogs a-top o' him" (B 101). (B 358) [Occasionally S., S.Midl, NEng, DARE]

do (one's) do: *v. phr.* [to do what comes naturally] "The fall of the year is when sweet-potatoes *does their do*" (A; J 2:359). [Chiefly S., S.Midl., DARE]

do': *n.* short for *door.* Rare. Also La., Ky. (A). (C 2) "Ef ye need light, open the do'" (MacGowan) (B 305). Do', Flo', Mo', Yo', Co'te, Nuss, are rare, except where mountains join lowlands (J 2:490). [Chiefly S., DARE] [K insists that all r's are pronounced (B 355)].

doated: [*part.* rotten timber.] Said of trees dead at the top. Also applied to lumber prepared from wood not exactly decayed but unsound to the extent of being not springy and tough enough (J 20:3). [Has English dialect authority according to Fox in J 2:489.] [See also **doted, dozed wood.**] [DARE has "doty" and "dozy" with this meaning, distribution S., S.Midl.]

doctor medicine: [*n. phr.* medicine] differentiated from home remedies (A). "Not herbs" (C 2). "My teeth are all rotted from takin' doctor medicine" (J 2:475). [S.App., DARE]

dodge: [1. *v.*] "to evade" (C 2). [2. *n.*, in the phrase,] **on the dodge.** Given to dodging or evading, especially the police. "His boy was sorter *on the dodge.*" Also Ky. (A).

dog hobble: [*n.* a low shrub, growing very thick; supposedly hunting dogs would get tangled (hobbled) in it, hence the name.] On Hazel Creek this name is given to the Hobble Bush or American Wayfaring Tree (*Viburnum alnifolium*). Elsewhere it is given to *Leucothoe* (Fox 229; Peterson 135; Mathews, *Wild-flowers*, 446; Mathews, *Trees*, 392) (J 1:66). [Chiefly S.App., DARE]

dog hook: [n., loggers' term; not defined, but used with **fid hook,** so apparently one of the hooks used to bind chains to logs.] "He [the teamster] examines the chains, lest they should part, and, above all, the objects watched more than any others, the 'fid hook' and the 'dog hook,' the former that it does not work out, the latter that it loose not its grappling hold on the tree" (Springer 107-108) (D 1). [N., NEng, GLakes, NW, DARE]

dog trot: [*n.* the open area between two cabins joined by a common roof.] The double log cabin has a space between, roofed, serving as dining-room most of the year. "Two pens with an entry between" (Miles 77). "In Ky. this entry is called a 'dog trot'" (MacClintock) (J 2:373). (J 2:601) [Chiefly S., S.Midl., DARE]

[common] domestic: [*n.* homespun or floursack cloth.] "Well, when they dressed up to come to church the men—grown men—'d have shirts made of this common domestic, with the letters AAA on their backs; and them barefooted, and some without hats, but with three yards of red ribbon around their necks" (B 312). [Entries in DA and DAE suggest a widespread usage. DARE limits the use to S., S.Midl.]

dominecker chicken: [*n.*] (from *dominica*—K) [the breed of chicken named Dominican after the order of monks, a black & white barred variety] A large white fowl, black-spotted. Also La., Ill., S.Car., Kan., Ky. (A). (J 2:371, 642o) [Scattered, but chiefly S.Midl., DARE]

dominecker gnat: [*n.*] a punkie [or biting midge; any of the family *Ceratopogonidae*] (A). (J 1:75, 2:597) [Also TN, DARE]

done: [1. *v.* variant of *did* in expressions like these:] "an' it done come true" (B 104). "He done me dirt" (B 371). [Montgomery suggests that those examples "could well be the intensifying *done* (sense 2)" [2. *v.* variant of *has/have*, as in "he done broke it," or in the following, which K treats as a "pleonasm" and today would probably be regarded as an intensifier:] "I done

done it" (have done it or did do it) (B 359). "I've done growed" (B 98) [Chiefly, S., S.Midl., DARE]

doney or **doney-gal:** [*n.*] (from *doña*) sweetheart (A). A queer term used by Carolina mountaineers, without the faintest notion of its origin, is doney (long *o*) or doney-gal, meaning a sweetheart. Its history is unique. British sailors of the olden time brought it to England from Spanish or Italian ports. Doney is simply *doña* or *donna* a trifle Anglicized in pronunciation. Odd, though, that it should be preserved in America by none but backwoodsmen whose ancestors for two centuries never saw the tides (B 363). (J 1:286, 2:603) [Chiefly S.App., DARE]

doodle-bug: *n.* the ant-lion [*Myrmeleon immaculatus*]; so called because it is said to emerge from its pit if one calls "doodle-bug, doodle-bug." Also La., S.Car., Ky. (A). (C 2; J 2:603) [S., S.Midl., DARE]

door shutter: [listed under "coinages" in J 2:601.] [S.E.Mo., DARE]

doset: *n.* dose. Also Ill., Ky. (A). "I tuk it all at one doset" (J 2:475). [Chiefly S., S.Midl., DARE]

dote: [1.] *n.* wood partly decayed by a fungus (A). "Cut into the dote" (J 1:53). (J 2:642) [2.] *adj.* **dotey** in Ky. (A). "That limb's dotey" (J 1:53). [3.] **doted** p.a. In Me., **dosey** (A). Partially decayed timber (Lewis & Clark 951) (D 1). [DARE lists examples from W.NC, KY, but also NEng, GLakes; see also **doated, dozed.**]

dottle: [*n.* "unburnt and partially burnt tobacco caked in the bowl of a pipe (Webster's Third).] "I wouldn't give the dottle of my pipe for it" (M[rs]. B[arnett].) (J 2:625). [We suspect that K recorded this for the quaintness of the saying or its feminine source rather than for any oddity he might have associated with *dottle,* which though hardly mainstream English is common enough among pipe smokers.]

double-bitt axe: [*n. phr.* two-edged axe, double-bit axe.] "both single and double bitt axes" (J 2:401). [ME, & NW, DARE]

double-teaming: [*v.t.* in fighting, to double up on someone, as in other sports.] There is no compunction about striking foul and very little about "double-teaming" (B 416). And there is no romance about a real mountain feud. It is marked by suave treachery, "double teaming," . . . and general heartlessness and cruelty (B 421). [Chiefly S., DARE]

doublings: [*n.*] In moonshiners' parlance, the liquor of second distillation is called the "doublings." It is in watching and testing the doublings that an accomplished blockader shows his skill, for if distillation be not carried far enough, the resulting spirits will be rank, though weak, and if carried too far, nothing but pure alcohol will result (B 135). [Chiefly S.Midl., DARE]

Dover's powder: [*n. phr.* a brand name of medicinal powder] used to treat colds (J 2:469).

do well by someone: [*v. phr.* to treat fairly in trading.] "He done me pretty well" [treated me fairly—K] (J 2:459).

down-go: *n.* decline in health. "I love strong coffee, but when I get on the down-go I cain't hardly come it." Also Ky. (A). "If [a man is] declining in health, he is on the down-go" (B 368). [S.App., DARE]

dozed wood: [*n. phr.*] rotten wood (J 14:80); such as is decayed by a fungus growth (D 2). Also **dozy** [*adj.*] So decayed as to be soft and useless: said of trees and timber (J 20:3). [See also **doated, doted.**]

draft: [*n.* a brook.] After close study of mountain speech I have failed to discern that the word draft is understood, except in parts of Virginia and Kentucky, where it means a brook (B 294). [Obs., DAE; chiefly App., DARE]

dram: [1. *n.*, loggers' term.] "These cribs are again bound together, though in a manner easily to be unloosed, into 'drams,' or 'bands,' sometimes called, each dram containing about 25 cribs; these drams bound together make up a 'raft'" (Fraser 340) (D 1). [2. a small liquid measure, most frequently of whiskey] "I ginerally, usually take a dram mornin's" (B 360). [Old fashioned, DAE; S.Midl., DARE]

drap, drapped: [1. *v.*, variants of *drop, dropped.*] Examples of a strong preterite with dialectal change of the vowel are . . . drap or drapped [drapped is weak] (B 358). "My new hulls [cartridges—K] fit loose in this old chamber and this one drap [dropped—K] out" (B 101). [2. *metaphor* to die] "Looks like he mought drap off, him bein' weak and right narvish and sick" (B 298). [S., S.Midl., DARE]

draw: *n.* drawing. "Are you making a draw of the fence?" (A). [W.NC, DARE]

draw bar: *n.* a removable bar in a fence (A; C 2). "You can meet me down at the draw-bars" (J 4:885). [Formerly NEng, now chiefly S.Midl., DARE]

drawed: [*v.* variant of *drew*.] A weak preterite supplants the proper strong one (B 358). [Esp. S., S.Midl., DARE]

dreamp', dreampt, or **dreamt:** [*v.*, variants of *dreamed*.] Rarely ever heard except among the illiterate" (C 3). "I dreamp' I seen a flock o' black sheep" (J 2:641). "Who dreamt him a good dream?" (B 85). [Chiefly, S., S.Midl., DARE; see also **dremp**.]

drean or **dreen:** [*v.*, variants of *drain*.] "He dreaned all the water out" (C 2). [**dreen** listed as English dialect by Fox (J 2:489).] (J 2:603) [Chiefly S., S.Midl, but occasionally NEng, DARE]

d'reckly: [*adv.* immediately; variant of *directly*.] "Them dogs, I'll get out there an kill 'em d'reckly" (J 2:371). "I'm comin' d'reck'ly" (B 351). [Chiefly S., S.Midl., DARE]

dremp: [*v.* variant of *dreamed*.] "Bill dremp that he seed a lot o' fat meat layin' on the table; an' it done come true" (B 103-104). [See also **dreamp'**]

drink: *v.i.* to discharge the function of drink. "Wonder if that water'd drink?" "That drinks right" (A). (J 2:642) [W.NC, S.W. MO, DARE]

drinkables: [*n.* drinks.] "cold drinkables" [from an advertisement in the Elizabethton, Tennessee, Carter Co. *News* 23 Aug. 1912] (J 2:436). [Though appearing in S. App., this may not be a specifically Smoky Mountain word.]

driv: [*v.*, variant of *drive*] a weak preterite (B 358). [This should be a strong preterite; "K got it backwards," as Montgomery notes, "or rather many of those he calls weak are actually strong, going back to Middle English preterite singular." Widespread, DARE]

drive: [n., loggers' term.] "The first business of the drive is to collect all these scattered timbers and 'boom' them into the main channel of the river" (Fraser 271, 331) (D 1). [N., esp. NEng, DARE]

drivers: [n. the men who drive or ride the timber downstream; loggers' term.] (Fraser, 331) (D 1). [DARE also lists "river driver"; the distribution is N., esp. NEng.]

droger: [*n.* a teamster; loggers' term, from Scots dial. "drogue"] (Springer 144) (D 1). [Widespread among loggers, DAE; formerly NEng, now widespread, DARE]

droll: [*adj.* whimsical or odd.] "He hed his droll way" (J 2:637). [A learned or bookish term in general use among mountaineers. DARE lists this term as English dial. common in S., S.Midl.]

drotted: *p[red]. a[dj].* dratted [euphemism for *damned*]. Also Ky. (A). K may have known of examples in which this functioned as an adjective, perhaps as in "that drotted dog!", but in the journal example that follows, it is adverbial.] "I'm too drotted tired. I'm nigh about giv out" (J 2:631). (J 2:603) [S., S.Midl., DARE]

drouth: [*n.* drought.] "This drouth is very severe; it's even killing the red oaks" (J 23:60). [Scattered but less frequently S., S.Midl., DARE]

drowned lands: [*n. phr.* "flooded bottom land" (E. Monteith)] "where the ground is low-lying, in swamp or marsh, the country on both sides is completely submerged, forming what are called 'lagoons' in the Southern states and in our back woods 'drowned lands'" (Fraser 281) (D 1). [Monteith's recognition suggests "drowned lands" is and was in use in the mountains, even if not the preferred term. DAE lists this as originally American, and the illustrative citations suggest a wide distribution; DARE too offers widespread listings.]

drug: [1. *past. part.* of *drag*, used conventionally] a strong preterite (B 358). [2. specifically, for "harrowed".] Sometimes no harrow was used at all, the plowed ground being "drug" with a big evergreen bough (B 37). "It arter be drug." ("In the mountains they hitch a horse to a log or a large piece of brush and, dragging this over the plowed ground, make shift to smooth it without a harrow" (MacGowan) (J 2:339). [Widespread, DARE]

drugs: *n. pl.*, variant of *dregs.* Also S.Car., N.Y., Ky. (A). [Chiefly S.Midl., DARE]

drummers: [*n. pl.* peddlers.] During "court week" when the hotels at the county seat are overcrowded with countrymen, the luckless drummers who happen to be there have continuous exercise in closing doors (B 293). [Originally American, widespread, DAE; widespread but chiefly S., S.Midl., DARE]

druse: [1. *n*] geode, or a rock covered with crystals. [2. *adj.*] **drusy** covered by or containing crystals (J l8:39).

dry-shod: [*adj.* dry-shoed, without getting one's feet wet.] "I *have* the faith, to walk over that river dry-shod" (B 345).

dude: [*n.* a man; a dandy.] "a slick-faced dude from Knoxville" (B 137). [Widespread, DARE]

duff: [*n.* a bread pudding boiled in a bag.] Upon our return we found the blackberry crop unharvested and had a bag pudding—"duff"—or what you call it (B 59). [Widespread, DAE; DARE lists as coastal NEng. Perhaps K was groping for a word here and settled on one that was from his own vocabulary but not necessarily one in local use.]

dum: [euphemism for *damn*.] "In one of Whit Hensley's traps, dum him!" (B 93).

dummern, pl. **dummerunses:** *n.* woman. "Uncle John Thomas always said dummern; he was born and raised in Mitchell Co. Lots of old people out there said it" (A). In Mitchell County, North Carolina, we hear the extraordinary forms ummern and dummern ("La, look at all the dummerunses a-comin'!") (B 353). [See also **'oman, wimmern, womern.**] [W.NC, DARE]

durn: [euphemism for *damn*.] "Durn this blow, anyhow!" (B 79). "We are too durned poor to do ary one or t'other" (B 122). [Chiefly S., S.Midl., DARE; see also **darned**]

dustin': [*vbl. n.* the smallest portion, a sprinkling of something] Marg walked five miles to the store with a skinny old chicken, last of the flock, and offered to barter it for "a dustin' o' salt" (B 33). [Chiefly S., S.Midl., DARE]

d'ye: [*abbrev.* do ye] "Now d'ye see?" (B 107).

dynymite: [*n.*, variant of *dynamite*] "That gal Omey ain't got a spoonful o' sense" (M.B.). "No, what brains she's got, if 't was dynymite, 't wouldn't blow her nose" (Bob) (J 2:637).

E

ear marks: [*n.* the cuttings made in pigs' ears for quick identification, like cattle brands; the following is a list of terms for registered marks with K's drawings:]

Ear-marks
1. Crop or Smooth-crop.
2. Slit, or Split.
3. Over-bit.
4. Under-bit.
5. Over half-crop.
6. Under half-crop.
7. Over-slope.
8. Under-slope.
9. Crop and slit.
10. Swallow-fork.
11. Round hole.
12. Thief-mark, or Grub (ear cut off close to head).
13. Crop, slit, and under-bit.
14. Over-slope and under-bit.
15. Poplar-leaf (swallow-fork, over-bit, and under-bit).
16. Crop and half-crop.

(J 2:367)

Ear-marks

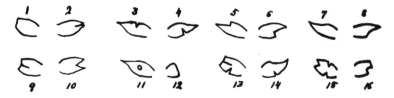

easin' powder: *n.* an opiate (A; C 2). "Cain't you-uns give her some easin'-powder for that hurtin' in her chist?" (B 298). [DARE labels it an analgesic, S.App., cf. **restin' powder** (C 2)]

Easter flower: [*n.*] mountain meadow rue [*Thalictrum polyga-mum*]—a frail elfin thing (J 1:67). [DARE asserts that this name is commonly applied to the daffodil in KY, NC.]

eat: *v.i.* [to taste.] "That eats good." General (A, J 2:429). "Won't you eat some tomatoes?" "They eat sorter" (J 2:428). "This poke salat eats good" (B 356). [Chiefly S., S.Midl., DARE. A related usage meaning "to feed" is cited in DAE: "This land is so good that two or three acres of it will 'eat a family.'" (Morley, *Carolina Mountains*, 1913)]

eddicated: [*adj.*, variant of *educated.*] "My father got all the corn out of his farm that the land would yield and he wasn't eddicated" (Ralph) (J 4:767). [NEng through S., DARE]

edibles: [*n.*] "foodstuffs" [from an ad in the Elizabethton, Tenn. Carter Co. *News*, 23 Aug. 1912] (J 2:436). [The source makes the currency of this in the Smokies dubious.]

edzact: *v.t.* to make precisely right. "Let me study this thing over: then I can edzact it" (A; J 4:765). Our schoolmaster, composing a form of oath for the new mail-carrier, remarked: "Let me study this thing over; then I can edzact it"—a verb so rare and obsolete that we find it in no American dictionary, but only in Murray [i.e. OED] (B 362-63). "Exactly (right)" (C 2) [S.App., Ozarks, DARE; DAE includes the adverb *edzactly*, marked collo-quial, with several citations from KY.]

eet: [*v.t.*, variant of preterite *ate*; from Fox's list] (J 2:489). [S., S.Midl., DARE]

eetch: n., variant of *itch*. "That's eetch-weed; it's good for toe eetch." Also La., Ill., S.Car., Kan., Ky. (A). (B 352) [Cf. **toe eetch,** which in the journals appears to be a synonym for **eetch weed.**]

ef: [*conj.*, variant of *if.*] "Ef ye need light, open the do'" (B 305). "Ef only He'd turn me into a varmint I'd run back tonight!" (B 307). (J 2:642) [Clearly a lowering of the front vowel is indicated here; suggesting a pronunciation as in *teflon;* not an eye dialect spelling.]

'em: [pron., contraction for *them.*] "of 'em that kem [to meeting]" (B 312).

endurin': [1.] *prep.* during. Also S.Car., Ky. (A). [Chiefly S., S.Midl., DARE] [2. *part.* long-lasting.] "the whole endurin' night" (C 2). (J 2:601) [S., S.Midl., DARE; DAE notes the first usage but not the second.]

enjoy: *v.t.* to make happy, [to] amuse. "I'll try to enjoy you, someway" (A; J 4:723). [In B the quote is explained:] Which, being interpreted, means, "I'll entertain you as best I can" (B 272). (C 2; J 2:642) [S.App., Ozarks, DARE]

ensure: *v.t.* to make sure provision for. "The best way to carry a pig is to put it in a tow sack with a hole cut for its nose ensurin' it to breathe" (A; J 2:437).

enthoritate: [*v.t.* to authorize] "The owner enthoritated Big Tom Wilson to sell it" (J 2:459).

entry: [*n.* the unenclosed hallway between the two rooms of a double cabin, also called a "dog-trot."] "A sagging clapboard roof covered its two rooms and the open space between them that we called our "entry" (B 76). [TN, S.App., DARE]

enurf: [*adj.*] variant of *enough*. (A)

'er: [*pron., cont.* for *her.*] "Nobuddy knew 'er death war expected" (Poole 258-61) (J 2:485).

evening: [*n.* afternoon.] Evening, in the mountains, begins at noon instead of at sunset (B 370). [Chiefly S., S.Midl., DARE; S., W., DAE]

every bit: [*adv.* often.] "[The bear] haster stop every bit, and fight" (B 81).

experience: *v.i.* [sic, the citation is a verbal noun] to acquire experience. "X had to begin all over again and do the experiencin' himself" (A). "Now, *I've* hed some experiencin' up hyur that'll do to tell about" (B 78).

expiry: [*n.* expiration] "the expiry of three months" (J 2:639). "And now, before the expiry of three days, you're plottin' agin me" (J 10:82).

extracize: *v.t.* to extract. "I've done extracized them" (A; J 2:641). "I've got a bone in my swallerer. Cain't you extracize it?" (J 2:475). [W. NC, DARE]

ey: In oaths: ey God, ey George. Also Ill., N.Eng. (as ey Gorry), Ky. (A). Ey God, a favorite expletive, is the original of egad, and goes back of Chaucer (B 361-62).

F

fact: [*n.* used in place of *assertions*, as in this comic exchange:] "Bill, you've been drinkin' and makin' a fool of yourself."/ "Old woman, these are facts that I deny" (J 2:637; 10:82).

faint: *n.* worthless residue in the "thumper" after distilling whiskey (A). [S.Midl., DARE]

fair: 1. *v.i.* to clear, of weather. "It may fair up and be a pretty week." Also S.Car. (A). "It may fair off by day" (C 2). "Oh, it faired up, an' I went a-plowin'" (J 3:1015). fair up (J 2:642). [DAE lists both "*fair off*" and "*fair up*" in this sense, along with an 1886 citation attributing them to S.usage; S., S.Midl., DARE]

fall out: [*v. phr.* to disagree, to dispute.] "Ever since they fell out" (J 4:855). "Him and Sam fell out and had a cuss fight" (J 4:853). [DARE does not list this term as dialectal, except in the sense of "faint."]

fall poison: [*n.*] *Amianthium muscaetexicum.* "Cattle sometimes are poisoned, as is supposed, by feeding on amianthium muscaetexicum; hence its name of 'fall poison'" (Gray) (J 2:363).

fanning-mill: [*n.* a device for separating grain from chaff.] "In some counties there is not so much as a fanning-mill, grain being winnowed by pouring it from basket to basket [the women fluttering bed sheets or aprons], after having been threshed with a flail" (Allen, "Cumberland") (J 2:350).

farewell: [1.] *n.* aftertaste. "That ain't got no bad taste; it has a leetle farewell to it 's though it had campfire in it" (A; J 2:475). archaic form (J 2:597). (J 2:642u) [Midl., DARE] [2.] **farwel** or **farwell** [is the conventional phrase of leave-taking; **farwel** listed in Fox (J 2:489).] "Giddep! I'll be back by in the mornin'"/ "Farwell!" (B 372).

fat meat: [*n.* fat back.] "Bill dremp that he seed a lot 'o fat meat layin' on the table; an' it done come true" (B 103-104). [Chiefly Midl., also S., DARE]

fat wood: [*n.* resinous pine wood.] The wasteful old-time way of producing tar was to collect "fat wood" and pine knots, put them in a hole in the side of a hill, and set fire to the top wood.

The tar trickled out through a tube at the bottom of the pit, into barrels fixed to receive it (J 25:169). [Chiefly FL, GA, DARE]

fault: *v.t.* to find fault with. "He took to faultin' her." Also Kan. (A). "Granny kept faultin' us all day" (B 356). "She kept a-faultin' me all day" (J 10:83). (J 2:597) [Chiefly S.Midl., DARE]

favor: [*v.t.* to treat indulgently.] "On the south side, whar the sun favors it" (J 2:342).

faze: [*v.t.* to affect; listed in Fox as "English dialect" (J 2:489).] (J 2:603)

feather into (one): *v. phr.* to attack, as with arrows piercing to the feather. "He feathered into him, feeding him lead (A). "Feathered into them!" Where else can we hear to-day a phrase that passed out of standard English when "villainous salt-petre" supplanted the long-bow? It means to bury an arrow up to the feather, as when the old chronicler Harrison says, "An other arrow should haue beene fethered in his bowels" (B 362). [S.Midl., DARE]

feather spring: [*n. phr.* a part of the cocking assembly of a gun.] "Then the dad-burned gun wouldn't stand roostered [cocked-K]; the feather-spring had jumped out o' place" (B 101).

feist: *n.* a fice [a small short-haired dog] (A). "A feist is one o' them little bitty dogs that ginerally runs on three legs and pretends a whole lot" (B 94). (J 2:603) [Citations in DA and DAE suggest a localization in S.Midl.; DARE suggests S., S.Midl.]

feisty: *adj.* [like a feist, lively, energetic.] "Feisty means when a feller's stuck on hisself and wants to show off—always wigglin' about wanting everybody to see him." Also Kan., Ky. (A). "You-uns won't be so feisty and brigaty atter this, will ye!" (B 94). "Feisty means when a feller's allers wigglin' about, wantin' ever'body to see him, like a kid when the preacher comes" (B 94). (J 2:642) [Chiefly S.Midl., DARE; DA cites K; cf. **brigaty.**]

fell down: [*past. part.* fallen.] "she's fell down and busted a rib inside o' her!" (J 2:462; B 299).

feller: [*n.* variant of *fellow*] (Old Pete on the porch) "I jes' *got* ter know who that feller is" (J 4:739). [Widespread, DAE]

felons: [*n. pl.* suppurative sore, especially of the fingertips] (J 19:19). [Chiefly S., Midl., DARE]

fer: [*prep.*, variant of *for.*] "What fer?" (M.B.) (J 2:642).

ferget: [*v.*, variant of forget] "Might as well stick your head in a swarm o' bees and ferget who you are" (B 302). [Possibly a simple instance of eye dialect, though we doubt it, judging from K's keen awareness of the condescension associated with such spellings. We rather suspect that K perceived this pronunciation—the first syllable rhyming with "fur"—to be a departure from mainstream usage—or at least from his pronunciation, which as a Northerner would have exhibited something closer to a back vowel in the initial syllable.]

fermenters: [*n.* listed among items confiscated in a raid on a still; in a letter from Chas. K. Beck, 22 Apr. 1921] (C 4).

fernent or **ferninst:** *prep.* in front of. (A). [Montgomery suggests this is usually glossed as "next to."] "Jest afore it got quite fernent me, I shot" (J 4:749). "as 'fernent the brick church'" (C 2). [Listed as English dialect in Fox (J 2:489).] (J 2:603) [Chiefly Midl., DARE]

ferro: [*n.*] In some places . . . the locust insect is known as a ferro (Pharaoh?) (B 369).

fer why: [*adv.* why.] "I swapped hosses, and I'll tell you fer why" (B 371; J 2:642). (J 2:605) [S.Midl., DARE]

fetch: [*v.t.*] "bring. Rarely used except among the most illiterate." (C 3). "Here, you, go down to the spring and fetch water" (B 84). [DARE lists the word as "somewhat old-fashioned."]

fid: [*n.* a hook; loggers' term.] "the 'fid,' which united the chain that bound the load [of logs]" (Springer 107) (D 1). [ME, DARE]

fid hook: [*n. phr.*, loggers' term.] "He [the teamster] examines the chains lest they should part, and, above all, the objects more watched than any others, the 'fid hook' and the 'dog hook,' the former that it does not work out,the latter that it loose not its grappling hold on the tree" (Springer 107-108) (D 1). [ME, Pacific N.W., DARE]

fiddle butt: [*n.* sounding board of a violin] (J 25:180).

fiddle strings: [*n. pl.* bow strings.] "Quill [Rose] used to make his fiddle-strings out of his wife's hair and play all night. After the hair got done stretching it made good strings" (J 2:457).

figger: [*v.t.* to calculate, variant of *figure.*] "All Skeets and Bushees, and married back and forth and crossways and upside

down till ev'ry man is his own grandmother, if he only knew
enough to figger relationships" (Day) (B 297).

find a calf: *v. phr.* to foal. Also Ky. (A). [Chiefly S., S.Midl.,
DARE]

fire board: [*n.* mantel] (J 2:603). [Chiefly S., S.Midl., DARE; as
opposed to "a board or screen used to shut off a fireplace when
it is not in use" (DAE); S.WV, W.Va, W.NC, N.SC, Kurath]

fire-coal: *n.* an ember (A). "Ants won't cross a fire-coal mark" (J
1:75). [Chiefly S.Midl., DARE]

firstest: [*adj.* superior, highfalutin.] Social distinctions there are
none. It is only in the valley lands that one hears of "The firstest
folks in Greenville" (J 4:713). [S.E. (Black), E.TN, W. NC, DARE]

fist-and-skull: [*adj.* fighting] "barehanded. 'They fought fist-
and-skull'" (C 3). [Chiefly S., S.Midl., DARE]

fit: [*pret.* of fight] a weak preterite supplants the proper strong
one . . . fit [for fought] (B 358). "Coaly [a dog] fit agin, all right,
and got his tail bit" (B 101).

fitified or **fittified:** p.a. [some examples from K are verbal
nouns.] Subject to fits; epileptic. Also Ky. (A). "He's fitified" (J
1:306). "him fittified and a fool by natur" (John Wilson) (J
10:83). "The fitified" (J 2:447). "He arrested . . . a boy, that was
scared most fitified and never resisted more'n a mouse" (B
170). "Mountaineers never send their 'fitified' or 'half-wits' or
other unfortunates to any institution in the lowlands" (J 2:603).
[Chiefly Midl., also S., DARE]

fitten: [*adj.* fit, suitable.] "That light bread ain't fitten to eat" (J
2:639,10:82). "A good name; it is fitten" (B 214). "It ain't fitten"
(J 4:737). (J 2:603) [Chiefly S., S.Midl., DARE]

fitty: *adj.* fit. "It ain't fitty fer hell." Tenn. (A; J 2:401). "The words
that man used ain't fitty to tell" (B 303).[S.App., DARE]

fix, fixing: [*v.* to plan, to get ready; listed under "words with
many meanings" (J 2:605).] "Well, come agin and fix to stay a
week" (B 372). "Are you-uns fixin' to move?" (J 2:336). . . . our
Snake-Stick Man, was "fixing for a good long drunk," as our
mountaineers so delicately phrase it (B 200). "Are ye fixin' to go
squirrelin'?" (B 356). [SAtl, Gulf States, DARE]

flag: [*n.* blue flag, the wild iris.] (*Iris versicolor*) [Flowers] May-
July. Violet blue. Root med[icinal]. (J 26:22). dwarf iris [now
considered a distinct species (Iris cristata)] (J 1:69).

flake stand: [*n. phr.* part of a distillery.] "One flake stand, part of property seized and destroyed in a raid on an illicit distillery" (letter from Chas. K. Beck, 22 Apr. 1921) (C 4). [S.App., DARE]

flander: [1. *v.i.* to splinter, to shatter, to break into pieces] "He threw a full fruit jar out o' the cyar."/ "How do you know it was full?"/ "Because it just bruk; it didn't flander" (J 2:639). [2. *n.* piece.] "Hit it a tap and, 'stead o' flattening, it busts to flanders" (J 10:83).

flea dope: [*n. phr.* insect repellant] (J 3:995).

fleshy: [*adj.* fat.] "She's a tol'able big, fleshy woman" (J 4:722; B 360). [S.Midl., DARE]

fling: [1.] *v.t.* to throw. (A). "A mountaineer does not throw a stone; he "flings a rock" (B 371). [2.] **fling up,** v. to vomit (A). "She'd been flingin' up all night" (J 2:475). [S.Midl., DARE]

flooding: [*part.* menstruating.] Mrs. C. wears no napkin, although flooding in season and out. "You can track her along the floor" (J 2:437). [Listed in DARE as Negro usage in LA, SC, also KY, IN.]

flush: [1. *adj.* even, congruent.] "The end of this plank was sawed off flush with the end of that one." [2. *adv.* evenly] "That box lid just fits flush with the top of the box" (C 3). [Not listed as dialectal in DARE, DA, or DAE]

fly mad: [*v.i.* to become angry; cf. "fly off the handle"] "What helped was that they'd fly mad sometimes and kill one another like fools" (B 312). "I don't know what the fraction was, but he flew mad about something (A). [W.NC, also KY, PA, VT, DARE]

fly-specked: [*adj.* soiled by flies.] "That dipper was all fly-specked when we bought it" (J 2:439).

folkses: [*n.* folks', people's.] "Them loggers jest louzes up folkses houses" (B 272). [S., S.Midl., DARE]

foller: [1.] *v.t.* [, variant of *follow*.] To do as a practice or custom. "He follers pickin' the banjer." "What do you-uns foller for a living?" Also W.Res.,Ill., N.Eng., Ky. (A). "What mought you-uns foller for a living?" (B 275). "We don't ginerally foller takin' in strangers" (B 272; J 4:723; [J 4:719 suggests the quote in some form is from Olmsted, 258.) (C 2). S.Midl., DARE] [2. *v.t.*, also variant of *follow*, but conventionally:] "My dogs can foller ary trail, same's hound" (B 81). "Follerin' a fellow around, pet pig style" (J 2:637). "We follered him clar over to the Spencer Place" (B 106). [3. *v.t.* to herd.] "He follers up his hogs, an' corn feeds them, an' gentles them up" (J 2:366). [With more on butchering, see J 2:443.]

fool: [1. *adj.*] foolish. "them fool-women" [listed with Chaucer words in Fox (J 2:489); widespread listings in DAE.] [2. *n.* a fanatic.] If one is especially fond of a certain dish he declares that he is a fool about it. "I'm a plumb fool about pickle-beans." Conversely, "I ain't much of a fool about liver" is rather more than a hint of distaste (B 367). [GA, DARE]

fool's gold: [*n.* pyrite] "You've seed what they call 'fool's gold' ain't ye? Hit's yaller and shiny and mocks gold right smart, but you hit it a tap and 'stead o' flattening, it busts to flanders" (J 10:83).[While this term is certainly not exclusively App., its presence in K's journals indicates its local currency during the period in which he collected—hardly surprising, considering the history of gold mining in the area.]

footin' it: [*v. phr.* hurrying.] "He's footin' hit as if the devil was atter him—" (B 130).

foot in hand, to take: *v. phr.* to walk. Also Ill., Ky. (A). "To walk to a place" (C 2). [S., S.Midl., DARE]

for a sample: [*prep. phr.*, variant of "for example"] "There's Jim Cody for a sample; he was principally raised in this country, and I've known him from a boy" (B 170).

forehanded: [*adj.* circumspect; looking or planning ahead; listed under "Habits. Manners" and then "Providence" with **full-handed** in J 2:642p] (J 2:603, J 6) [OED's first citation for this usage is 1650, but it notes that the term is "Now only U.S," where it does not enjoy a wide currency; chiefly NEng, DARE; cf. **full-handed**]

foreparents: *n. pl.* forefathers (A). Ancestors (J 2:601). "My foreparents war considerably Scotch" (J 1:304). [B 429 reads "principally Scotch."] (J 2:642p) [Chiefly S.Midl., DARE]

fotch: [*v.*, variant of *fetch*] "We gutted him [the bear], and left him near the top, to fotch in the mornin'" (B 107). [Also the preterite forms:] fotch or fotched (B 358). [S.Midl., DARE]

fotch-on: *adj.* brought-on, q.v. [store-bought; K uses "imported."] Also Ky. (A; C 2). "Damn this fotch-on kraut that

comes in tin cans" (J 2:419; B 359). (J 2:601) [Chiefly S.Midl.,
DARE]

fotch up: [*v. phr.* raised, or as purists would have it, reared.]
"*Good* la! whar was you fotch up?" (B 94). [K tells an anecdote
about a mountaineer who drank pea soup, thinking it was
chocolate; then exclaimed:] "That's what I was fotch up on" (J
3:971). [DARE lists this term as Scots, N.English dialect, includes examples from KY, AR.]

foxfire: [*n.* phosphorescence; a folk etymology] (J 2:604).
[Chiefly S., S.Midl., DARE]

fox grape: [*n. phr.* any of several native grapes with a foxy flavor.]
"If it rains on the first day of June, the fox grapes get knotty"
(Schuler, Dillsboro, [NC]) (J 2:671). [In lists of seasonal
changes, K notes:] August: Fox grape. First ripe, Aug-Sep.
Brownish purple. (J 26:39). Sept. 19, on Tuckaseegee [River]
fox grapes dropping; have been good for past two weeks (J
1:69).

fraction: *n.* ruction. [also rupture < ME *fraccioun* < L *fractio* (to
break)] "I don't know what the fraction was, but he flew mad
about something" (A). "I don't know how the fraction begun."
Fraction for rupture is an archaic word, rare in literature,
though we find it in *Troilus and Cressida* (B 362). (J 2:642)
[S.Midl., DARE]

frail: *v.t.* [flail?-K] "He frailed him well." Also Ill., S.Car., Ky.
(A). To beat with a brush (C 2). (J 2:603) [S., S.Midl., DARE; DAE
registers the same uncertain association with "flail."]

fraish: [*adj.*, variant of *fresh.*] "This butter hain't fraish" (J 2:429).
"The sign was spang fraish" (J 4:749). "I've larned now whar
they're [the bear] crossin'—seed sign a-plenty and it's spang
fraish" (B 94). [Esp. S.Midl., DARE]

franzy: [adj.,] "variant of *frenzy,* but used in the sense *wild* or *out
of (one's) head* due to sickness, as fever, etc. 'He has been awful
sick for several days and has been franzy most of the time'" (C
3). [Montgomery notes the example is an adjective, so it is
probably a variant of frantic, rather than frenzy, as Bird suggested; chiefly S., S.Midl., DARE]

fray: [*n.* a serious fight.] "There's been a fray on the river." He
meant fray in its original sense of deadly combat, as was fitting

where two men were killed (B 362). [Chiefly S.Midl., DARE; another instance of a literary or learned word found in the active vocabulary of the App. mountaineer.]

fried backings: [*n. phr.* a taffy-like concoction.] Prepared by boiling the backings of the still with ginger and sugar. "And it's good too" (J 4:847).

fringebush: [*n.* fringe tree (*Choinanthus virginica*); flowers] May-June. White, fragrant. Root-bark med[icinal]. (J 26:22). "In May, beautiful blossoms—bark of root possesses tonic for those suffering from exhausting diseases." (Asheville *Citizen*, 22 Jan. 1928) (J 2:480). [Chiefly S., S.Midl., DARE]

friz: [*v., past tense,* variant of *froze*] "The cattle all huddled up a-top o' each other and friz in one pile, solid" (B 78). (B 358; J 2:642) [Chiefly S., S.Midl., DARE]

frog, also **toad frog:** [*n.* a toad.] (J 1:77). In the Smokies a toad is called a frog or a toad-frog (B 369). (J 2:649) [Chiefly S., S.Midl., DARE]

frog stool, also **mushyroom:** [*n.* a toadstool.] A toadstool is a frogstool (B 369). (J 1:71; 2:603) [Chiefly S., S.Midl., DARE]

frolicksome: [*adj.* agitated, disturbed.] "Things 'ud get frolicksome ginerally." Said of a feud (J 3:911).

from: [*prep.* since.] "I've knowed him from a boy" (B 170).

fruit: [1. *n.* apples.] "We have lots of fruit this summer, but no peaches" (C 1). [2. *n.* apple sauce.] "Fruit means apple-sauce" (J 2:421). "We noted at the tables of this region a singular use of the word fruit. When we were asked, 'Will you have some of the fruit?' and said 'Yes,' we always got apple sauce" (Warner) (J 2:421). [Chiefly S.Midl., DARE; see also **sass**]

full: [*v.i.* to grow full.] "The moon fulls tonight" (J 1:38). [Confronted with a "furriner" who stuffed himself at dinner,] the landlady giggled an aside to her husband: "Git the almanick and see when that feller'll full!" (as though she were bidding him look to see when the moon would be full) (B 326). [The "landlady" speaks to "Bob" and uses "full up" in J 2:423.] (J 2:605) [DAE contains an example of this usage taken from Morley's *Carolina Mountains* (1913). Chiefly S., S.Midl., DARE]

full-handed: *adj.* well supplied, well to do. "He was a full-handed man—had a-plenty." Also Ky. (A; J 1:262). Having plenty of money (J 2:601). (J 2:642; J 6) [S.Midl., DARE]

funk: *n.* an offensive smell. "Open the door and let the funk out" (A; J 2:438). archaic (J 2:597). Chiefly S.Midl., DARE]

fur: [1. *v.i.* to be coated or become fuzzy.] [Sled] runners are usually made of natural sourwood crooks . . . [since sourwood] wears very smooth and does not fur up nor splinter (B 42). [2. *adj.* variant of *far*] "Bill sung out, 'Is it fur down thar?' and I said 'Purty fur'" (B 106). [3. *prep.*, variant of *for*] "She hit a miss-lick with an axe, and cut her fut fur a-plenty" (J 2:475).

furder, furdest: [*adj.*, comparative and superlative degrees, variants of *farthest/furthest*.] "We caint go no furder" (J 1:322). "Bushnell's the furdest ever I've been" (B 23; J 1:200).

furrin: [*adj.*, variant of *foreign*; but applied to anything exotic.] "other odd bric-a-brac interesting to 'furrin' eyes" B 318). "a big furrin dog" (B 80). [Esp., S.App., DARE; cf. **furriner.**]

furriner: [1.] *n.* anyone from outside the mountains. Also Ky. (A). They call all outsiders "furriners" (B 16). Whether you come from Boston or Chicago, Savannah or New Orleans, in the mountains you are a "furriner" (B 17). A native of the Carolina tidewater is a "furriner" in the Carolina mountains (B 185). (C 2; J 2:597, 642) [Esp. S.App., DARE]

fussin': [*part.* overly fastidious.] "He who would take pains to make a workmanlike job . . . would be ridiculed as 'fussin' around like an old granny-woman'" (B 316).

fust: [*adj.*, variant of *first*.] "Fust thing I knowed" (J 2:641). "They'd fust-place ask you some questions" (B 118). [Cf. **hind-side-fust**]

fusty: [*adj.* stuffy or musty.] Such a windowless cabin often smells very fusty and damp (J 2:373).

fut: [*n.* variant of *foot*.] "I stove a nail into my fut" (J 2:475). [Probably not an eye dialect spelling, judging from K's sensitivity to such things; the spelling perhaps signals a mid-central vowel, so that the word would rhyme with *but*.]

G

gab: [*n.* idle talk] (J 2:642).

gaily: *adv.* well. "The folks is *gaily*" (A). "I hope the folks with you is gaily" (B 359). [Originally Scots, now chiefly S.Midl., DARE]

gal: [*n.* variant of *girl.*] "The decorations of the room [pages from papers and magazines—were] the work of the 'gals' " (Vincent 13-14) (J 2:642). "Well, if I'd a-been that gal, I'd a-got me a forty-some-odd and shot enough meat offen that feller to feed a hound-dog a week" (Mrs. Davis) (J 4:841). [DAE lists as a "vulgar or dialectal variant" with a wide distribution.]

Gall-of-the-Earth: [*n.*] lion's foot (*Nabalus serpentarius*). [Flowers] July-Oct. Cream-color or yellowish. (J 26:35). [Cf. DAE, where it is listed as the *Prenanthes serpentaria.*]

galliant: [1. *adj.*] variant of *gallant* (A). [2. *v.*] **g'lantin:** They're g'lantin' (gallanting) around. (Young couple out riding) (J 2:642). [DAE has two citations, both from the nineteenth century, one from NEng., the other from Black S. speech; chiefly S., S.Midl, DARE.]

galluses: [*n. pl.* suspenders.] (M[rs]. B[arnett].) "What you think Adam'd do if he was to come here and find everything looking like a back-house?" / (Bob) "I reckon he'd go to takin' his galluses down" (J 4:763). [Colloq., widespread, DAE; widespread, but esp. S., DARE]

galvanize: *n.* nickel plating. "The *galvanize* wore off my pistol" (A; J 2:401 adds: "or watch"). (J 2:601) [W.NC, KY, DARE]

gamble: [*n.* chance.] "I bid two on the gamble of catching a trump" (J 4:755).

gamecocks: [*n.* fighting cocks.] "I landed right in the middle of them, bear and dogs, fightin' like gamecocks" (B 106). [Listed in both DA and DAE with widespread citations.]

gant: (gaent) [1.] *adj.* [lean, slim.] Variant of *gaunt.* [2.] *v.t.* [to slim down.] "*Gant* them cattle up; get the grass out of them so they can travel." Also Kan. (A). "The colt's all ganted up" (C 2). [DA and DAE list "*gaunt*" as a verb without the particle; DARE

offers many citations from across the map; apparently, originally NEng, but moved S. and W..]

gant-lot: *n.* an enclosure for cattle, to prevent their fattening on
grass. Also N.Eng., Ky. (A). A fenced enclosure into which
cattle are driven after cutting them out from those of other
owners. So called because the mountain cattle run wild, feeding only on grass and browse, and "they couldn't travel well to
market when filled up on green stuff: so they're penned up to
git *gant* and nimble" (B 93, note). (J 2:361, 601) [Chiefly S.App.,
DARE]

gapped open: [*part. phr.*, comic metaphor for] (yawning) "I jest
set here gapped open all the time" (M.B.) (J 2:631).

gaum, gawm, gawn: [1. *n.* "a greasy mess" (Webster's Third). "I
want to go to Asheville as bad as you, but blamed if I can up
and leave everything in a gaum. This house must be cleaned"
(M.B.) (J 4:763). "I can't leave everything in a gawm" (J 2:438).
2. *v.* to smear with a sticky substance (OED).] If the house be in
disorder it is said to be all gormed or gaumed up (B 368).
"gawn" (J 2:603). [Chiefly S., S.Midl., but also NEng, DARE; see
also **gorm**]

gee and haw: [*interj.* from the commands to horses to turn right
(gee!) and left (haw!); in context it appears to mean conflicts,
conflicting orders] "Tired of the everlasting 'gee and haw'" (J
27:1d). [Chiefly S., DARE]

gentle: *v.t.* to render tame [or make gentle] "He follers his hogs,
corn-feeds them, and *gentles* them up." Also N.Eng. (A; J 2:366
reads "Dilly Welsh follers up his . . ."). "To feed, as to gentle
wild turkeys" (C 2). The backwoodsman does not want "critters that haffter be gentled and hand-fed" (B 43). [Esp. S.Midl.,
DARE]

gettin' it on (someone): [*v. phr.* to show malice toward (someone).] Malice, "getting it on" someone (J 10:5).

giddep: [*interj.* command to a horse] (B 372).

gift of the gab: [*idiom*, a way with words.] "They all had the gift of
the gab" (J 2:637).

gilt: *n.* a female shoat. (General among hog-raisers—R.S.F.) (A;
B 369).

gimcrack: [*n.* a knickknack, something more showy than useful.]

The most kyanized old woodsman that you ever saw always lugs along some gimcrack that he is half ashamed of in public but idolizes in private (J 27:1a).

gimlet: [*n.* a tool shaped like a corkscrew.] "You ain't got as much sense as 'd lay on the p'int of a gimlet" (J 10:82; J 2:637 attributes the quote to M.B. with these changes: "She didn't have as much sense as would . . ." [Though "gimlet" is not a localism, it is also not a word found in the active vocabulary of many people; its presence here may reflect the popularity of the saying as a whole.]

gin: [*conj.* if, whether.] "My face gets so snaggy, gin I go a week without shavin'" (J 1:274). "Ax the woman gin you can git a bite" (J 4:723; [B 271-72 reads:] "I'll ax the woman gin she can git ye a bite.") (J 2:642) [OED lists this word as Scottish and dialectal, possibly related to *given* in the conditional sense, "given that . . ." Chiefly S.App., DARE]

gi'n: [*v.* variant of *given*,] a weak preterite (B 358). [But note the preceding entry.]

ginerally: [*adv.*, variant of *generally*.] Mrs. B says . . . "Mis' Whiteside's neck was ginerally as black as a pot" (J 2:439). (B 80) [This is probably not a case of eye dialect spelling; K was very sensitive to the kind of condescension that such spellings betrayed. Most likely it is indicative of the merger of /i/ and /e/ before /n/ in S. speech, something that a Yankee like K, who probably distinguished between "pin" and "pen," would have noticed immediately.]

gineration: [*n.*, variant of *generation*.] "They married through and through till the whole gineration nigh run out" (B 311-12). [See note regarding pronunciation in preceding entry.]

ginseng: [*n.*] herb (*Panax quinquefolia*). [Flowers] July-Aug. Greenish. Root pseudo-med[icinal]. Leaves make pleasant tea. (J 26:34). "It cheers the Heart even of a Man that has a bad Wife, and makes him look down with great Composure on the Crosses of the World" (Byrd 210-11) (J 2:354). [See also **sang**]

git, gittin': [1. *v.t.*, variants of *get, getting*.] "Git up, pup!" (B 75). "Whar's that brekfust you're yellin' about?" / "Hit's for you-uns to help *git!*" (B 84). "She's in the field, up yan, gittin' roughness" (B 112). [2. *v.i.* to become.] "I gits a better and better Christian ever' year" (B 347). [3. *vbl. n.* portion.] "You can git ye one more gittin' o' wood up thar" (B 357) [S.App., also AR, MO, DARE]. [4. *v.* to be allowed.] "I want to git to stay all night." "Can I git?" (J 4:723).

gittany: [*n.*, probably a variant of *jittany*, a nickle, q.v.; it is simply listed, not defined in J 2:642.]

give: [*n.*, variant of *gave*.] "I see they give Bryan a lot of reception when he kem back from the other world" (B 17). [Esp. S., S.Midl., DARE]

give down: *v. phr.* to admit, confess. He'll *give* it *down* at last." Also Ill. (A). "To confess" (C 2). [W.NC, DARE]

give out: [1.] *n.* announcement. "I didn't hear no *give-out* at meetin'." Also Ill. (A; B 357) [S.App., DARE] (J 4:775, 2:642) [2. *v. phr.*] "become exhausted. 'I can't work long without givin' out' " (C 3) [S., S.Midl., DARE] [3. *v.t.* to make an announcement] "Phil's Ann give it out to each and every that Walt and Layunie'd orter wed" (B 372).[S., S.Midl., DARE]

gizzard: [*n.* the stomach; a comic metaphor.] "it cut him to the gizzard—and soon he went upstairs lookin' like a sheep-killin' dog" (J 4:785). [DARE's earliest citations are from GA, later ones from as far away as Pacific N.W.]

glass: [*n.* lookingglass, mirror.] "He's so homely, he has to take a bracer afore he can look hisself in the glass." (J 10:82).

glass weed: [*n.* glass wort (*Salicornia bigelovii*).] Toe eetch . . . also called glass weed or water weed, q.v. (J 2:481).

glimpsh: *n.* [,variant of] *glimpse* (A). [W.NC, DARE]

glory: [*v.t.* to brag about, to celebrate.] "I'm a hillbilly, all right, and they needn't to glory their old flat lands to me" (B 386). [S.App., DARE]

glunch, as in **glunch o' sour disdain:** [*n.* a look, appearance.] Dyspepsia . . . accounts in great measure for the "glunch o' sour disdain" that mars so many countenances (B 296). [The phrase appears in both Burns and Scott; Scots dial (OED).]

gnat smokes: [*n. phr.* fires lit to chase away insects.] (J 1:75) [E. KY, DARE]

go: [1. *v.* to weigh.] "And he'll go a good two hunderd, that bear" (B 107). [2. *v.* to start.] "I reckon he'll go to takin' his galluses down" (Bob) (J 4:763). (J 2:642) [Chiefly S., S.Midl., DARE]

gobbler: [*n*. male turkey.] "I was callin' a gobbler when this fool thing [a hen turkey] showed up" (B 91).

gobs: [*n*. lots, a lump or mass, especially a mouthful.] "Every morning I cough up just gobs o' snuff" (J 4:745). [Scattered except in the S., DARE]

goddamighty: [*exclamation,* variant of *god almighty!*] "My goddamighty, Mam, thar's the boogerman—I done seed him!" (B 24).

god's biscuits: [*n*. stones; comic metaphor.] (J 4:853)

goin's on: [*gerund phr.* things happening, improprieties.] "I never seed sich goin's on!" (J 4:737). (J 2:642)

goin' to meetin': [*v. phr.* attending church.] They certainly have put a damper on frolics, so that in very many mountain settlements "goin' to meetin'" is recognized primarily as a social function and affords almost the only chance for recreation in which family can join family without restraint (B 340). [Widespread, DAE]

golleroy: *n*. the dottle of a pipe; also called **pipe-guts** (A). "I wouldn't give the golleroy of my pipe fer it" (J 10:82). (J 2:601) [W.NC, DARE]

goober: [*n*. peanut (*Arachis hypogaea*).] (J 2:607) [S., W., DAE; widespread, but chiefly S.E., DARE]

gooder/goodest: [*adj.*, comparative and superlative, better/best] "That gooder o' us 's all gone [dead] now!" (J 2:483). "That's the goodest" (J 2:641).

Good-man: *n*. God; child's term. (A) (J 4:775) [Midl., esp. S.Midl., DARE]

goozle: *n*. [guzzle?-K] throat. (A) "openin' her mouth till you could might' nigh see down her goozle . . ." (J 4:759). [Chiefly S., S.Midl., DARE]

gorm: [*v*. to make a mess.] If a house be in disorder it is said to be all gormed or gaumed up (B 368). "Hit's all gormed up" (J 2:438). (J 2:642) [See also **gaum**]

go-way bag or **go-'way sack:** *n. phr.* satchel (A). [listed along with:] "suggin," "habersack," "poke," "sack o' meal" (J 1:327f). [W.NC, WV, FL, DARE]

go-way stuff: [*n. phr.* dried rations easily transported] rice, oatmeal, etc. (J 2:429)

grabble: *v.i.* to dig up a few of the best (potatoes) and smooth back the dirt. Also Ill., Kan. (A; B 368 adds "without disturbing the immature ones"). "To take out with the hands, as potatoes, from the hill—pushing the dirt back" (C 2). "grabble 'taters" (J 2:359). (J 2:599, 603; J 6) [Chiefly S., S.Midl., DARE]

grade: [*v.i.* to proceed on an incline, to incline (Webster's Third)] "The trail grades around the top" (J 1). (J 2:642q)

grain: [*n.* a small amount.] "The only medicines we-uns has is yerbs, which customarily ain't no good 'thout a leetle grain o' whiskey" (B 121). (J 2:601) [Esp. S.Midl., DARE]

grand climacteric: [*n. phr.* sixty-third year of life; multiples of seven and nine were considered fateful years in a person's life; therefore, the 63rd year (7 x 9) was especially so and designated the "grand climacteric" (C 4).]

granny doctor: [n.] any obstetrician. [Most commonly, just mid-wives. K seems to be evasive here; no male doctor would have liked being called "granny"] (A). (J 2:601) [W.NC, KY, SC, DARE]

granny woman: [n. grandmother, old lady.] Few houses are thoroughly chinked and he who would take pains to make a workmanlike job of chinking would be ridiculed as "fussin' around like an old granny-woman" (B 316). [Listed as a pleo-nasm, B 360.] (J 2:592) [Chiefly S., S.Midl., DARE; chiefly NC, WV, Kurath]

gran'sir' or **grandsir:** [n. grandfather; also as an honorific title.] "Hit was thataway in my Pa's time, and in Gran'sir's, too" (B 160). "Old gran'sir' Pilkey" (A). We will hear an aged man referred to as "old Grandsir'" So-and-so (B 364-65). (J 2:597) [Chiefly NEng, S.Midl., DARE; NEng, Kurath]

grass: [*n.,* metaphoric expression for *spring*] "Three year ago, come grass." "From now til grass" (J 2:629). [See also **come grass, come June**]

grass-gutted: [*adj.* fattened, bloated.] "If I'd a chance to eat apples one week, I'd be as pot-bellied as a little grass-gutted pig" (J 2:428)

gredge: *n.,* variant of *grudge* (A). "They had a gredge atwixt them" (J 4:853). (Bawley Joe Welch) "He has a gredge at all creation, and glories in human misery" (Bob) (J 2:637; B 296). [S.App., DARE]

green out: *v. phr.* to swindle (A). "I got a good one on him—greened him out bodaciously" (J 2:459, 10:82). "Sim greened him out bodaciously" (to green out or sap is to outwit in trade) (B 368). (J 2:642) [S.Midl., DARE]

Grin an' Go 'Foot: [a social game or "play party" game, played where dancing is not permitted] (B 338).

grindin' rock: *n.* grindstone [whetrock] (A). "He sharpens tools on a grindin'-rock or whetrock" (B 371). "Time lost going to a neighbor's to borrow a tool or to use his grindin' rock" (J 2:401). (J 2: 601) [DAE lists "grinding stone" as obs.; DARE lists "grind rock" also with a distribution of S., S.Midl.]

grit: [1. *n.* pluck, spunk] "Won't this [being mauled by bear] spoil [the dog] for hunting hereafter?" / "Not if he has his daddy's and mammy's grit" (B 94).[DAE lists as slang and provides evidence of a wide distribution.] [2. *v.*, variant of *grate*] (B 352). [Chiefly S., S.Midl., DARE; see also **gritted, gritter**]

gritted: [*past part.*, variant of *grated*.] "In winter if the mills froze up, corn was boiled and gritted. Not so palatable, but 'an ever-present help in time of trouble'" (J 2:403).

gritted-bread: [*n.* bread made from grated corn] (J 2:597). When maize has passed from the soft and milky stage of roasting-ears, but is not yet hard enough for grinding, the ears are grated into a soft meal and baked into delectable pones called gritted-bread (B 365). [Chiefly S.Midl., DARE]

gritter: [*n.* machine for grinding corn. There are several kinds, and Kephart has furnished the following drawings:]

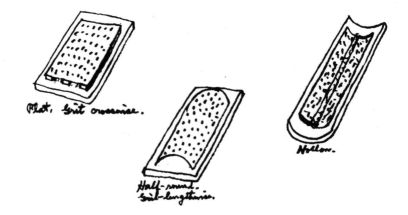

(J 2:403)

grouch: [*n.* bad disposition.] "That give him a grouch" (J 1:75; 18:61). [Widespread, DARE]

groundhog: [*n.* preferred to woodchuck (*Marmota monax*).] "We had things served piping hot on the table, soon after daylight: hot corn bread, hot coffee, and hot *groundhogs*" (B 229). [Widespread, but esp. Midl., DARE; see also **whistle-pig.**]

ground ivy: [*n.*] (*Glecoma hederacea*) [Flowers] March-May. *Plant med[icinal]* (J 26:11). "That'll break up the hives when nothing else won't" (J 2:481). (J 1:67)

ground squirrel: [*n.* chipmunk (*Tamias striatus*).] (J 26:56). [DAE's earliest citation is from Lawson's *Carolina* (1709); chiefly Midl., S., DARE]

growed: [*v. pret.* of grow.] "I wish t' my legs growed hind-side fust . . . so's I wouldn't bark my shins!" (B 102). (B 358) [Chiefly S., S.Midl., DARE]

grub, grubbed: [*v.t.* to remove stumps and roots.] "I've cl'ared me a patch and grubbed hit out—now I can raise me two or three severe craps!" (B 36). "What is the hardest work you ever did?" I asked Mrs. Barnett. "Grubbin', and splittin' rails, and carryin' them up a mountain side as steep as that one thar" (J 1:294).

gryste: [*n.* archaic variant of *grist*, grain for grinding.] Red grains of corn being harder than white ones, it is a humorous saying in the mountains that "a red grain in the gryste [grist] will stop the mill" (B 133). (J 2:453) [DARE also lists "grice" with a S.App. distribution.]

gum: 1. *n.* a hollow log. (A) "A hollow log—as in bee gum, ash gum" (C 2). 2. [*n.*] barrel. "I'm goin' to put my ashes into that gum." Also Ky. (A). [DA includes four citations; usage seems limited to S. and S.Midl. DARE lists as exclusively S.App. when it refers to a beehive; enjoys wider distribution when refers to a hollow log.]

gumming: [*v. pres. part.* teething.] 15 months' [old] Eddie sitting on a pile of muck and "gumming" a jagged fragment of a whiskey bottle. The mother nonchalantly looking on and saying to us, "Ain't he a sight?" (J 2:435).

gump: [*n.* an epithet of undetermined meaning.] "What a Gump he is!" MacG[owen]. (J 2:619). [The capitalization of the term suggests perhaps a character like Andy Gump in the cartoon strip of that name.]

gun-stick: [*n.* a notched staff used for steadying a long rifle.] "Yes, they are [scoundrels]; plumb ornery—lock, stock, barrel, and gun-stick" (B 169). (J 2:401) [DARE offers citations from NC, TN, and SC, but defines the term as a ramrod; our local informants, however, hold for the definition as we have given it above.]

guttered: [*past part.* having run-offs like gutters.] "a spring branch guttered by washouts where there used to be pools" (J 23:43).

gwine: [*v.*] There are many corrupt forms of the verb, such as gwine for gone or going (B 358). "Stranger—meanin' no harm—*whar* are you gwine?" (B 275; J 4:738 uses "where" and gives speaker as Bill Morris). [Also **a-gwine:**] "I ain't a-gwine to" (J 2:589).

gyarb: [*n.*] variant of *garb*. Also S.Car., Ky. (A). "See the gyarb them children's in" (J 1:278). (J 6) [Aside from the palatalization evident in this and in the two succeeding entries, note the relatively bookish or literary quality of this word—not something one expects in the usual active or spoken vocabulary.]

gyard: [*n.*, variant of *guard*] (C 2).

gyarden: [*n.*] variant of *garden*. Also S.Car., Ky. (A). (J 2:359) [Cox adds:] "Charleston, S.C." (C 2)

H

haar or ha'r: [*n.*, variants of *hair*] haar (hair) (B 352). "Hit'll make the ha'r slip from a mule" (J 2:367). "He bit a hole under the foreleg, through hide and ha'r, clar into the holler, so t' you can stick your hand in and seize the bear's heart" (B 107). (J 2:642)

hack: *v.t.* to annoy, nettle. "That joke hacks Steve to this day." Also Ky. (A). [Chiefly S., S.Midl., DARE]

haffter or **hafter:** [*v*. variants of *have to*.] "When I move, all I haffter do is call up the dog an' shet the door" (J 2:336; B 36 reads "put out the fire and call the dog.") "You cain't foller up on hossback, but hafter do your own runnin'" (B 80). [Midl., S.Midl., DARE]

haid: [*n*., variant of *head*.] "My haid's a-swimmin'" (J 2:642). [Esp. S., S.Midl., DARE]

hain't: [*v. phr.*, variant of *ain't, have not*.] "'Twa'n't (so and so) fer he hain't got no squar'-headed hobnails" (B 130). "But if he hain't, you'll know his Jane" (J 4:722). [Chiefly N.E., S., S.Midl., esp. App., DARE]

half-pop: [*n*.] uncle (Indian expression) (J 3:1050)

half-wit: [*n*. a silly, or imbecilic person.] "Mountaineers never send their "fitified folks" or "half-wits," or other unfortunates, to any institution in the lowlands" (B 296). (J 2:642; J 6) [Certainly this term had currency outside App., but K's use of quotation marks here suggests that to him at least it represented mountain speech.]

ham-meat: [*n*. ham.] a pleonasm (B 360). "That ham-meat's spoilt" (J 2:419). "'Ham-meat' is for the most part fried in irregular pieces, which float about in a flood tide of grease" (Vincent 10-11) (J 2:425). [S.Midl., DARE]

hampered: [*v*.] shackled or jailed (B 370). [Archaic, OED]

hand-fed: [*v. phr.* to be fed by hand.] "Critters that haffter be gentled and hand-fed" (B 43).

handily: *adv*. readily. "You couldn't handily blame him." Also Ky. (A; J 2:641; B 371). (C 2) [S.App., DARE]

hand-towel: [*n*. towels used to dry hands.] Wetting face and hands and wiping dirt off on towels; one towel a week. "Hand-towel" (J 2:435).

handwrite: [*n*. variant of *handwriting*.] "Here's a letter fer ———; whose handwrite do you say that is?" (Granville's wife) (J 4:739). [S., S.Midl., DARE]

hang: [*v*. to persevere, to hang in/on.] "A plumb cur, of course, cain't foller a cold track—he just runs by sight; and he won't hang—he quits" (B 80-81).

hant or **ha'nt:** [*n*. ghost, variant of *haunt*.] "If he ain't a hant, what is he?" (J 18:56). "He looked like he'd seed a ha'nt" (J 2:635).

"I'd believe he's a hant if 't wasn't for his tracks—they're the biggest I ever seen" (B 91). The hills would return no echo, for the cry came from a riotous "ha'nt" (B 376). (J 2:603) [Chiefly S., S.Midl., DARE] [also in **ha'nt bait:**] "She's as ugly as ha'nt bait" (Ledford) (J 2:625).

hardness: *n.* ill feeling. "Likely to git up right smart o' hardness between 'em." Also Ky. (A; J 4:853). If [a man] and his neighbor dislike each other, there is a hardness between them; if they quarrel, it is a ruction, a rippit, a jower, or an upscuddle—so be it there are no fatalities which would amount to a real fray" (B 368). [Chiefly App., DARE]

hard pushed: [*v. phr.* hard up,] destitute: "I ain't that hard pushed yet" (J 3:985; B 327). [Esp. NEng., DARE]

harness marks: [*n. phr.*] expressions produced by prolonged use of a function, habit of life, etc. [comic metaphor] (J 12:102)

has: [*v.*, nonstandard variant of *have*] "Several trees has been wind-throwed and busted" (B 77). (C 1)

haster: [*v. phr.*, variant of *has to.*] "[The bear] cain't run away—he haster stop every bit, and fight" (B 81). (C1) [Cf. **hafter.**]

hatefuls: [*n.* pests, hateful things.] "Them bugs—the little old hatefuls!" (B 357). [S.App., DARE]

he and **she:** male and female beasts: "a bearing she," "The old he." "I heered the old she poppin' her teeth" (J 4:749). [DARE lists numerous citations from eastern seaboard.]

(in) head: [*n.* (in) mind; listed under "Words Used in a Peculiar Sense" and followed by a note: "compile variants of *think, intend* (J 2:642)] "I had in head to plow to-day, but hit's come on to rain" (B 371). "He had in head to do it" (J 2:641)

heading: [*n.*] extemporized pillow [loggers' term] (Hubbard 43) (D 1) [S., S.Midl., DARE]

head-lice: [*n.* different from body lice; frequents head of host (*Pediculus humanus capitis*)] (J 2:435).

head-swimmin': *n.* vertigo [dizziness, possibly a migraine] (A). "I was sick that day with a head swimmin'" (J 2:475). "Looks like he mought drap off, him bein' weak and right narvish and sick with a head-swimmin'" (B 298). [Listed under "coinages" in J 2:601.; W.NC, WV, DARE] [See also **swim (in the haid).**]

head wrappins: [*n.* scarf, bandana?; listed under "coinages" in J 2:601.]

heap: [*adj.* many, a lot.] Heap o' folks [was] contemporary with the *Canterbury Tales* (B 362). "Heap o' folks thinks. . ." (J 2:641). "I've traveled about the country, been to Asheville wunst, and to Waynesville a heap o' times" (B 120). "He sets a heap o' store by you" (J 2:611). [Chiefly S., S.Midl., DARE]

heap-sight: [*intensifier* much.] "I'd a heap-sight rather hunt" (J 4:749). "I'd a heap-sight ruther ketch me a big old 'coon for his hide" (B 386). (J 2:601) [See **heap**]

hearn: [*v.*, variant of *heard, have heard.*] "I hearn tell. . ." (J 2:367, 491). [See also **heerd, heern**]

hearten up: [*v.*] "to brighten." (C 2)

hearty: [*adv.*, variant of *heartily.*] "You cain't eat hearty, nor sleep good o' nights" (B 386).

heatin' stoves: [*n.* wood stoves.] "I do like a fireplace; none o' yer heatin'-stoves for me" (J 2:439).

heavy-footed: *adj.* gravid. (A). [K's use of this learned word in his definition is fastidious; he means pregnant.]

he-balsam: *n.* blackspruce (A). Spruce is he-balsam, balsam itself is she-balsam (B 369). (C 2) (J 1:59, 71; 2:601) [W.NC, DARE]

hed: [*v.* variant of *had.*] "I wish t' we *hed* roasted the temper outen them trap-springs, like we talked o' doin'" (B 93). "Whut do you-uns know about windstorms? Now, *I've* hed some experiencin' up hyur that'll do to tell about" (B 78). "He hed his droll way" (J 2:637).

heepe: [*adj.* variant of *heap,* q.v.; listed as Chaucer word in Fox (J 2:489).]

heerd, heered, hyerd: [*v.*, variants of *heard, have heard.*] " 'heerd, hyerd [are both] used by Normal school pupils regularly outside the classroom' (Joe Morgan of near Asheville) 6 July 1926" (C 11). "Ain't you never heered them call my name?" (J 2:641). "They've heered tell about the judges; and they've seed the revenuers in flesh and blood" (B 120). (J 2:367) [See also **hearn, heern**]

heern: [*v.*, variant of *heard.*] "I heern tell you was one o' them 'sperts" (B 351). [See also **hearn**]

heft: [*n.* weight.] "The main heft is on yon side" (J 2:641).

hell: [*n.* an extremely thick growth of rhododendron or laurel; listed under "Country—Landscape" in J 2:642.] A "hell" . . . is a thicket of laurel or rhododendron, impassable save where the bears have bored out trails (B 375). [Esp. S.App., DARE; see **slick, woolly-head, yaller patch.**]

hellaballoo: *n.* [ruckus, hubbub.] Variant of *hullaballoo*. Also Kan., Ky. (A). "They made a big hellaballoo" (J 4:847). "Well, you needn't to make sich a hellaballoo about it" (J 10:82). [Scattered but less frequently S., S.Midl., DARE]

hell and gone: [*n. phr.* the remotest distance.] ". . . and lit out for hell an' gone." "It's me for the high hills of hell an' gone" (J 23:82).

hellin' around: [*v. phr.* wild partying.] Jake came to town, some months later, and proceeded to make merry after the fashion that our lumberjacks call "hellin' around" (B 209).

hell-roarin' bunch: [*n. phr.* a wild gang.] I asked a woods boss . . . why the [lumber]men were treated so . . . like convicts. He answered: "If you had to run a hell-roarin' bunch like mine, you'd know why. Their idea of conversation is an argument; their idea of argument is a rumpus. I can't afford that where there's two-hundred dollars' worth of crockery lyin' handy" (B 233).

Hell's banjer!: [*exclamation.* Speaking of revenuers:] "Hell's banjer! they don't go prodjectin' around lookin' for stills" (B 171). [S.App., DARE]

hemlock: [*n.* a low growing shrub, *leucothoe*.] What the mountaineers call hemlock is the shrub leucothoe (B 369). Near my cabin: swamp dogwood, . . . "hemlock" (leucothoe), galax (J 1:67). Women and children did better, in the days before Christmas, by gathering galax, "hemlock" (leucothoe), and mistletoe, selling to the dealers at the railroad, who ship them North for holiday decorations (B 41). A boy who was gathering "hemlock" told me with evident pride that "some of them go to London, England" 30 Nov. 1904 near Medlin (J 2:358; cf. B 41).

hender: [*v.*, variant of *hinder*.] (B 352) [Perhaps this spelling represents K's awareness of the merger of i and e before n in most S. and S.Midl. speech.]

he'p: [*v.*, variant of *help*.] "I wanted somebody to he'p me" (J 2:641). [S., S.Midl., DARE]

her'n: [*pron.* hers.] "A heifer o' her'n" (J 2:641). [Montgomery suggests the apostrophe here used is superfluous since this is not a contraction; [chiefly S., S.Midl., NEng, old fashioned, DARE]

het up: [*part. phr.* heated up, exhausted.] "Finally he [the bear] gits so tired and het up that he trees to rest hisself" (B 81). "They was all het up" (J 4:853). (B 358) [Somewhat old fashioned, widespread, DARE]

hick'ry: [*n., abbrev.* for hickory stick, specifically as used in punishment, in whipping.] The oft-heard threat "I'll w'ar ye out with a hick'ry!" is seldom carried out (B 334; J 1:298). [Chiefly S., S.Midl., DARE]

hicky: [*n.*] a thing for which no name is known. 'Do you see that little hicky turnin' round? That's what cuts the twine'" (C 3). [SC, WV, PA, DARE]

hiddenest, hiddenmost: [*adj., supl.,* the most well-hidden; covert] "It's the hiddenest place you ever seen" (J 3:1001). (J 2:642) "I found a patch of sang in the hiddenmost place you ever seen" (J 1:81).

hide-out: [1.] *n.* a hiding place (A). (J 2:601) [2. *v.* to hide out from authorities like the revenuers.] "Hide out—as 'hide out the horses'" (C 2). I have heard a deputy sheriff admit nonchalantly, on the stand, that when a homicide was committed . . . he advised the slayer to take to the mountains and "hide out" (B 414). When men are "hiding out" in the laurel, it is the women's part, which they never shirk, to carry them food and information (B 419).

high-ball: *v.i.* to decamp. "I'll make him high-ball out o' here (A). "Lit a nag and high-balled out o' there" (J 4:723). (J 2:601) [DARE lists wide distribution, mentioning railroading origin; cites definition proposed by K above.]

hill-billy: *n.* a mountaineer; humorous or depreciative. Also La., Kan., Ky. (A). "I'm a hill-billy, all right, and they needn't to glory their old flat lands to me!" (B 386). (J 4:763) [Widespread but esp. S.Midl., DARE]

hill o' corn: [*n. phr.* the small mound in which a few kernels of corn are planted.] "Many's the hill o' corn I've propped up with a rock to keep it from fallin' down-hill" (B 35).

hind-side-fust: [*adv.,* in reversed order, back to front.] "I wish t' my legs growed hind-side-fust."/ "*What* fer?"/ "So 's 't I wouldn't bark my shins" (B 102). [DARE lists this quotation from K. with its citation for "hindside-before, " which it says is widespread but less frequent in S., S.Midl. Perhaps "hind-side first" is now the preferred usage.]

hippin': *n.* a diaper, breech clout. Also Ill. (A). [As evidence of uncleanliness:] Hogs and chickens running through the house; dishwater spilled from back door to be waded through; yard littered with tin cans and pairings of fruit and vegetables; peach pomace at Stileses; unwashed "hippins" (J 2:435). [Scots dial., chiefly S., S.Midl., DARE]

hirelin': [*n.* hireling; someone who will do anything for pay.] "I ain't nobody's damn hirelin'!" (J 3:985). [DARE lists "hireland" for KY, TN, defines as "sharecropper."]

hisself: [*pron.*, variant of *himself.*] [The bear] "trees to rest hisself" (B 81). "He's so homely he has to take a bracer afore he can look hisself in the glass" (J 10:82). "That road winds around till a feller meets hisself, nearly" (J 1:322). [Chiefly S., S.Midl., DARE]

hist'ry: [*n.*, variant of *history*] He was fond of the expression "hist'ry says" so-and-so, and he considered it a clincher in all matters of debate (B 160). [For many speakers such a rendering might be merely eye dialect, but we suspect that K's N. dial. called for three syllables in this word and that he perceived the syncopation he heard as App. dial.]

hit, hit's: [*pron.* it, it is.] Our highlander often speaks in Elizabethan or Chaucerian or even pre-Chaucerian terms. His pronoun hit antedates English itself, being the Anglo-Saxon neuter of he (B 361). [Listed in Fox] (J 2:489). [On being asked if he rotated crops, a farmer responded:] "La, no! By that time the land would be so poor hit wouldn't raise a cuss-fight" (B 36). "Hit's gittin' wusser" (B 77). "I'm goin' to wash my feet." / "I wouldn't wash more 'n one tonight, Sairy, hit might make you sick" (J 2:437). "Bears . . . is all left-handed. . . . Hit's the left paw you wanter look out fer" (B 102). In some cases an unconscious sense of euphony seems to govern, as "Hit looks like it" (J 2:490).

hitched: [*past part.*; used metaphorically, like a horse standing outside in bad weather.] "Uh—looks like I could stand hitched all night [if not invited inside]" (B 272).

hoarsed up [*adj. phr.*, variant of *hoarse*.] "I'm kinder hoarsed up and cain't hardly talk" (J 2:475). [NH, VT, DARE]

hobble: [v.i.] to limp, to walk with difficulty. "Mrs. Frizzle on Pant'er Creek had a lame man [husband] who could barely hobble about." (J 1:294).

hobble bush: [*n.*] dog hobble (*Viburnum alnifolium*). [Flowers] May-June. White. Devil's Shoestrings, Tangle-legs. (J 26:26). [Esp. NE, DARE]

hobbledehoy: [*n.*] awkward stripling (J 1:272). "He was a hobble-dehoy of 16." (J 1:288).

hobnails: [*n.* short, broad-headed nails, used in shoes to prevent wear or slipping.] [The mountains are so steep] "goin' down, a man wants hobnails in the seat of his pants" (B 21). "He hain't got no squar'-headed hobnails" (B 130).

hog fat: [*adj.* fat as a hog, excessively fat.] In the Smoky Mountains the black bear, like most of the trees, attains its fullest development, and . . . it occasionally reaches a weight of 500 pounds when "hog fat" (B 97). [DARE lists a quotation from Oklahoma in which the expression is applied to humans.]

hoggin': *vbl. n.* [sic; probably *v.* or *pres. part.* is more accurate] Scratching (A). "He useter get up agin a post forty times a day to scratch his back, an' if anybody ast him what he was a-doin', he'd say, 'I'm a-hoggin'.'" (M.B.) (J 2:441).

hog-killin' time: [1. *n. phr.* late fall or early winter, when it first gets cold enough that meat will not spoil quickly.] At "hog-killin' time," the poorest live in abundance (B 326). [2. *n. phr.* by extension of the above, a particularly good time] "My goodness! if we didn't have a hog-killin' old time that night—two banjers and a fiddle" (M.B.) (J 4:761). [Chiefly S., S.Midl., DARE]

hog rifle: [*n.*] a squirrel rifle. The stress falls on *rifle* (A). There is a class of woodsloafers, very common here, that ranges the forest at all seasons with single-barrel shotguns or "hog rifles," killing bearing females as well as legitimate game, fishing at night, even using dynamite in the streams. (B 69). (J 2:401) [S.App., DARE]

hog-wallow: [*n.* a muddy place where hogs lie to cool themselves. In notes on mountain houses, K writes:] weeds in front and hog-wallow in rear (J 2:375). [Elsewhere in the same vein:] Hog wallow stinking under porch. Wife churning on the porch. Ten-year-old girl combing lice off her hair within two feet of churn (J 2:437).

hold or hold to: [*v.* to adhere to or to follow, to believe.] "She holds to the Babtis' and him to the Methodis' " (J 4:775). [In response to a man's claim that the dog is man's best friend, because it will starve for its master, a woman (probably M.B.) responded:] "I allers did hold it was a mighty triflin' sort o' man 'd let either his dog or his woman starve" (J 2:642). [Ozarks, DARE]

holdin' co't: [*v. phr.* courting. [Although the cabin door almost always stood open,] "when yo're a-holdin' co't and sech-like maybe you'll want to shet the do' sometimes—" (J 2:376).

holler: [1.] *n.* the visceral cavity. "I got wet to the *holler*" (A). [The dog] "bit a hole under the fore leg, through hide and ha'r, clar into the holler, so t' you can stick your hand in and seize the bear's heart" (B 107). [S.App., DARE] [2. *n.* a shout.] "He give a keen holler" (J 2:642). [Chiefly S., S.Midl., DARE]

holler tooth: [*n. phr.* a tooth containing a cavity.] "I've burnt my holler teeth out with a red-hot wire" (B 302).

holp: *v.t.* to help. "I axed him to *holp* me out." Also Ky. Pronounced *hôp* by the younger generation. Both in S. Car. In La. also *hvlp* (A; J 2:641). [Listed as Chaucerian term in Fox] (J 2:489). In mountain vernacular the Old English strong past tense still lives in begun, drunk, holped . . . Holp is used both as preterite and as infinitive: the *o* is long, and the *l* distinctly sounded by most of the people, but elided by such as drop it from almost, already, self (the *l* is elided from help by many who use that form of the verb) (B 357-58). (C 2)

holt: [*n.* hold.] Take a-holt (J 2:641). "Like the nigger that had a holt of the bull's tail, I didn't have time to chat" (J 4:763).

holy laugh: [*n. phr.* a form of religious ecstasy or hysteria, depending on your point of view.] I saw two Holiness exhorters . . . one of them shouting and exhibiting the "Holy laugh" (B 345). [S., S.Midl., DARE]

holy tone: [*n.* a gutteral sigh used for rhetorical emphasis among some preachers.] "So the ah or uh of the preacher's "holy tone"

(J 2:589). "Oh brethren, repent ye, and repent ye of your sins, ah; fer if ye don't, ah, the Lord, ah, he will grab yer by the seat of yer pants, ah, and hold yer over hell fire till ye holler like a coon!" (B 341; J 4:779).

hone: *v.i.* to desire with craving. "He jes' *hones* atter it." Also Kan., Ky. (A). "Boys, I did hone fer my dog, Fiddler, an' the times we'd have a-huntin'" (B 386). hunger (J 6). (J 2:603) [Chiefly S., S.Midl., DARE]

honeysuckle: [*n.* flame azalea (*Rhododendron calendulaceum*).] (J 2:359) [Scattered, but esp. S., S.Midl., DARE]

hootin': [*v.* to move like a hoot-owl in a square dance; part of the call; comic.] "First couple cage the bird with three arms around. Bird hop out and hoot-owl in; three arms around and hootin' agin" (B 338).

hoot-owl in: [*v.* to place one male partner (hoot-owl) from two couples inside the circled arms of the other three people in a square dance step; see **hootin'**.]

hooty-big owl: [*n.* probably a big hoot-owl.] "There's a hooty-big owl out there in the yard" (J 4:56).

horse sorrel: [*n. phr.* probably *Trifolium arvense*—Pittillo.] (Not sheep sorrel, which sometimes is used as a substitute) Plant with clover-like leaf, sour like sorrel, small yellow flowers; grows in gardens, sometimes as high as one's knee. [K tells of its use as cure for cancerous growths when mixed in a pewter bowl—the acid left is the agent.] (J 2:481). [See also **rabbit clover.**]

horse-throwed: *p.a.* [sic, *past. part.*, thrown by a horse] "Ever since I was *horse-throwed*" (A; J 2:475). "Pringle's a-been horse-throwed down the clift, and he's in a manner stone dead" (B 299). [S. App., Ozarks, DARE]

hoss: [*n.*, variant of *horse*.] "I've seed hit blow, here on top o' Smoky, till a hoss couldn't stand up agin it" (B 77).

hossback: [*n.* horseback.] "Bear-fightin' in these mountains . . . you cain't foller up on hossback, but hafter do your own runnin'" (B 80).

hounds: [*n.* long-eared hunting dog of a variety of breeds.] "Hounds has the best noses, and they'll run a bear all day and night, and the next day, too; but they won't never tree—

they're afeared to close in" (B 81). "He could talk a hungry hound off a meat wagon" (J 2:637).

how come or **huccum:** [*inter. adv.*, why?] (C 1) (J 2:603)

howdy do: [a greeting, variant of *how do you do?*; also used as the name of a square dance step:] "Right hands across and howdy do?" (B 338). [Chiefly S., S.Midl., DARE]

howsomever: [*conj.* however.] "Howsomever, they is but one thing that will come here" (J 3:951.24). [Scattered but chiefly S, C.Atl, S.Midl., DARE]

huckleberries: [the following list appears to designate varieties of berries common to the mountains; usually "huckleberry" refers only to the genus *Gaylussacia*, which has ten larger seeds; "blueberry" refers to any of the genus *Vaccinium*, which has more, but smaller seeds (Pelham Thomas):] dangleberry (*Gaylussacia frondosa*), high bush huckleberry (*G. resinosa*), bush huckleberry (*G. dumosa*), mountain blueberry (*Vaccinium pallidum*), squareberry (*Vistaminenia*), farkleberry, Tree huckleberry (*V. arboreum*) (J 26:27). [see **hurtleberry**.]

huk-uh: [*interjection*, variant of *uh-huh*, yes.] He rolled his quid and placidly answered: "Huk-uh; when I move all I haffter do is put out the fire and call the dog" (B 36).

hull: [1. *n.* bean pod.] Beans dried in the pod, and then boiled "hull and all" (B 366). [Chiefly S., S.Midl., DARE] [2.] *n.* Applied [metaphorically] to cartridge shells. Also Ky. (A). "I went to shoot up at him, but my new hulls [cartridges—K] fit loose in this old chamber" (B 101). "How many hulls you got?" (hunting term) (J 4:749). [Chiefly S.Midl., DARE] [3. *adv.*, variant of *whole*.] "He had a hull raft o' money" (J 2:641).

hunderd: [*n.*, variant of *hundred*.] "a hunderd pound" (J 2:366). "He must weigh two hunderd and fifty" (B 91). [Chiefly Atl, S.Midl., & S., DARE]

hunkers: [*n.* haunches; buttocks.] "[Revenuers] set at home on their hunkers till some feller comes and informs" (B 171). [Chiefly Midl., S., DARE]

hunky-dory box: [*n.*] a portable camp cupboard—for utensils and foodstuffs (J 18:34).

hurt: [*adj.* burned, overdone; comic understatement in the expression,] "Them 'taters ain't hurt a-bein' done" (M.B., returning sweet potatoes to oven.) (J 2:642, 429).

hurted: [*v.*, nonstandard form of *hurt.*] (B 385). [Chiefly S., S.Midl, but esp. S.Atl, DARE]

hurtin': [1.] *n.* a pain. Also Ill. (A). "As a hurtin' (pain) in the side" (C 2). "Cain't you-uns give her some easin'-powder for that hurtin' in her chist?" (B 298). [2. needing; wanting.] "There's a lot o' folks around hyur [or here] hurtin' for lard, and I ain't got none" (Pete Laney) (J 2:461, 487). [S., S.Midl., DARE]

hurtleberry: [*n.*, variant of *whortleberry*] (J 14:80). [See also **huckleberry.**]

hyar, hyeh: [adv. variants of *here*] "From hyar to the railroad is seventeen miles" (B 122). "But I'm hyeh to tell you they're the most *uncouth* cooks I ever saw in my life." (Whaley on mountain cooking) (J 2:461). [See also **hyur.**]

hyep, hyep, hyep: "(like turkey yelp)—Call to scattered dogs through the hills after hunt, at nightfall." (Native huntsman) (C 1).

hyur: *adv.*, variant of *here.* Pronounced *hyeh* only in calling a dog [though the quote given above appears to contradict this.] Not local [i.e. not restricted only to the mountains] (A). "Thar's lots o' folks a-hurtin' around hyur for lard" (B 32; J 2:461). "You've scrouged right in hyur in front of the fire" (B 75). "Yes, th'r's a right smart seenyuh around hyur" (J 1:7). "This is good, strong land, or it wouldn't hold up all the rocks there is around hyur" (B 36). [See also **hyar, hyeh.**]

I

idgit: [*n.*] half-wit (J 1:306).

I'd tell a man!: [exclamation] With the stress [on *tell*], is simply a strong affirmative (B 360).

if so be: [*conj. phr.* if.] "I'll name it to Newt, if so be he's thar" (B 371).

ill: *adj.* ill-natured, vicious. "That feller's *ill* as h————." [A; J

2:637 reads "ill (vicious) as hell."] "Hit's the younger [dog] that's ill," by which he meant vicious (B 80). "ill-natured, as 'Ill as a hornet'" (C 2).

ill-convenient: *adj.* inconvenient (A; J 2:603).

illude: [*v.*] to play tricks on, cheat, mock, snare. Rare. (J 3:1007).

impertinent: [*adj.* annoying.] "I had an impertinent tooth in my upper jaw" (J 2:475).

Indian physic: [*n.*] Bowman's root (*Porteranthus trifoliatus*). [Flowers] May—July. White and reddish. Root substitute for ipecac. (J 26:24). Emetic, used especially in treatment of milk-sickness (J 2:473). [DAE's earliest citation is from *Flora Virginica* (1743).]

Indian sanicle: [*n.* white snakeroot (*Eupatorium rugosum urticaefolium*); contains poisonous alcohol tremefol, soluble in milk fat] also deerwort, boneset [usually a different plant, *Eupatorium perfoliatum*], white snakeroot, rich weed: cause of milk sickness (J 2:473).

Indian tobacco: [*n.*] lobelia (*Lobelia inflata*). [Flowers] July-Nov. Light Blue. Plant med[icinal], emetic & poisonous. (J 26:35). "In midsummer . . . the *Lobelia inflata* or Indian tobacco comes. . . . Leaves and tops are a drug for asthma," Asheville *Citizen*, 22 Jan. 1928 (J 2:480). [DAE suggests wide distribution.]

Indian turnip: [*n.*] jack-in-the-pulpit (*Arisaema triphyllum*). [Flowers] April-July. Purple, brown, and green. Root edible, dessicated, acrid raw (J 26:16). Indian Turnip, pared, sliced, dried, and powdered in a mortar is said to cure phthisic (J 2:481). [DAE citations from Eastern seaboard]

indignant: [*adj.* indigent; a malapropism.] "You get any help from the railroad Brotherhood?"/ "I was on the indignant list" [indigent list] (J 2:639).

ingons: "*n.* onions. (Mrs. K.) Mark of old settlers. 22 July 1926" (C 11).

in reason: [*adv. phr.* rightly.] "I knowed in reason she'd have the mullygrubs over them doin's" (B 371).

instanter: [*adv.* more quickly.] "No, my boy, that liquor goes down your own throat instanter" (B 65).

instid: [*adv.* instead; listed in Fox as Chaucer word] (J 2:489).

insurance: [*n.* proof, surety.] (J 2:603)

in trust: [*n.* money paid for the use of money, interest] "He paid in trust on what he borrowed" (J 2:459).

ipecac: [*n.* popular emetic, used to treat milk sickness among other illnesses.] "First puke 'em out with lobelia, or Indian physic, or ipecac." Then large doses of apple brandy and honey, until drunk. Then sweet oil to open the bowels (J 2:473) [DA citations suggest Midl., S.Atl. distribution.]

iron-rustin': [*v.* staining with rust.] "That old can that I've been washin' in is iron-rustin' my clo'se" (J 2:417). Iron rust (J 2:592).

is: [*v.* frequent substitute for **are**] "Bears . . . is all left-handed" (B 102). "Much of my jars is in use" (C 11).

is't: [*contraction* for *is that*] "The reason is't we know them men" (B 170).

ivy: [*n.* mountain laurel (*Kalmia latifolia*)] Laurel is [called] ivy, and rhododendron is laurel (B 369). (J 1:71) [DA has citations from VA, NC, TN, ME; NEng only, Kurath]

J

jamboree: [*n.* a great meeting; used in place names.] Jamboree (Pike, Ky.) (J 26:80).[DA, DAE suggest a wide distribution.]

jape: *v.i.* to copulate. Oxf.E.D. and W[ebster] mark it *Obs.* (A; J 4:843).

jaybird: [*n.* bluejay (*Cyanocitta cristata*.)] "He's as antic as a jaybird when he takes the notion" (A).

jedgmatically: [*adv.* judiciously, but with evasive connotations, "as far as I can tell."] "Jedgmatically, I don't know." [A response to a question about a person's being a moonshiner.] (B 117).

jedgment: [*n.,* variant of *judgment.*] "It's my opinion and jedgment" (J 18:29).

jellico weed: [*n.*] angelica (A). " 'Jellico weed' taints a hog's flesh so that you can smell a hog that has eaten it 'if he is wild and bristles up'" (J 1:67). [See also **angelico**]

jerkin': [*vbl. n.* drying (of meat).] Meat-scaffold Branch is where venison was hung up for 'jerkin' (B 374).

jerks: [*n.* contortions of the body.] Men and women at the camp-meetings fell victims to "the jerks," "barking exercises," erotic vagaries, physical wreckage, or insanity, to which the frenzy led (B 344). [KY, DAE]

jest: [*adv.*, variant of *just.*] "jest nacherally" (B 78). "Jest this-away" (B 122). [See also **jist**]

jine: [*v.t.*, variant of *join.*] "She jined the Holiness People" (J 4:775). "He grabbed a laurel to swing hisself down by, but the stem bruk, and down he come suddent, to jine the music" (B 106).

jinglin': [*part.* causing a noise, portending gossip.] "You can hear the news jinglin' afore he comes within gunshot" (B 276).

jint: [*n.*, variant of *joint.*] "With his nose out o' jint" (B 94). " 'Bout as long as the jint of yer thumb" (J 23:85).

jist: [*adv.*, variant of *just.*] "This stuff Johnny has is jist as wuthless" (J 10:83). "The road was jist in a slosh" (J 1:322). (J 14:80) [See also *jest.*]

jiste: *n.*, variant of *joist*. General (A; J 2:377).

jittany: *n.*, variant of *jitney* [a nickle] (A). [Listed under "money terms" on J 2:459, under "coinages" on J 2:601; see also **gittany**] [DA lists as slang, widespread]

job: *v.t.*, variant of *jab*. Also Ill., Ia. (A). "Job that wood into the stove so it won't fall out on the floor" (J 2:429).

John Henry: [normally a signature name: "write your John Henry," it appears to have become a comic substitute, as in this condemnation of mountain cooking:] "The height of their ambition is to cook everything in grease, and as quickly as possible. . . . I'll be John Henry if I ain't cured" (Whaley) (J 2:423). [DA lists former but not latter.]

Johnnycake: [*n.* cornmeal bread.] Johnnycake Br[anch]. (McDowell, W.Va.) (J 26:85). [DAE associates the term with NEng, but DA suggests distribution has spread.]

joner: [*n.* disreputable person, one who causes bad luck] (J 2:603).

joree bird: [*n.* eastern towhee (*Pipilo erythrophthalmus*).] I could hear the *t-wee, t-wee* of "joree birds" (towhees) which winter in the valleys (B 90). [Possibly to suggest etymology, K added a note after listing "Joree-bird" (J 1:73) among S.App. fauna: "*Joree-bird* /Bartram (Travels, p. 357) mentions a Cherokee village of 'Jore' and the 'Jore' mountains 'said to be the highest land in the Cherokee country,' and the 'Jore' River or Creek, near Charleston [Bryson City—K] 'which is a considerable branch [Tuckaseegee?—K] of the Tanase." (J 26:54) [DA, DAE suggest S. distribution.]

jower, jour: *n., v.* quarrel. Also Ill., Kan., Ky. (A). If [men] quarrel, it is a . . . jower (B 368). ". . . the smell o' the woods, and nobody bossin' and jowerin' at all" (B 386). "He kept on and on jouring about the matter till I got plumb sick" (C 3). [Also MO, DAE]

joyful: [*adj.* rich, productive.] "That Thunderhead's a joyful place for sarvice-berries (Louis) (J 2:433). "Keerless Knob is a joyful place for wild salat" (B 375).

juberous: *adj.* dubious. Also Ill., Kan., Ky. (A). "It looks juberous" (J 2:641). "doubtful" (C 2) (J 2:603) [S.App., DA]

jue: [*adj.*, variant of *due*.] (B 352)

juggle: [*n.*] "a junk or slab split off in hewing a log square" (D 1).

jump: [*v.t.* to extract a tooth with a hammer.] "A man who knows how can jump a tooth without it hurtin' half as bad as pullin'" (B 301). [See also **tooth jumping.**]

K

kag: [*n.*, variant of *keg*] Kag for keg [was] the primitive and legitimate form (B 362). [See also **cag.**]

keeck: *v.*, variant of *kick* (A).

keen: [*adj.* sharp.] "He give a keen holler" (J 2:642).

keer, keerful, keerless: *n., adj.* variants of *care, careful, careless.*

Also Ky. (A). [Listed under "shiftlessness" in J 6; used in placenames:] Keerless Knob, Greenbriar, W.Va. (J 26:84). (J 2:642; B 352)

kem: v., variant of *came*. Also Ky. (A). "They kem up from the river" (J 2:641). "I see they give Bryan a lot of receptions when he kem back from the other world" (B 17). (B 307)

kentry: [*n.*, variant of *country*.] "Borned in the kentry and ain't never been out o' hit" is all that most of them can say for themselves (B 429).

ketch: [*v.t.*, variant of *catch*.] "He made a lunge to ketch the hog" (J 2:367). (Bob) "Wish t' I had a pair o' white wool socks." (M.B.) "What fer?" (Bob) " 'Cause the fleas get all tangled up in 'em so's they caint hop, an' a feller can see good on the white to ketch 'em!" (J 2:642)

ketch a breath: [*v. phr.*] "catch a breath ([to] see or move about in cleared space.) 'You can ketch a breath near 'bout up to Henson's now, down in that river bottom since the weeds has been cut down' (Mrs. H.) 9 July 1926" (C 11).

ketchin': [*pres. part.* contagious.] I knowed in reason if I stayed thar a day longer I'd git down with some ketchin' townsickness" (J 1:322f).

kin: [*v.*, variant of *can*.] "If I kin help it." 20 Feb. 1922 (C 6).

kinder: [*adj. phr.*, variant of *kind of*.] "I'm kinder hoarsed-up and caint hardly talk" (J 2:475).

kindlin': [*n.* small pieces of wood used for starting fires.] "Several trees has been wind-throwed and busted to kindlin'" (B 77). [Widespread, DAE]

kindly: [*adv.* kind of, rather.] " 'That sets kindly crooked.' (Mrs. Crawford) 9 Aug. 1926" (C 11).

kinfolks: [*n.* relatives.] "They was kinfolks" (J 1:304). (J 2:603)

kittle: [*n.*,] variant of *kettle*. General (A; J 2:367). (J 6)

kiver: [1. *n.* cover.] "Blankets and coverlets, known as 'kivers,' come in considerable numbers from the household looms." (J 2:451) "From [ropes strung above the beds] hung linsey dresses and store clothes, and now and then a bright 'kiver,' a pair of winter boots, strings of dried apples, bunches of yellowish-green tobacco and other odd-looking articles." (Vincent, "Pawnshop") (J 2:375). "You ain't got enough kiver on the bed"

(C 3). In many homes you will still find the ancient spinning wheel, with a hand-loom on the porch and in the loft there will be a set of quilting frames for making "kivers" (B 319-20). (J 6) [2. *v.t.* to cover. That bear was] "kivered with fat, five inches thick" (B 96). [An interesting instance of umlaut still in operation.]

kiver patterns: [*n. pl.* cover or blanket patterns.] "[Patterns] are made of cotton warp, and the woof has two shuttles, one carrying the white cotton and the other the wool." [These are not the same as quilting patterns, though perhaps later imitated. The following are mentioned as favorite patterns by Mrs. Robinson: chariot wheels and church windows, dogwood blossom and running vine, cat track, log cabin, blooming leaf, young man's fancy, rose in the wilderness, castle city.] (MacClintock) (J 2:451).

knob people: [*n.* mountaineers. A reference is made to the quarrelsomeness of knob people.] (J 4:857)

knock: [1.] *v.i.* to box, to spar. [2.] *n.* **knocker** [fighter] (A). "a practiced knocker" (B 141). (J 2:642) [Both DA and DAE attest to this usage.]

knocked dead: [*adj. phr.* knocked out.] "He was knocked dead for a while" (J 2:475, 519).

knock-fight: *n.* fisticuffing (A). He was "a practiced knocker" . . . "a master hand in a knock-fight" (B 141). (J 2:605)

knowed: [*pret. v.* knew.] "I've knowed him from a boy" (B 170). "I knowed in reason" (B 371). (B 358)

knotty: [*adj.* gnarled, dried-up.] "If it rains on the first day of June, the fox grapes get knotty" (Shuler, Dillsboro [NC]) (J 2:671).

knucks: [*n.* brass knuckles, used in fighting.] (J 4:857). [see **brass knucks.**]

konkus: [*n.*] "There is a cancerous disease peculiar to the pine tree, to which lumbermen give the name of 'conk' or 'konkus' " (Fraser 99) (D 1). [NEng, DAE]

kraut: *v.t.* [to make sauerkraut.] "I don't do like old Mis' Posey, *kraut* my cabbage whole" (A; J 2:429). "Mrs. Barnett and I, in one day, cut up 100 lbs. of cabbage and 'krauted it' all, the cutting being done with a 1 lb. tin coffee can, every now and then hammering the edge smooth on a round stick" (J 2:419). "Kraut, which is the sole contribution to highland speech of those numerous Germans (mostly Pennsylvania Dutch) who joined the first settlers in this region, and whose descendants, under wondrously anglicized names, form to-day a considerable element of the highland population (B 363-64).

kukluxing: [*vbl. n.* behaving like someone in the Ku Klux Klan. Going armed] "was a necessity in the old Indian-fighting days, and throughout the kukluxing and white-capping era following the Civil War" (B 415). [Both DA and DAE list this verb form with citations from S., Midl.]

kyanized: [*adj.* from kyanite (?): enameled, tough.] The most kyanized old woodsman that you ever saw always lugs along some gimcrack that he is half ashamed of in public but idolizes in private (J 27:1a). [This may well be K's term rather than a genuine token of App. speech.]

kyarpet: [*n.,*] variant of *carpet* (A). "Also Charleston, S.C." (C 2)

L

La, law, lawd: [interj.; euphemisms for Lord] "Good La!" (B 85). "Yea, la!" (B 277). "La, no!" (B 36). Laws-a-mighty me! Law bless my heart! Laws-a-mercy! (J 2:607). "Laws-a-marcy, how it does hurt!" (B 303). "I'm a-waitin' fer Jim Johnson, and with the help of the Lawd I'm goin' to blow his damn head off" (B 347).

lagoon: [*n.*] "Where the ground is low-lying, in swamp or marsh, the country on both sides is completely submerged, forming what are called 'lagoons' in the Southern states and in our back woods 'drowned lands.'" (Fraser 281) (D 1). [See also **logon.**] DAE lists this term with the above meaning; the citations suggest a S.E. distribution.]

laig: [*n.*] variant of *leg*. Also W.Res., Ill., Ia., Kan., Ky., N.Y., (A). [Also] **lag** (C 3). (C 2)

landing: [*n.*, place for logs "which have been slid into a pile at the bottom of a hollow and which will remain there until they are loaded onto a train" (E. Monteith).] "A 'landing' is a term used by lumbermen to denote a place cleared of bushes and trees on the bank of a stream or pond, to which the logs cut in the winter are hauled, in anticipation of the spring floods." (Hubbard vii) (D 1). [Both DA and DAE include this lumbering term as of NEng origin.]

lap: [1.] *n.*, variant of *lop*. The drooping portion of a fallen tree (A). [2. n.] "A treetop left on the ground after logging is called the lap" (B 369-70). "Lap: That part of the tree left after the saw[n] log has been taken off" (C 2). (J 2:603) [DAE defines as "a twig or branch trimmed from a tree, a fallen piece of timber."]

larned, l'arnt: [*v. pret.* learned.] He l'arnt better nex' time" (J 2:641). "I've larned now whar they're crossin' " (B 94). (J 10:83)

larnin': [*n.* information.] "I reckon he'll pick up some larnin' in the next two, three days" (B 80).

'lasses: [*n.* molasses.] Sorghum patches, "lasses" (J 2:421). ["humorous, colloquial," DA, DAE]

lath-open bread: Bread made from biscuit dough, with soda and buttermilk. The shortening is worked in last, instead of with the milk. The bread is baked in flat cakes; when broken edgewise, it parts readily into thin cakes longitudinally (A). "Lath-open bread denotes that it opens into lath-like strips" (B 367). (J 2:601)

laurel: [*n.* rhododendron.] Laurel is ivy, and rhododendron is laurel (B 369). (J 1:71) [DA confirms usage.]

laurely: [*adj.* covered with laurel.] "The Tennessee side of the mountain is powerful steep and laurely" (B 79). The Tennessee side [from Clingman to Guyot] is simply the Devil's own country, steeper, rockier, more thorny, and "laurely," and with fewer trails of any sort, than any other region I know of (C 10).

lavish: *n.* plenty. "If anybody wanted a history of this county for fifty years, he'd git a lavish of it by reading that mine-suit testimony" (A; B 357).

law: [1. *v.t.* take to the law or courts.] "If they planted rainbow [trout] in a stream of mine I'd law 'em thru every court in the land" [quoted from "one old man" by Walter Ponchot, letter of 18 Jan. 1928] (C 7). "If he or a kinsman be involved in 'lawin'' with a member of some rival tribe." (B 394). [2. *interj.*; euphemism for Lord] "Law bless my heart" (J 2:607). [See also **La.**]

lay: [*v. i.* lie.] "A man cain't lay cluss enough to you to to keep warm" (B 103). [Montgomery notes that "this is what most Americans use."]

lay hands on: *v. phr.* to carry (a corpse) as a pall bearer does. (A) "I had to lay hands on the corpse" (J 2:483). (J 2:642)

lay off: *v. phr.* to purpose without attempting [to procrastinate]. "I've laid off and laid off to do that, an' now I've never got it done." Also Ill., Ky. (A; B 371; J 1:256). (J 2:642p) [Colloq., but no locale indicated in DA.]

lay out: [*v. phr.*; two meanings are still in use locally and we are not sure which K may have been recording: 1. to avoid, to stay out of, as in "to lay out of school," i.e. to "skip" school; NC, W.VA, Kurath; and 2. to prepare a corpse for burial; the term is simply listed in J 2:603.]

lay-over: *n.* trap, dead-fall. "That's a lay-over to catch meddlers." In La., *laroes catch meddlers* (A; J 2:642, 4:739).

lay up against: [*v. phr.* hold against, hold responsible.] "Oh, we-uns don't lay *that* up agin the Government!" (B 123). [listed DA, DAE]

layway: [*v.t.* to waylay; listed under "inverted words" with *lessun* and *peckerwood* in J 2:605] A busybody . . . is likely to be run out of the country or even "laywayed" and silenced forever (B 413). "Then mebbe his brother would layway you" (J 3:911). And there is no romance about a real mountain feud. It is marked by suave treachery, "double teaming," "laywaying," "blind-shooting," and a general heartlessness and brutality (B 421).

lead: [*n.* ridge.] There are few "leads" rising gradually to their crests. Each and every one of these ridges is a Chinese wall magnified to altitudes of from a thousand to two thousand feet, and covered with thicket (B 20). (J 6, 2:603)

leader: [*n.* tendon] "He cut one of the leaders on his wrist." (C 3).

leaf-hoppers: [*n. pl.* (*Jassidae*). They] eject a spray from the anus. Where there are many of them, if the tree be shaken, there will fall what seems to be a light shower of rain. Hence the "weeping tree mystery" in Texas (J 23:85). [See also **wildmire**; DA, DAE suggest NEng origin.]

least: [*adj.* smallest.] "Them's the least hooks I ever seen" (J 4:751). [Both DA and DAE state that the term has become standard in American birdlore to describe the smallest of a kind, e.g. "least bittern."]

leather breeches: [*n. phr.*] green beans dried and cooked in the pod (A; J 2:419). Beans dried in the pod, then boiled "hull and all," are called leather-breeches (this is not slang, but the regular name) (B 366). (J 2:597, 601) [W.NC; DA uses this quotation from K.]

leetle: [1. *adj.* little.] "Whar one o' our leetle sleds can't go, we haffter pack on mule-back or tussle it on our own wethers" (B 123). [Note the frequency of the combination **leetle-grain**: apparently, a little bit] "yerbs . . . ain't no good 'thout a leetle grain o' whiskey" (B 121). [On hearing that George Washington enforced a whiskey tax, an old man said,] "Waal, I'm satisfied now that Washington was a leetle-grain cracked" (B 161). [2. *adv.*] "I'll take a leetle more" (J 2:429).

leg bail, to give: *v. phr.* to abscond. "He give em leg bail an' lit out fer home." Slang, not [just] local (A). (J 2:601, 4:883)

leist: [*adj.*, variant of *least*; perhaps this spelling suggests a slightly lowered vowel quality.] (J 6)

leowzin': [*pres. part.* lousing, lazying.] (J 2:642p) [See also **louze**.]

lepte: [*v.*, variant of *leaped*; listed in Fox (J 2:489) and possibly intended to convey the preference for leapt over leaped, i.e. the older verb form.]

le's: [*contraction* for "let us."] "Le's be movin'" (B 98).

less'n, lessun: [1.] *conj.* "unless" (C 2). [Listed under "inverted words] with "peckerwood" and "layway" in J 2:605.] "Men don't do nothin' fer amusement, lessun they chaw terbacker." Also Kan., Ky. (A). "Hit takes three days to make the round trip, less'n you break an axle, and then it takes four" (B 123). [2. *prep.* in less than] "Let ary thing go wrong in the fam'ly—fever, or snake bite, or somethin'—and we can't git a doctor up hyar less'n three days; and it costs scand'lous" (B 121).

let grass go to seed: [*v. phr.* to delay, to procrastinate] "The

judge'd right up and want to know why you let grass go to seed
afore you came and informed on them" (B 118).

lettuce: [*n.*] "*Saxifraga erosa,* a common plant, is eaten by the
natives as a salad, and is known as 'lettuce.'" (Gray) (J 2:433).

lettuce bed: [*n.*; listed under "coinages" in J 2:601 and under
"country landscapes" in J 2:642o, this appears to be a metaphor, used to describe the appearance of rhododenron "slicks"
as seen from above.]

lick: [*n.* one stroke with an axe or hammer.] Granville says that a
man cannot strike as true a lick with a bent-handled axe as with
a straight handle, and that the former blisters and cramps one's
hands (J 2:401). "They cut around the gum, and then put the
nail at jest sich an angle, slantin' downward for an upper tooth,
or upward for a lower one, and hit one lick" (B 302).

lick log: [*n.*] a notched log used for salting cattle (B 374). [DA, DAE
include as S., Midl.]

lickety cut: [*adv.* very quickly, lickety split] "going lickety-cut
down the hill" (J 10:56). [DAE.]

lie-bill: *n.* perversion of libel. Also Kan. (A). "I'll swear out a lie-
bill agin him" (J 4:887). "An' him a Baptis' preacher an' my son-
in-law! I knocked a hole with him in the Chatooga [sic] River
big enough to drown a cow in, an' now he goes a-lyin' and a-
lie-billin' me!" (J 4:855).

lief, liefer: [*adv.* soon, likely.] "I'd about as lief jump into a
pant'er den in my shirt-tail" (J 4:855). "Liefer as not, that's not
so" (J 2:642). [See also **liv.**]

life everlasting: [*n.* possibly pearly everlasting (*Gnaphalium ob-
tusafolium*] Life everlasting is smoked for catarrh (J 2:481).

light: [*n.* embers.] At bedtime the coals are covered up on the
hearth with ashes so as to keep a "light" for starting the
morning fire, and the house remains unheated all night (J
2:373).

light a rag: *v. phr.* to decamp. "I lit a rag for home." Also S. Car.
(A). "He lit a rag fer home" (B 371).

light and hitch: [*v. phr.* an invitation to visit; alight and hitch your
horse.] "Howdy, Tom: light and hitch" (B 372). "light and
hitch" (J 4:723).

light bread: [*n.* white bread.] "Brother Ponder—I can prove to

you by the Book that light bread ain't fitten to eat. . . . It says in
the Book o' Numbers: 'our soul loatheth this light bread'" (J
2:639). (J 10:82, 2:639) [S., DAE]

light wood: [*n.* resinous splinters used for starting fires.] Pine
knots for "light wood" (J 2:405). [DA lists *lighterd* as S. for *light
wood*. Kurath suggests more common in E.NC than in W.NC.]

like as if: [*phrasal conj.* for example.] Local locution (J 2:592).

like of: [*n. phr.* something like.] "By God, I was *expectin'* to hear
the like o' that!" (B 300).

like to: [*adv.* almost.] "It like to kill him." "He like to died" (J
2:475). "Them two preachers like to had a ruction" (J 4:853).
"My leg like to killed me" (B 303; J 2:471). "He like to broke his
neck" (J 2:603).

linger on: *v. phr.* to be ailing. "I 'low Mr. Brooks is takin' the fever.
He's jis been a *lingerin' on* for two or three days." Also La., Ill.
(A). "ailing day after day" (C 2).

lingister: *n.* interpreter. Also *linkister, linkster*. Also Ga. and Fla.
(A). Also *leingister* (J 2:642). In our county some Indians always
appear at each term of court, and an interpreter must be en-
gaged. He never goes by that name, but by the obsolete title
linkister or link'ster, by some lin-gis-ter" (B 364). (J 2:603) [DAE
suggests Midl., and S.Midl.]

linsey: [*n.* homespun.] ". . . But women wear 'linsey' gowns of
their own making." (Vincent, "Frontier") (J 2:447). [Midl., DAE]

listed: [*pred.adj.* striped. "That's a *listed* pig" (A; J 2:367). a striped
[animal] is listed (B 369). (J 2:603)

lit: [*v. pret.* of *light*, in the sense of to hurry, to speed] "He riz an'
knocked me down with his left paw, an' walked right over me,
an' lit up the ridge" (B 101). "I tuk my fut in my hand and lit
out." "He lit a rag fer home" (B 371).

little bitty: [*adj. phr.* small.] "A feist is one o' them little bitty
dogs" (B 94). "A small, little bitty hole" (B 359-60).

liv: [*adv* likely, willingly, variant of *lief*.] "I'd as liv do one as the
other" (J 10:84).

loafer: [1.] *v.i.* to loaf. "That dog's jist *loaferin'* about, up an' down
this road" (A). "Yea, la! I'm jist loafering about" (B 277; J 1:256).
[2.] *n.* **loaferer** (A). "He's nothin' but a loaferer" (J1:256). (J
2:371; B 351) [Cf. **brogue.**]

lobelia: [*n.* (*Lobelia inflata*)] an emetic [especially in the treatment of milk sickness.] (J 2:481). (J 2:473) [See also **Indian tobacco.**]

lock: *n.* joint. "The pain's way back in the *lock* o' my jaw" (A; J 2:475 adds: "just raisin' the devil"). (J 2:462o)

loden: [*n.* waterproof wool cloth.] Leggings should be of woolen cloth, preferably of "loden" (J 27:1m). [This may be K's term and not a genuine token of App. speech.]

logging crews: [K listed what he apparently considered a typical crew in a logging camp in J 2:642y. Under] "Camp": Camp Foreman, Time Boss, Cook, 2 Cookees, Commissary Clerk, Blacksmith, Saw Filer, Lobby Hog—Shit Slinger; [under] "Cutting Crew (7)": Push (measures & bosses), 2 Sawyers, 1 Chopper, 1 Knot-humper, 1 Ringer, 1 Spudder; [under] "Bark Crew": Push, Rawhiders, Teamsters; [under] "Ball-hooting Crew": Push, Ball-hooters; [under] "Skidding Crew": Teamsters, Grab-drivers, Landing Men; [under] "Road Crew": 1 Road Monkey (dynamites and improves); [under] "Swamping Crew (chop out road)": Buck Swamper (boss), Swampers; [under] "Train Crew": Engineer, Fireman, Loader, Top-loader, Tong-sticker, Train manager, *Co.*; [and the final entry] Scaler.

logging swamp: [*n. phr.*; lumberman's term.] " 'Logging swamp' is the building of the [logging] road" (Springer 84, 97) (D 1). [DAE defines this term as "a swamp from which logs are obtained," but the accompanying quotations agree better with our definition.]

logon: [*n.*, loggers' term.] " 'Logon,' probably a derivative of 'lagoon,' means a very shallow arm of a stream or pond, where lilies and grass grow profusely" (Hubbard vii) (D 1). [See also **lagoon.**]

long-sweetening: [n.] "Coffee and tea (if sweetened at all), they mollify with home-made sorghum molasses, which they call 'long-sweetening,' or with sugar, . . . 'short sweetening' " (Allen, "Cumberland") (J2:243) (J 2:601). [DAE's earliest citation of this term is from NC, but later ones range through Midl., M.W.]

lookout: [*n.* outlook, opinion, concern.] "Ef they's ary man in this aujience thet don't agree with me, thet's his lookout, an' not mine" (J 4:779). [Another "inverted word."]

louse around: *v. phr.* to play the parasite (A). [See also **louze.**]

louse-comb [*n.* a fine-toothed comb for removing lice.] "We ain't got no comb, but a little bitty louse-comb" (J 2:438).

louze, louzin': [1. *v.* to loaf, lazying around; listed under "laziness" (J 6).] "I don't see no use in jist louzin' around" (J 1:256). [See also **louse around.**] [2. *v.* to louse up, mess up.] "Them loggers jest louzes up folkses houses" (B 272). (J 2:642p) [See also **leowzin'.**]

love: *v.t.* to like; applies to taste in food. "Do you *love* pickle-beans?" Also O., Ia., Kan., Ky. (A). Your hostess, proffering apple sauce, will ask, "Do you love sass?" . . . It is well for a traveler to be forewarned that the word love is commonly used here in the sense of like or relish (B 367).

'low: [1. *v.t.* to allow, purpose, intend.] "I 'lowed to go to town" (J 2:641; cf. B 371). "I 'lowed to git me a plug o' tobacco" (J 2:461). [2. v.t. to believe, to assert] "I 'low I've done growed a bit atter that mess o' meat" (B 98). "I 'lowed I'd lost it" (J 2:641). "No, I 'low I won't" (J 4:749).

low-downest: [*adv.* worst, dirtiest.] "That's the low-downest thing a feller can do" (J 10:83). [S., W., DAE]

low wine: [*n. phr.*] singlings. The liquor of first distillation ("low wines" of the trade) which moonshiners redistill at a lower temperature to make whiskey (A). [Five gallons of low wine is listed among items confiscated in a raid on an illicit distillery.] Letter from Chas. J. Beck, 22 Apr. 1921 (C 4). [S., W., DAE]

luzzuries: [*n. pl.*, variant of *luxuries.*] "Certain luzzuries that people wants, and they're bound to have them" (J 2:639).

M

main: [*adj.* indisposed; variant of *mean;* K notes dialectal pronunciation in J 2:603.]

mainly: [*adv.* sickly; variant of *meanly*;] K lists under "quaint idioms" in (J 2:642.]

make: *v.t.* to achieve. "I can't *make* a crap (crop) on such land." Also Ill., Ky. (A). "To accomplish, as 'make a crop'" (C 2) [DA and DAE suggest distribution from NEng through S.Midl.]

make brags: [*v. phr.* to boast.] "They could make their brags about it the longest day they live of how they done him up" (J 4:858). "He made his brags" (J 2:642).

make nor meddle: [*v.phr.*] "I won't make nor meddle." (MacG[owan]) = I will have no part in it. Cf. "Will you never cease from making and meddling?" (Stevenson, *Ballantree* 188; *Black Arrow* 38) (J 2:611).

make out: [*v. phr.* to prosper; listed under "dialectal idioms" as:] makin' out (J 2:649). [S.Midl., DAE]

male: *n.*, used attributively, in affectation of sexual propriety, in combinations [such] as, **male-brute,** bull; **male-hog,** boar. Also Kan., Ky. In Ill., also **male-cow,** bull (A). Male-brute and male-hog are used as euphemisms (B 369). (J 2:607)

man: *v.t.* to master. "You can't hardly *man* that [tough steak—K], can you?" Also Ky. (A). He was wild drunk, but I thought I could man him" (J 10:84). (C 2)

mankind: [*n.* (generic) man.] Quintuple negative—"I ain't never seen no *man*kind of no kind do no washing'" (J 2:591).

mandrake: [*n.* May apple root (*Podophyllum peltatum*)] "Not long since, too, during a scarcity in corn, a local storekeeper told the people of a county to go out and gather all the mandrake or 'May apple' root they could find. . . . Fifteen tons were gathered and at three cents a pound the whole county got its seed corn" (Allen, "Cumberland") (J 2:354).

manners: [*n. pl.* expected conduct.] "It is 'manners' for a woman to drudge and obey" (B 332). (J 2:642)

(in a) manner: [*prep. phr.*; this appears to be an idiom that is a shortened form of "in a manner of speaking," that seems to soften the expression or word that follows it:] "Molly was in a manner stone-dead the next mornin.'" "Blamed if my eyes ain't in a manner out" (conjunctivitis). (J 2:475).

man-person: *n.* man (A). a pleonasm (B 360). (J 2:642)

man-power: *v.t.* [to use human muscle power, perhaps with some ironic cf. to horse-power.] "Let's we-uns *man-power* that log out o' the road" (A; J 2:592). And then, with handspikes, "man-power the log outen the way" (B 32).

many's: [*contraction* for *many is.*] "Many's the hill o' corn I've propped up with a rock to keep it from fallin' down-hill" (B 35).

mar: [*n.* dental pulp, possibly from *marrow.*] "I've burnt my holler teeth out with a red hot wire. The wire'd sizzle like fryin.'" / "Kill the nerve?" / "No, but it'd sear the mar so t' it wouldn't be so sensitive" (J 2:470; B 302).

marcy: [*n.*, variant of *mercy.*] "It'd be a marcy if he was to die" (J 2:475).

mark: [*v.t.* to note, remember.] "Fellers, you want to mark whut you dream about tonight" (B 83).

marked man: [*n. phr.*] Whoever has the reputation of being a dangerous man to cross—the 'marked' man, who carries his life upon his sleeve, but bears himself as a smiling cavalier—he is the only true aristocrat among a valorous but primitive people (B 393).

marm: [*n.* mother.] "maw," "mammy," "marm" [listed under "childhood" in J 1:298; obs. except in U.S., vulgar, OED; see also **maw;** cf. **daddy**]

mash: [*n.*, variant of *mesh.*] "Your gear wheels ain't in mash" (C 3).

mast: [*n.* nuts, such as acorns and chestnuts, and especially as accumulated on the forest floor.] "But the mast, sich as acorns and beech and hickory nuts, is mostly on the Car'lina side" (B 79). "How's the mast this year?" / "Better'n common." / "Plenty of chestnuts?" / "Yes, there's several" (J 2:361). "If it rains on the 17th of July, there will be no chestnut mast" (Bob) (J 2:671). [DAE lists examples ranging from NY through IN.]

master: [1.] *adj.* big, powerful. "He was the *masterest* bear-fighter I ever did see" (A; J 4:749). "He was a master brute" (J 4:749). "I mind that in 1862 . . . there come a master cold spell" (J 1:38). "It's the master place you ever seen—a shut-in shore enough" (J 1:81). "That Nantahala is a master shut-in, just a plumb gorge" (B 357). "On the night or eve of 'Old Christmas' (12th Night), Jan. 6th, . . . the cattle in the stable kneel down and pray. One informant positively asserted . . . she found the cows kneeling on the ground and making 'just the masterest moanin'" (Mooney 98) (J 2:671). [2]. adv. [powerfully, or in an extreme manner,] Masterfully. "He laughed master" (A; J 4:749).

maw: [*n.* mother.] "I don't know; maw, she knows" (B 112).

maypop: [*n.* fruit of the passion flower (*Passiflora incarnata*); sometimes the flower itself] (J 1:71) [See also **apricot**]

meadow mouse: [*n.* field mouse (*Microtus pennsylvanicus*)] (J 26:56).

mean: [*adj.*, probably used conventionally, but also in the archaic sense of being unwell, indisposed; listed under "diseases"] Old Davis "too mean" to get up (J 2:469). [See **meanness**]

meanness: [1. *n.* indisposition; listed as nonstandard dialect in J 2:603 and under "traits, disposition" in J 2:642p.] "Cur'ous that the meanness'll come over a feller thataway" (J 2:642). [2. n. probably ignoble, sordid, but possibly used in sense of "stingy."] "Where there's meanness born and bred in the bone, hit'll shore break out" (J 2:637).

measle: *v.i.* to catch measles. [We suspect that K may be slightly off here; to grow measly also alludes to an infestation of larval tapeworms in the muscles and tissues, a disease more common with domestic animals than the viral disease.] "The old cow *measled,* and she died last spring" (A).

measurin' stick: [*n. phr.* probably a yardstick: "We always used this for yardstick, but never for ruler" (Galskis), but from the context below, very likely used to make coffins:] "Well, is anybody dead? I see you've got your measurin' stick" (Mrs. John Thomas) (J 2:483).

meat: [1.] *n.* usually understood to mean "pork" (A). "Meat" invariably means pork; very seldom see beef or mutton (J 2:419). "Meat—usually pork" (C 2). (J 2:240, 369) [2.] v.t. to serve as meat. "Them bear'll *meat* his fam'ly all winter." (A; J 4:749). "That bear'll meat me a month." (B 356).

mebbe: [*adv.*, variant of *maybe.*] "Mebbe I better be a-stepping" (J 2:642). "Taxes cost mebbe three cents on the dollar. . . . But revenue costs a dollar and ten cents on twenty cents' worth o' liquor; and that's robbin' the people with a gun to their faces" (B 120). (J 2:592)

meetin': [*n.* a church service.] They told me that a certain blue-eyed girl thought that black eyes were "purtier" and that she actually changed her eyes to jet black whenever she went to "meetin'" or other public gathering (B 313). [DAE lists examples ranging from NEng through Midl.]

meetin' folks: *n. pl.* congregation (A). (J 2:603, 4:775)

meet up with, met up with: [*v.t.* in courtship, to find] a woman to [one's] taste: "I guess he's met up with him a woman" (J 1:286).

melt: [*n.* spleen.] Then came the four men, empty-handed, it seemed, until John slapped a bear's "melt" (spleen) upon the table (B 106). "Melt" (J 4:749).

mess: [*n.* a serving, portion.] "I 'low I've done growed a bit, atter that mess o' meat" (B 98). [NEng, S.Midl. DAE]

midder-man: [*n.*, variant of *middleman*.] (J 2: 603)

middlenight: [*n.*, variant of *midnight*.] (J 2:603)

might' nigh: [*adv.* mighty near, nearly.] "I come might' nigh doin' it" (J 2:641). "Might' nigh see down her goozle" (J 4:759). [Describing the steepness of the mountains, people say,] "Goin' up, you can might' nigh stand up straight and bite the ground" (B 21).

mile: [*n.* the singular form is used in plural contexts:] "'two mile' Mrs. K. 8/5/26" (C 11)

milk-sick: [1. *n.* milk-sickness, a disease of cattle now believed to be caused by cattle eating white snakeroot. It can be passed on to humans.] A more mysterious disease is "milk-sick," which prevails in certain restricted districts, chiefly where the cattle graze in rich and deeply shaded coves. If not properly treated it is fatal both to the cow and to any human being who drinks her fresh milk or eats her butter (B 303). Never called milk-sickness (J 2:473). Milk from a cow that is infected will not foam. It turns silver black. "Old Mis Posey always keeps a silver quarter in her churn" (J 2:473). [2. adj.] The extraordinary distaste for fresh milk and butter or the universal suspicion of these foods that mountaineers evince . . . may have sprung up from experience with "milk-sick" cows (B 304). Milk-Sick Mt. (White, Tenn.) Milk-Sick Cove (Swain Co., N.C.) (J 26:79). (J 2:601) [Midl., M.W., DAE]

milk-sick doctors: [*n.*] mountaineers who made a specialty of treating "milk-sick" disease (J 2:601).

mill toll: [*n.* payment for the use of a mill, made by leaving a

portion of the grain with the miller rather than cash.] The toll is
⅛; "This mill is like many, alike simple in construction, where
neighbors deposit their toll of grain, turn on the water, and
grind their own meal." (Carrington) (J 2:453).

mimic: [1.] *n.* likeness. "That [photograph]'s a fair *mimic* of him"
(A; J 2:641). "It's a fair mimic of silver" (J 10:83). [2.] v.t. to
represent. "That *mimics* him right smart" (A). Mimic or mock
[are used] for resemble (B 370). (J 2:642)

mincy: *adj.* fastidious in eating (A). picky (J 2:642). [Dauncy is
defined as] "mincy about eating," which is to say fastidious,
over nice (B 363). "She's mincy; she won't eat nothin'" (J 2:601,
642p) "She's mincy about eatin'" (J 2:429) [See **dauncy.**]

mind: [1. *v. t.* to remember.] "I mind one time when. . ." (J 2:641).
"I mind that in 1862 (it was the time of the war) there came a
master cold spell" (J 1:38). "I mind about that time, Doc; but I
disremember which buryin'-ground they-all planted ye in" (B
78). [2. *n.* inclination,] to have a mind to do a thing: Bob Cook
had a "mind" to try a corrosive sublimate tablet, thinking it
"might cure my headache" (J 2:469). (J 2:642)

misery: [*n.* pain.] "He's got a misery in his back" (J 2:475).

miss-lick: *n.* a false blow. Also Ill., N.Y., Kan. (A; C 2). "Old
Uncle Neddy Carter in Madison Co. (N.C.) went to jump one
of his own teeth out, one time, but he missed the nail and
mashed his nose with the hammer. He mashed his wife's nose
the same way, by a miss-lick." (Bob) (J 2:471). "She hit a miss-
lick with the axe" (J 2:475). (J 2:601) [Also DAE]

mistress: *n.* Mrs. "Now, *Mistress* Cook, get me a little hot water"
(A; J 2:475). A married woman is not addressed as Missis by the
mountaineers, but as Mistress when they speak formally, and
as Mis' or Miz' for a contraction (B 364).

mixtry: [*n.*, variant of *mixture*.] (J 2:603)

mizzle: [*n.* sweat.] "Dry up the mizzle from his moistened brow"
(Springer 130) (D 1).

mock: *v.t. to* mimic, q.v. Also Ill. (A). Mock [is used] for resemble
(B 370). "They mocked 'em right smart" (J 2:641).

moderate: [*adv.* moderately well.] "How you doin'?" / "Jist moderate" (J 4:74).

molasses: [*n.*,] always plural. "Pass me them molasses" (B 371).
[See also **'lasses.**]

mommick: [1.] *v.t.* to ruin by bungling. "That was a waste of timber, Uncle Bill; they jist *mommicked* it up" (A). (J 2:603) [2. n.] If the house be in disorder . . . things are just in a mommick (B 368).

moniment: [n. visual reminder; archaic form of monument < *monere*, to remind] It was just the "moniment" of a little ridge, meaning the image, the simulacrum. This is Spenser's usage." [Murfree, *The Ordeal*] (J 2:497).

moon-calf: *n.* in mountaineer's superstition, a shapeless thing, without life, that a steer causes in a cow by worrying her (A). I had supposed that . . . moon-calf had none but literary usage in America, but we often hear [it] in the mountains . . . moon-calf in its baldly literal sense that would make Prospero's taunt to Caliban a superlative insult (B 361).

moonrise: [n. the rising of the moon above the horizon.] (J 2:629)

moonshine: [1. *n.* whiskey distilled illegally, i.e. by night or moonshine. 2. *v.* to make such whiskey.] Our terms moonshiner and moonshining are not used in the mountains (B 126). [If not used, the term was obviously understood:] "the main reason for this 'moonshining' as you-uns calls it, is bad roads" (B 122). [Midl., S.Midl., DA and DAE]

mought: [*v.* variant of *might*; pronounced "mowt" (B 358).] "What mought yo' name be?" (J 4:739). "What mought you-uns foller for a living?" (B 275). [To illustrate mountain pride, K records a story in both J and B of a young boy caught gaping at the Biltmore Estate, who, when challenged, "What do you want?" responded that his Dad] "said if I liked it he mought buy it for me" (J 3:1023; B 328).

moughty: [*adv.*, variant of *mighty*.] "I tell yeou hit teks a moughty resolute gal ter do what that thar gal has done" (J 3:1025; B 468).

mountain boomers: [*n.* mountain people, used as a comic metaphor.] They call themselves mountain people, or citizens; sometimes humorously "mountain boomers," the word boomer being their name for the common red squirrel which is found here only in the upper zones of the mountains (B 281; J 4:763). [Midl., S.Midl., DAE; see **boomer.**]

mountain dew: [*n.* moonshine whiskey, usually slightly stronger than our contemporary commercial soft drink.] The maker of "mountain dew" has no other instrument [for testing it] than a small vial, and his testing is done entirely by the "bead" of the liquor (B 135). [So. mts, DAE]

mountain meadow rue: [*n.*] (*Thalictrum clavatum*) [Flowers] May-June. White. (J 26:24). [See also **Easter flower.**]

mountain oak: [*n. Quercus montana.*] Ascending above the zone of 3,000 feet, white oak is replaced by the no less valuable "mountain oak" (B 54).

mountain tea: [*n.* collective name for various herbal teas.] "Another beverage is 'mountain tea,' made from the sweet-scented goldenrod and from wintergreen—the New England checkerberry" (Allen, "Cumberland") (J 2:423).

mowin' blade: [*n.*] scythe. Also Ky. (A). (C 2; J 2:401, 601, J 6)

much: [1.] *v.t.* to make much of. "She *muched* the chaps greatly" (A). A verb will be coined from an . . . adjective: "Much that dog and see won't he come along" (pet him, make much of him) (B 357; J 2:371). [See also **mutch.**] [2. *intensifier* very] "Your name ain't much common" (B 371). [3. *pron.* many] "much of my jars is in use" (C 1).

mule: [*v.t.* to abuse; listed in section on quarreling.] "He muled my critter. He fed my dog pounded glass and killed him" (J 4:893).

muley-hawed: [*adj.* stubborn (Harry Rice).] "You needn't be so muley-hawed about it" (4:855, 10:83). [Listed under "factitious words" in J 2:601.]

mullygrubs: [*n.* emotional upset or disturbance.] "I knowed in reason she'd have the mullygrubs over them doin's" (B 371). [Cf. **narvish.**]

muscle: [*v.t.* to move, to shove.] "We can muscle this log up" (B 356).

mushyroom: *n.* mushroom (A; J 2:642o; C 2).

musicianer: *n.* musician (A). (C 2)

mutch: [*v.i.*] "call with lip sounds. 'I mutched to my dog to come to me.' 'He mutched to his horses and they pulled the wagon out of the hole'" (C 3). [See also **much.**]

mutter: *v.t.* to mutter to (one) (A).

my own self: [*pron.* distinctive in adding the intensifier, own; since this construction may appear in many dialects, K is apparently drawing attention to its unusual frequency, to its

use in contexts which in other dialects would not elicit its use.]
(B 122). [Cf. **your own self.**]

N

nabel: [*n.*, variant of navel.] Hillsmen say nabel (B 352). "I et till
my nabel stuck out like a pot-leg" (M.B.) (J 2:428).

nachelly, nacherally: [*adv.*, variants of *naturally.*] "I'd jes nachelly
a-shot him" (J 2:642). "The wind sprung up . . . a blow that jest
nacherally lifted the ground" (B 78).

nare: [*adv.* never; contracted: ne'er.] Simply the right pronunciation of ne'er (B 353). Nare nuther (never another) (J 2:649). [Cf.
nary]

narves: [*n. pl.* nerves.] "And hit's wearin' on a feller's narves" (B
140).

narvish, nervish: *adj.* nervous (A). "He mought drap off, him
bein' so weak and right narvish and sick with a head-swimmin'" (B 298). "Of course, I'm weak yit and right nervish" (J
2:475).

nary: [*quantifier* not any, none.] Nary is ne'er a, with the *a* turned
into a short *i* sound (B 353). "There ain't nary bitty sense in it" (J
2:641; 4:853; B 351). Nary one (J 2:642). "Nary one of us nursed
our mammy; we was every one of us raised on can milk" Mrs.
Barnett (J 1:288) Without nary (J 2:642). (C 1) Triple negatives
are common. "I ain't got nary none" (J 2:591). [See also **neer**]
[NEng, DAE]

natur: [*n.*, variant of *nature*; pronounced "nay tour."] "Hit's agin
natur to put up with sich as that" (J 10:83). [Cf. **pictur**]

neck of the woods: [*n. phr.* area. They'd ask] "what you-uns was
doin' in that thar neck o' the woods" (B 118). [Americanism,
colloq., DAE]

needcessity: [*n.*, variant of *necessity*] (J 2:607).

Needle's Eye: [*n. phr.* a "play-party" social game] (B 338).

neer or **ne'er:** [*adv.* never.] *Nare* is simply our own corrupt spelling of *neer*, and *nary* is *neer-a* (J 2:491). [See also **nare**]

neighbor: [*v.t.* befriend.] "I know in reason I cain't neighbor him" (J 4:731, 853). (J 2:599)

neighbor-people: [*n.* neighbors; listed as a pleonasm on B 360.] "All the neighbor-people" (J 4:731). (J 2:642p)

nesties: *n. pl.* nests (A). The ancient syllabic plural (B 359). "The hens make their nesties in the deep weeds" (C 2). [Cf. **beasties**]

nex': [adj. next.] "He l'arnt better nex' time" (J 2:641).

nicely: [*adj.* well] "My folks are nicely, thank you'" (C 1).

nigger: [*n.* Negro.] "Hyur's yer old nigger woman" (B 93). "I b'lieve in treatin' niggers squar'." Nigger-skull Mt. (Jackson, N.C.) (J 26:82). I have never heard a Carolina mountaineer say "niggah" (J 2:488). [K insists that r is always pronounced.]

nigger in the woodpile: [*n. phr.* hidden agenda.] "I suspected a nigger in the woodpile" (B 93). [S., W., DAE]

nigh: [1. *adj.* near.] "Take the nigh cut" (C 1). "The nighest State dispensary, even, is sixty miles away" (B 121-22). Nigh Way Br[anch]. (Buchanan, Va.) (J 26:84). [2. *adv.* nearly.] "I come might' nigh doin' it" (J 2:641). "I'm nigh breechless!" (B 92). "That wasn't nigh all the ups and downs they had" (J 2:640). "They married through and through till the whole gineration nigh run out" (B 311-12).

nine bark: [1. *n.*] (*Opulaster opulifolius*) [Flowers] June. White or purplish. (J 26:31). [2. n.] downy hydrangea (*Hydrangea radiata*) also called "ninebark" [Flowers] June-July. White. Bark med-[icinal]. (J 26:31) [W.NC, DAE]

nipety-tuck, nickety tuck: [*n. phr.* living marginally; variants of *nip and tuck.*] Also N.Y. (A). "It's just nickety tuck with 'em" (J 1:238). [Listed under "poverty"] (J 6). [Clearly related to *nip and tuck*, widespread colloquialism, DAE, DA]

nod a wink: [*v. phr.* to signal.] "I seed you nod him a wink" (J 10:83).

no-count: [*adj.* worthless] "He's a no-count triflin' feller" (J 1:256). [S., DAE]

noction line: [*n.* equinoctial line (or circle); celestial equator] equinoctial (J 14:80).

nohow: [*adv.* anyhow (through negative concord); in no way.]

Then Budd Sockwell chimed in that "if it was time for Snow to die, he couldn't be saved nohow, and if it wa'n't time he would be saved anyhow" (J 3:981). [Revenuers] "use their authority to abuse people who ain't never done nothin' nohow" (B 170). Quadruple negative—"He ain't never done nothin' nohow" (J 2:591).

noise: *v.t.* to make the sound of. "Any kind of thing he ever heered tell of, he can *noise* it" (A; C 2 adds "to mimic" and "Daniel as mimic"). (J 2:462)

North and South: [*n.* a kind of flower] (J 1:71).

notion: [*n.* inclination; "to take a notion" = to decide.] "I've tuk a notion to quit" (Bob) (J 1:296).

not much: [*adv.* not very (well).] "I'm not much" (J 10:83).

nuss: [*n.* variant of *nurse*] (J 2:475, 642s).

nuther: [*adv.* variant of *neither*.] "I didn't nuther" (J 4:853, 10:83).

O

obleege: [*v.*, variant of *oblige*.] "But now things has got so 's I've obleege to spend three hours a trip, worryin' my way to sich a fur-off panter-den of a place as this!" (J 26:63). "I was might' nigh obleeged to" (J 2:641).

(have) oblige: [*v.phr.* "to have an obligation," must.] "We have oblige to take care on him" (B 359). "Well, I have oblige to go" (J 10:83). (J 2:642).

offen: [*prep.*, variant of *off of*] (J 2:367).

oil cloth: [*n. phr.*] the universal table covering (if any) in the mountains: "At Boone, N.C., the flies would have carried all the food from the dining-room table (for flies do not mind eating off oil cloth, and are not particular how food is cooked), but for the machine with hanging flappers that swept the length of it" (Warner 37) (J 2:441). [Widespread, DAE]

old Grandsir' (So-and-So): [a polite form of address] We will hear an aged man referred to as "old Grandsir'" So-and-So (B 364-5).

Old Hundred: [*n.* the hymn, used as a benediction.] "Well, it's time to sing Old Hundred and go home" (J 10:83). [J 2:642 adds: "(Defeated at cards)," suggesting a comic liturgy.]

old man: [1. *n. phr.* husband.] A woman, learning that her un-armed husband was besieged by his foes, seized his rifle . . . rushed past the firing-line, and stood by her "old man" (B 419).[Widespread, DAE] [2. *epithet*] In the last house up Hazel Creek dwelt "old man" Stiles (B 327). [Colloquial, DA]

Old Ned: [*n. phr.* fat pork.] "Bill, hand me some Old Ned from that suggin o' mine." Old Ned is merely slang for fat pork (B 75). [S., DAE; TN, DA]

Old Wind-maker: [*n. phr.* comic epithet for God.] "Old Wind-maker's blowin' liars out of North Car'lina" [The implication is that this would take a very strong wind!] (B 78-79).

old woman: [*n. phr.* wife.] "Whar's your old woman?" (B 278). Louis: "My old woman throws up laziness to me sometimes, but I don't git mad—it's *the truth*" (J 1:256). [Vulgar, colloquial, DAE see also **the woman.**]

'oman or **ooman:** [*n.* woman. See also **dummern, ummern, womern**] (J 2:603).

on: [*prep.*, variant of *of*] ". . . to take care on him" (B 359). "Well, I jes' hardly can't make a meal out on bad biscuits" (M.B.) (J 2:642). [See also **outen.**]

once't: [*adv.*, variant of *once.*] "I shot a . . . bird once't" (J 4:56). "I went out to the river oncet a-visitin'" (Lily Calhoun) (J 4:745).

one: [*pron.*] short for *one or the other.* "He either went to Medlin or to Bradshaw's, *one.*" Also Ill., Kan. (A). either——— or———, one (J 2:642). "Sam went to Andrews or to Murphy, one" (B 371).

one more time: [*n. phr.* a good time.] "We had one more *time*" means a rousing good time (B 360). "Well, if we didn't have one more *time* (at a dance) (J 2:611).

one-time: *adj.* single. "Tore up for *one-time* bandagin'" (A; J 2:642).

onless: [*conj.* variant of *unless.*] ". . . onless he's trapped" (B 102).

onliest: [*adj.*, unusual superl.: (most) only] (J 2:591).

onpias: [*n.*, variant of *capias*, q.v.; a subpoena] "Well, Virg, I got a onpias for you. I hate it, but you know I've got to do my duty" (J 4:885).

onry: [*adj.* ornery, irritable.] "You onry cuss" (J 10:82). "Jim's an on'ry cuss" (J 2:637). [DAE suggests NEng origin. DA includes quotations from IN, S.W.]

ort, orter: [*aux. v.* ought, ought to,] corrupt forms (B 358). "You hadn't orter a-told" (B 85). "You orter heered his tushes pop" (J 4:749). (No alarm clock) "What's the use when a feller'd orter have a good crowin' rooster" (Bob) (J 2:399). [See also **arter.**]

ournses: [*pron.* our.] "Pap made liquor jist up the branch back o' ournses house" (J 26:63).

outen: [*prep.*, variant of *out of*] "you'll git some o' that meanness shuck outen you" (B 80). Then, with hand-spikes "man-power the log outen the way" (B 32). "I wish t' we *hed* roasted the temper outen them trap-springs (B 93). "Come outen thar!" (J 2:641). "Outen, with the phrase out of there" (C 1). (J 2:603)

outlandish: *n.* foreigners collectively (A). A traveler . . . asked a native of the Cumberlands what he would call a "Dutchman or a Dago." The fellow studied a bit and then replied: "Them's the outlandish" (B 17). "Foreigners." (C 2) [Note, however, this is listed under "Forms not Heard in NC" (J 2:642x).]

outs: [*n.* enmity, especially in the phrase "at the outs," i.e., at odds with.] "She's at the outs with Iley" (J 4:853; 2:603).

outsharp: *v.t.* to outwit (A). "He outsharped them" (J 2:459). "The bear outsharped us" (B 106). "I wouldn't be surprised if the bear'd outsharp them yit" (J 4:749). (J 2:603)

outsider: *n.* bastard (A). A bastard is a woods-colt or an outsider (B 368).

outsmart: [*v.t.* to outwit.] (J 2:603). [See also **green out**]

oven: [*n.* can refer to a Dutch-oven.] (J 2:403).

overhet: [*past. part.* overheated] By the time they had corralled him they were "plumb overhet" (B 143-44).

P

pack: [*v.t.* to carry.] "She packed it acrost the mountain" (C 1). [According to Frost, *pack* for *carry* is an Anglo-Saxon survival.] (J 24:22). [Chiefly W., DAE]

paling: [*n.* picket.] "The clothes were stretched on the sharp points of the garden paling to dry" (Jones) (J 2:417). [DAE suggests S. usage; Midl., S., Kurath.]

pallet: [*n.* makeshift bed on the floor.] "I got lots o' bed-kivers. We'll jest make a pallet on the floor" (J 2:399). "I lay on a pallet on the floor for over a month" (B 303). [S., S.Midl., Kurath]

pan'ter: [*n.* panther.] Wolves and panthers used to be common here, but it is a long time since either has been killed in this region, albeit impressionable people see wolf tracks or hear a "pan'ter" scream every now and then (B 99). [Also:] **pan'ter den** (J 2:642). "I'd about as lief jump into a pan'ter den in my shirt-tail" (J 4:855, 10:83). "Sich a fur-off panter-den of a place" (J 26:63). (J 26:56) [DAE citation from KY]

paperstring: *n.* twine. (A; J 2:601)

parch: [*v.t.* to toast under a dry heat.] "It's like parchin' coffee: you wanter let anything else go to hell and think about nothin' but coffee" (J 10:82).

pardners: [*n.*, variant of *partners.*] "Him and me war pardners" (J 2:641). [Vulgarism, DA]

particulars: (ptiklərz), *n. pl.* perishable foodstuffs (A).

passel: [*n.* parcel, a general collective.] "A passel of children" (J 1:298). (J 2:642) [DAE suggests S.Midl.]

pasteboard soles: [*n. phr.*; cardboard used as a temporary sole for a shoe worn through; in the quote it may be more a generic term, an early protest against shoddy "synthetic" substitutes.] "Pasteboard soles and chewing gum heels" of women's shoes (Bob) (J 2:449).

patch: [1. *n.* small field.] sorghum patch (J 2:421). "I've cl'ared me a patch . . . " (B 36). [2. *v.t.*, comic usage for repair] "Reckon I'll haffter patch them shoes with a new pair" (Bob) (J 2:449). [3. *v.* to be similar or comparable to someone or something; colloq.;

cf. "not a patch on," DAE] "I'm not a patchin' to . . ." (Fox) (J 2:641). [DAE suggests S.Midl.]

paten'pail: [*n.*, variant of *poteen:* whiskey; loggers' term for the bucket used to carry booze to lumbermen on drives.] "holds 10-12 quarts" (Fraser 308) (D 1).

Paul Pry: [*n. phr.* a peeping Tom] (J 9:102).

payrole: [*n.*, variant of *parole*] "out of the pen under payrole" (J 2:639).

peaked: [*adj.* ill, run-down, pronounced with two syllables.] "I'm feelin' sorter peaked" (J 2:475).

'pear: [*v.i.* to appear.] "I don't 'pear to have no stren'th left" (B 299; J 2:476). "'Pears like"—"looks like" (J 2:641).

peart, peert, pearty: [*adj.* healthy, cheerful;] peart [was] contemporary with the *Canterbury Tales* (B 362). [K probably follows Fox; the list of terms from Fox includes "peert" on J 2:489.] "Powerful peart." / "W'y, you're pearty" (J 2:641). "A tall, peart sort of a gal, wearin' a vascinator" (J 2:637). "Powerful peart old man" (J 2:631). (J 2:597).

pearten up: *v. phr.* to become lively or cheerful. Also Ky. (A). "To brighten." (C 2) "Pearten up, honey!" (J 2:641). (J 2:597)

peazzer: [*n.*, variant of *piazza;* defined as a porch, but may have been understood, Montgomery suggests, to mean plaza] "The clothes were stretched on the sharp points of the garden paling to dry, or on the 'peazzer' rail, whence they occasionally blew down in the night and the dogs slept on them" (Jones) (J 2:417).

peckerwood: [*n.* woodpecker; listed as an "inverted word" in J 2:605.] The woodpecker is turned around into a peckerwood (B 369). Peckerwood Ck. (Clay [Co.], N.C.) [S., DA] (J 26:76). (J 1:73; C 1)

peep o' day: [*n. phr.* dawn.] Also **crack o' day** (J 2:629).

pee wee: [*n.*] phoebe (J 26:54, 56). [Peterson distinguishes between a wood peewee (*Contopus virens*) and the Eastern Phoebe (*Sayornis phoebe*). We are not sure whether the same distinction would have been made by K's informants; it might have been and he was unaware of it.]

pen: [1. *n.*, comic metaphor for a house.] "Why lordy! . . ." remonstrated Doss Provine over a question of matching boards and battening joints, "ef you git yo' pen so almighty tight as that you won't git no fresh air" (B 305). [2. *n.* abbrev. for *penitentiary.*] "They'd only get a month or two in the pen" (B 118-19).

Pennyroyal: [*n.*] (*Hedeoma pulegiodes*). [Flowers] July-Sept. Pale purple. Foliage fragrant. Plant med[icinal] (J 26:35). [Cf. below.]

penny-royal pills: [*n. phr.* pills made from pennyroyal oil;] abortifaciants: knitting needle, self-operated; "penny-royal pills." "Borax and rye liquor will knock one out right now" (J 4:841).

pen-point: *n.* pen. Not [just] local (A; J 2:603).

peppergrass: [*n.* the common plant (*Lepidium apetalum*); listed among plants used as greens] (J 2:433).

perpendic'lar: [*adj.* extremely steep, variant of perpendicular] "These ridges is might' nigh straight up and down, and, as the feller said, perpendic'lar" (B 360; J 2:642).

Peruvian: *n.* wild red cherry [*Prunus pennsylvanica*]. (A; C 2) (J 1:59, 71; 2:601)

pet pigs: [*n. pl.* pigs that are] "corn-fed around home, and get fat" (J 2:367). In some of these places you will find a "pet pig" harbored in the house (B 323).

pheasant: [*n.* ruffed grouse] (J 26:54).

pickle-beans: [*n.* beans preserved in vinegar.] "Do you love pickle-beans?" (J 2:429).

pick my flint: [metaphor for "get ready"; literally to clean the flint on a gun before refiring] "Well, I'll pick my flint and try again" (J 10:82).

pictur: [*n.*, variant of *picture*; we suspect what K records is a pronunciation like /pɪktər/ comparable to the general nineteenth-century pronunciation of *nature* as /neitər/, as recorded of Emerson and Webster, and quite distinct from the twentieth-century and northern /pɪkčər/ and /neičər/.] "the women folks's seed his pictur" (B 120).

pie: [*n.*] A pie means a sort of fruit pot-pie or cobbler, made with plain biscuit dough, and often it is served not merely as the *pièce de resistance* but as the whole meal (J 2:421).

piece: [1. *v.t.* to sew a quilt with pieces of cloth.] Women who are breaking their health and spirit over a thankless tub of suds ought surely to turn their talents to better account, ought to be

designing and weaving coverlets . . . or "piecing" the quilt
pattern now so popular (B 459). [2. v.t. as a comic metaphor: to
enlarge a garment, suggesting a pregnancy:] "She had to piece
her apron string" (with child) (J 2:642). [Not originally American, DAE.]

pieded: *p.a.* pied, piebald (A). A spotted animal is said to be
pieded (pied) (B 369). "He had a Jersey cow that was pieded" (J
2:361). (C 2)

pie-peaches: [*n.*] Natives [are] fond of canned peaches, but only
buy the "pie-peaches" of cheapest grade, and then only when
uncommonly prosperous. Luncheon at cross-roads store [included as one item] pie peaches so hard and woody that one
suspects they were made synthetically out of wood pulp and
coal-tar flavors (J 2:421).

piggin': [*n.* a small pail, esp. a wooden one having a handle made
by a single stave longer than the others, DAE] "washin' sissles
in a piggin'" (MacGowan) (J 4:763). [DAE suggests S.Midl.
distribution.]

pinchin' times: [*n. phr.* hard times.] Even to families that are
fairly well-to-do there will come periods of famine . . . called
"pretty pinchin' times" (B 323-24).

p'int: [1. *v.i.* point.] "You go along a battlefield, right atter the
action, and you'll find most o' the dead faces pintin' to the sky"
(B 102). [2. *n.*] "place its squar p'int agin the ridge of the tooth"
(B 301).

p'int-blank: [*adv.* certainly, exactly; K misleadingly suggests that
the phrase] is a superlative or an epithet [The examples that
follow are neither.]: "We jist p'int-blank got it to do." / "Well,
p'int-blank, if they ever come back again, I'll move!" (B 360; J
2:641). [In the second sentence, the phrase may have the force
of an epithet, but we think it is, semantically, the equivalent of
"certainly."] "That beer tastes p'int-blank [exactly] like a mad
bumblebee smells" (J 2:421). (J 2:605, 642)

p'intedly: [*adv.* certainly; possibly immediately or directly.] "a fat
woman was bad enough, but a fat man ort p'intedly to be led
out and killed" (B 287).

pissabed: [*n.*] yellow, bell-shaped [flower] (J 1:69).

pitch: [*n.*, loggers' term.] "The word 'pitch' refers either to the resinous mixture used on canoes, to a small water-fall, or to the height of a stream" (Hubbard vii) (D 1). [K's list of loggers' terms includes entries for both the second and third meanings given by Hubbard, above, suggesting both were common in N.C.] "Upon a favorable and early start, with a good 'pitch of water' [i.e. proper water level] may depend the whole success of the log drive" (Fraser 271) (D 1). small waterfall (D 1). [DAE suggests NEng usage.]

pizen: [1. *n.*, variant of *poison*; K appears to suggest a pronunciation like /paizən/ rather than /pɔɪzən/.] "It squirts out a streak o' pizen that hits you in the eye" (J 23:85). [2. *v.*, past. part.] "So, to be good law-abiding citizens, we-uns must . . . pay express rates on pizened liquor" (B 122). "Oh, sometimes hit's some pizen old bum who's been refused credit" (B 171).

pizen-vine: [*n.*] poison ivy. [In Ill., also **poison-vine.**—K] (A). Stump-water (rainwater) is supposed to be good for ivy-poisoning ("pizen-vine") (J 2:471). (J 2:642o) [DAE contains two citations from NC.]

plant: [*v.t.* to bury; comic analogy.] "I disremember which buryin' ground they-all planted ye in" (B 78). [DAE lists as slang; citations suggest it was widespread.]

play-party: *n.* party; entertainment. Also Kan. (A). "Play-parties" are held, at which social games are practiced with childlike abandon: Roll the Platter, Weavilly Wheat, Needle's Eye, We Fish Who Bite, Grin an' Go 'Foot, Swing the Cymblin, Skip t' m' Lou (pronounced "Skip-tum a-loo") and many others (B 338). Most of the mountain preachers nowadays denounce dances and "play-parties" as sinful diversions, though their real objection seems to be that such gatherings are counter-attractions that thin out the religious ones (B 340). [S.IL, DA]

play-pretty: *n.* plaything (A), toy (J 1:298). "Here's you a play-pretty" (C 2). Also **play-pritty:** small gourds (C 1). Dried gourd used as a noise-maker for children to play with (J 2:597). Also **play-purty:** toy. The children have few toys other than rag dolls, broken bits of crockery for "play-purties" (B 333).

play shut-mouth: [*v. phr.* be silent.] "Them roosters take a round o' crowin' and then play shut-mouth for a while" (J 2:371).

pleasure: [*v.t.* to give satisfaction.] "I wouldn't pleasure them enough to say it" (B 356; J 4:853).

pleurisy root: [*n. phr.* the orange milk-weed, butterfly weed (*Asclepias syriaca*).] Asheville *Citizen*, 28 Jan. 1928 (J 2:480). [VA, AL, DAE]

Plott hound: [*n.* a locally developed but famous breed of fine bear-dogs.] I've been told that the Plott hounds are the best bear dogs in the country (B 80).

plug: [*n.* a pressed cake of tobacco.] "I 'lowed to git me a plug o' tobacco" (J 2:461). [DAE suggests a widespread usage.]

plumb: [1. *adj.* outright; complete, full.] "Them hogs are plumb pets" (J 2:367). "A plumb cur, of course, cain't follow a cold track—he just runs by sight" (B 80). "It was plumb night by that time" (B 106). "You're a plumb fool" (J 4:853). "You plumb rogue" (J 10:82; 2:637 reads "He's a plumb rogue"). [2. adv. completely, altogether] "Yes, they are; plumb onery—lock, stock, barrel, and gun-stick" (B 169). (J 2:642) [DAE suggests originally S.Midl. but has spread westard.]

pneumonia fever: [*n.* pneumonia] (C 1) (J 2:477).

pock: *n.* pox. Also W.Res. (rare), Ill. (A). syphilis: "He had the pock." (K.H. The C's Lumber Camp) (J 2:477).

poil: [*n.*] hair, pelage (Lewis and Clark 1011) (C 2).

poke: [*n.* bag] Her husband returned, bearing a little "poke" of corn meal (B 273). "suggin'" "Habersack" "poke" "sack o' meal" [roughly synonymous] (J 1:327f). (C 1) (J 2:597)

poke, poke shoots: [*n., n. phr.*] used as greens, never eaten raw (J 2:433). Poke Patch C[ree]k. (Cumberland, Tenn.) Poke Patch (Deep Creek, Swain Co., N.C.) (J 26:75).

poke suppers: [*n.*] A substitute for the church fair is the "poke supper," at which dainty pokes (bags) of cake and other home-made delicacies are auctioned off to the highest bidder. Whoever bids-in a poke is entitled to eat with the girl who prepared it, and escort her home. The rivalry excited among the mountain swains by such artful lures may be judged from the fact that, in a neighborhood where a man's work brings only a dollar a day, a pretty girl's poke may be bid up to ten, twenty, or even fifty dollars (B 338-39). Sometimes sold for as much as $50 (J 4:755).

polecat: [*n.* skunk (*Mephitis mephitis*); at present some use "polecat" only for the spotted skunk (*Spilogale putorius*) to distinguish between the two species."] Polecat Cove (Marshall, Ala.)

Polecat Br[anch] (Estill, Ky.) (J 26:82). (Bob) "What do you call that stuff?" / (I) "Oil of citronella." / (Bob) "Smells like oil of polecats a-fightin'" (J 4:763). [DAE contains two citations from NC; S., S.Midl., Kurath]

political speakin': [*n.*] a political gathering (J 3:453).

poll-parrot: [*n.* a parrot.] "He can talk more and say less than a poll-parrot" (J 2:638, 10:82).

pomper: *v.t.*, variant of *pamper* (A).

pone: [1.] *n.* lump; swelling. "A *pone* came up on her side" (A; J 2:475). "Old Uncle Bobby Tuttle's got a pone come up on his side (B 298). [2. *n.* a small oval loaf of corn bread] "a cake, as a corn pone" (C 2). "I gather the corn, and shuck hit and grind hit my own self, and the woman she bakes us a pone o' bread to eat" (B 122). [DAE citations for this second meaning suggest S.Midl. distribution; Midl., S., Kurath.]

poor do: *n.* scrapple (A). The old Germans taught their Scotch and English neighbors the merits of scrapple, but here it is known as poor-do (B 366). meat: poor do (J 6). (J 2:601) [DA contains the above citation.]

poor whites: [*n.* impoverished white people; the expression never had much coinage in the mountains where everyone was more or less poor.] Poor whites had nothing to do with settling the mountains (B 433). Lowland "poor whites" became "pine-landers" or "piney-woods people," "sand-hillers," "knob-people," "corn crackers" or "crackers" (B 433). [K thought none of these terms applied to mountain people:] however poor they may be in worldly goods, [they] are by no means "poor white trash" (B 397-98).

pop: [1.] *v.* to gnash. "I heard the old she *poppin'* her teeth" (A; J 4:749). "You orter heered his tushes pop" (J 4:749). (J 2:642; B 81) [Could this be the origin of "pop goes the weasel"?] [2. *v.t.* to serve; to surprise someone with something] "I popped it to him" (J 4:749). "She didn't do a thing but popped him with a warrant" (J 4:749).

pop-crackers: *n. pl.* fire-crackers (A). (J 2:601)

pop-skull: *n.* bad whiskey. Cf. Kentucky **bust-head** (A). "If we git [liquor] sent to us from outside the State it has to come by express—and reg-lar old pop-skull it is, too" (B 122). [Adulterated whiskey was known in the mountains as] "pop-skull," "bust-head," "bumblings" (B 137). (J 2:601)

pore: [*adj.* poor, miserable.] "Stay on, stranger; pore folks has a pore way, but you're welcome to what we got" (B 274). "Poor young one!" M.B. to Eddie Crisp (J 1:298). [Listed among archaic terms in Fox, J 2:489.]

'possum: [*n.*, variant of *opossum* (*Didelphis virginiana*).] Possum Jaw C[ree]k (Smyth, Va.) 'Possum Trot (near Rome, Ga.), Possum Trot C[ree]k. (Yancey, N.C.) (J 26:84). [S.Midl., S., DAE]

posties: *n. pl.* posts (A). old syllabic plural (B 359). [Cf. **beasties**]

pot-tails: *n. pl.* the residue in a moonshine still after the backings are run off (A). (J 2:601)

pot-bellied: [*adj.* rotund, like a pot] (J 2:428).

pot-taters: [*n. pl.* joking pronunciation for boiled potatoes.] "They ain't pot-taters till they're boiled" (J 2:428). [The implication is that before cooking (in a pot) they are just plain old 'taters!]

pounding barrel: [*n.*] "The washing was done in tubs on a slab bench by the wall. The men's working garments were beaten in a pounding-barrel; the other clothes were rubbed between the hands" (Jones) (J 2:417). [DAE suggests both NEng, GLakes usage.]

pounding-mill: [*n.*] a mortar and pestle mill run by water from a spout that alternately fills, lowers, and spills out of a box fixed to the end of a walking beam opposite to the pestle (A). [An "extraordinary improvement" over the hand-mill, the pounding-mill] consists of a pole pivoted horizontally on top of a post and free to move up and down like the walking-beam of an old-fashioned engine. To one end of this pole is attached a heavy pestle that works in a mortar underneath. At the other end is a box into which the water flows from the elevated spout. When the box fills it will go down, lifting the pestle; then the water spills out and the pestle's weight lifts the box back again (B 365-66). "A water mill to pound meal from corn by means of a box on a long beam which pounds when it fills with water" (C 2). [The mills gave names to creeks on which they were located:] Pounding Mill Run, Buchanan Co., Va.; Randolph and

Teague Counties, W. Va.; Pounding Mill Branch, Pike Co., Ky.; Allegheny and Tazewell Counties, Va.; Pounding Mill Creek, Cleveland Co., N.C. (J 2:453; cf. 26:74,77). (J 2:601)

pow . . . pow: *interj.* bang: imitative of the explosion of a gun. Also Ga. (A). [Montgomery notes, properly, that this was in very general use.]

power: [1.] *n.* religious ecstasy. "She had the *power*. Also Kan., N.Y. (A). "religious fervor" (C 2) [2. n., with collective force:] "many. 'A power of chestnuts this year'" (C 2). A power [means] much (B 370). "I thought a power of him" (J 4:727).

powerful: [1. *adj.* strongly inclined, bent upon.] "The White-sideses, you know, is powerful people to go to church" (J 2:439). [2. *adv.* very.] "Not so powerful much" (J 2:641). "Is it dinnertime?" "Ain't powerful long, I wouldn't think." (J 2:642). "The Tennessee side of the mountain is powerful steep and laurely" (B 79). "'Tain't powerful long to dinner, I don't reckon" (B 372). (J 2:642)

pra'ar: [*n.*, variant of *prayer*; the pronunciation indicated by the spelling is approximately that of *prior*.] (J 4:775)

praar-book: [*n.* prayerbook.] Lyin' John (whose "mouth ain't no praar-book, if it *does* open and shet") (B 276; J 10:643 identifies this as John Cable).

practiced knocker: [*n.* an expert pugilist.] He was what a mountaineer described to me as "a practiced knocker," . . . "a master hand in a knockfight" (B 141).

preacher-man: [*n.* preacher;] a common pleonasm (B 360). (J 2:592)

praise-God: [*adj.* holy.] "Then Pete stood up with a sorter praise-God smile on his face" (J 10:82; J 2:637 attributes the quote to HK).

principally: [*adv.*] for the most part. "Jackson County, whar I was principally raised" (J 2:640).

prise: [*v.t.* to pry.] "Le's prise this rock up" (J 1:322). [This older usage is apparently preferred to the modern back formation.]

prodject: [1.] *v.i.* prospect. "I'm just *prodjectin'* around." Also S. Car. (A; J 4:734; B 277). "Hell's banjer, they don't go prodjectin' around looking for stills" (B 171). [2. v.] "to tamper with" (C 2). [3. a euphemism for gossiping; cf. **brogue:**] There is somebody who makes a pleasure of gathering and spreading news, . . .

announcing his mission by indirection. . . . "Oh, I'm jes' prod-jectin' around" (B 276-77). [S., DAE]

proffer: [*v.t.* to offer.] "He proffered to fix the gun for me" (J 2:641). [An instance of a literary term in general use.]

prong: [*n.* branch of a stream; especially at the juncture where two branches meet—coming out like prongs] "Tuk right down the bed o' Desolation, up the left prong of Roaring Fork, right through the Devil's Race-path" (B 91). "He went up the left prong of the river" (C 3). [S., DAE]

protracted meetings: [*n. phr.* revival meetings] (J 4:859). [DAE, DA suggest wide distribution.]

proud: *adj.* pleased. "I was *proud* to hear from you." Also Ky. (A). (C 2)

public works: [*n. phr.*] any job (B 381). Louis said: "Before public works came in here 50¢ a day was the wage for hard labor, such as splitting rails. Now it is 75¢ a day. Lumbermen now pay 40¢ a thousand for cutting soft woods, such as poplar, cucumber, and ash; 50¢ to 60¢ for hard woods." Few of the men on Little River got over $1.00 a day and board. (J 2:463). (J 2:642q)

puke: [*v.t.* to make sick.] "A lettuce salad with mayonnaise or French dressing would 'nigh puke 'em'" (J 2:421).

pullers: [*n.* forceps; tooth pullers.] The only "tooth-pullers" in the settlement: a pair of universal forceps (B 34). pullers (J 2:471) [See also **tooth pullers.**]

(like) pullin' teeth: [*n. phr.* difficult or painful.] "Old man Proctor allers *will* have a good, big fire, and, by George, hit was just like pullin' teeth to come away from it" (J 4:735).

punkies: [*n. pl.*] gnats (J 19:bc1). [DA suggests U.S. origin.]

punkin: [*n.*, variant of *pumpkin;* especially common in place names, like Punkin Run, Madison, Ky.; Punkintown C[ree]k, Jackson Co., N.C.; see the lists in J 26:75-81.]

purty, purtier, purtiest: [1.] *n.*, variant of *pretty.* Plaything. Also Ill., Ky. (A). [See also **play pretty.**] [2. adj. pretty] They told me that a certain blue-eyed girl thought that black eyes were "purtier" and that she actually changed her eyes to jet black [with jimson weed] whenever she went to "meetin'" (B 313). "That's the purtiest quilt (J 2:541). [3. adv. somewhat] "Bill sung out, 'Is it fur down thar?' and I said, 'Purty fur'" (B 106).

put the case: [*v. phr.* to give an example.] "I put the case this away" (J 3:951-24). [A bookish term in general use.]

putt: [*v.t.*, variant of *put,* rhymes with *but.*] "Where did you putt it?" (J 2:641).

put on: [*v. phr.* to pretend?; listed under "Ailments" in J 2:642s and under "Dialectal Words; Unknown to Standard" in J 2:603.]

pyerch: *n.*, variant of *parch* (A). [Cf. **cyard.**]

Q

quantum: [*n.* portion, amount.] It is quite impracticable for a blockader to age his whiskey. In the first place, he is too poor to wait; in the second place, his product is very small, and the local demand is urgent; in the third place, he has enough trouble to conceal, or run away with, a mere copper still, to say nothing of barrels of stored whiskey. Cheerfully he might "waive the quantum o' the sin," but he is quite alive to "the hazard o' concealin'" (B 136).

quar: [1. *adj.* variant of *queer;* different] Foreigner, outlander, it is all one; "different," we are, "quar," to the mountaineer (B 17). Also **quare** (J 2:642p). [2. *adj.* unusual, intoxicated] "That makes me feel the quarest (cannabis)" (J 2:475).

quern: [*n.* hand-mill.] The ancient quern or hand-mill [is] jocularly called an arm-strong-machine (B 365).

quile, querl, quorl: *v.i.* to coil. "A dog *quiled* up in the leaves." Also Ky. (A). [J 2:625 adds:] Him, he's as satisfied & drowsy as a dog quiled up in the leaves" (HK). "I'd rather be a man in chains than a dog quiled under the house!" (J 23:77). Variously pronounced [as spellings above may suggest] (B 365). [DAE suggests U.S. origin.]

quillaree: [*n.* wood thrush (*Hylocichla mustelina*)] (J 26:55). Perching bird nearly as large as a robin. Brown dove-like head,

brown back and wing coverts, whitish throat and breast with
dark dots. Twitters in low, dove-like tone (J 1:70).

quilt patterns: [*n. phr.*; a list follows, contributed by M.B.:] "Old
Maid's Puzzle," "Friendship," "Seven Stars," "Hangin' Star,"
"Ocean Wave," ("That's the purtiest quilt I might' near ever
seen"), "Sunflower," "Bear's Paw," "Save-all" (There's not a
thread of the cloth left when you're through cuttin' out), "Half-
brick," "Palm Leaf," "Oak Leaf" (all patch work), "Lazy Gal"
(easy to make because you take the scraps just as they came
and quilt them in), "Log Cabin," "Irish Chain," "Double Irish
Chain," "Nine Diamonds" (J 2:541).

quit: [*v.t.* to abandon, leave.] "Let a bear take to a gang o' hogs
an' he'll never quit 'em" (J 4:749).

quite: [*adv.* almost, about.] "Jest afore it got quite fernent me, I
shot" (J 4:749).

quorl: *n.* coil, whorl. "The *quorl* of sang roots" (A; J 2:354).

R

raar or **ra'r:** [*v.* to roar] Men, women and children drink whiskey
in family concert. . . . when I protested that raw whiskey
would ruin the infant's stomach, the mother replied . . .
"Why, if there's liquor about, and she don't git none, *she jist
raars!*" (B 138). [In J 2:471 K uses this quote (spelled "jest ra'rs"),
but attributes it to John Walker's wife while she was feeding
raw onions to a three month's babe. The quote is followed by
the observation (apparently incorporated into the "quote" for
the book):] Often I have seen these mothers give raw whiskey
to babes that were still at the breast. The liquor was fresh
"moon shine" that was above proof, and it would fairly stran-
gle a man unaccustomed to that peculiarly fiery brand, but it
was given the babes, a spoonful at a time, without a drop of

water, and I never saw one of them bat an eye. [See **rar.**]

rabbit clover: [n., plant, like sorrel; probably rabbit-foot clover (*Trifolium arvense*); see **horse sorrel**] (J 2:481).

rabbit-skin soil: [*n. phr.* a comic metaphor for thin, poor soil] (J 2:342).

race: *n.* a little stick or bar, as "a *race* of ginger" (A; J 2:428). a little stick or root (C 2). "Can I borry a race of ginger?" means the unground root—you will find the word in *A Winter's Tale* (B 365). [DAE contains *race ginger*.]

raelly: [*adv.*, variant of *really*; probably rhymed with *tally*] "I ain't right clar in my mind as to B.M. raelly ownin' that property" (J 18:29). "What we-uns calls the cur, in this case, raelly comes from a big furrin dog that I don't rightly know the breed of" (B 80).

raft: "*n.* abundance "There was a raft of children at play" (C 1). "He'd a hull raft o' money" (J 2:641). (J 2:642u) [Colloq., DAE]

raft up, rafting up: [*v., part.* to make, or making rafts of timber; loggers' terms] [Timber is] "rafted up to go down the Ottawa in 'cribs'" (Fraser 340) (D 1). [In spring] "during the 'rafting up' process, that is, the binding together of the single pieces of square timber into 'cribs,' each containing about twenty-five sticks [logs] . . . for up to this point the timber has been floating in the streams in loose single sticks" (Fraser 334-35).

rain crow: [*n.*] yellow-billed cuckoo [*Coccyzus americanus*] (J 26:54). "You're cookin' old rain-crow" (J 10:84).

raise, raisin': [*v., vbl. n.* to bring up (children), upbringing] "Right thar you deny your raisin', Jim" (Miles) (J 2:641; 10:82). "Jackson County, whar I was principally raised" (Louis) (J 2:640).

rammick: [*adj.*, variant of *rammish;* like a ram: rank, lustful?; listed as a "coinage" in J 2:600.]

ramp: *n.* rampion; the wild garlic of the mountains [*Alium tricoccum*] (A). (J 2:603)

rar: [v.i. variant of *rear*] "I do love, of a winter night, to build a good log fire, and jest rar' back and eat big apples!" (M.B.) (J 4:735). "He r'ard around on one leg" (J 23:82). [See **raar.**]

(to have a) rather: *v. phr.* to have a preference. Also Kan. (A). [In B 357, K introduces a passage from the journals as follows:] An old lady quoted to me in a plaintive quaver, [and then continues with the journal entry:] " 'It matters not, so I've been told,/ where the body lies when the heart grows cold.' But a body has a rather about where they'd be put." (Bob's mother) (J 2:483). [B also "corrects" this to read: "person . . . he'd . . . "].

ratsbane: [*n.*] crisped bunch-flower. Resembles hellebore. (J 1:69)

rave: [*n.* railing of a sled; loggers' term, taken from a footnote in Springer, 105] (D 1).

rawhide: *v.t.* to carry on one's back. "I *rawhided* that sack acrost the mountain" (A; J 1:322f). [Listed as a] coinage, as verb (J 2:601).

razor-back: [*n. phr.* a sharp ridge.] For Sugarland Mountain is, in fact, a "razor-back" ridge, rising 1,500 feet above its corresponding valley, and running for about eight miles down from the Smoky divide, without a single gap along the crest (B 231).

read: [*v.i.*, to contain, to tell about.] "Bob, what does that book read about?" (J 2:641).

read after: *v. phr.* to read. "You write the nicest English I ever *read after.*" Also S.Car. (A).

(in) reason, (I know): [*adv.* in this context, rightly, for sure] "I know in reason he will" (J 2:641). (J 2:642) [See also **in reason.**]

receptions: [*n. pl.* parties.] "I see they give [William Jennings] Bryan a lot of receptions when he kem back from the other world" (B 17).

reckon: [*v.i.* to think, suppose.] "I reckon it can stand one more night of it" (B 77). "She got, I reckon, about the toughest deestric' in the ceounty" (B 468). "Whut you reckon ails me?" (B 299). (J 2:603)

recollect: [*v.i.* to remember.] "I don't seem to reecollect" [sic] (J 2:641). "I recollect you-uns said every one o' them miles was a thousand rods long" (B 122).

reco'nize: [*v.t.*, variant of *recognize.*] "I didn't reco'nize you" (J 2:639).

redbird: [*n.* eastern cardinal (*Richmondena cardinalis-cardinalis*)] "Pretty as a redbird and prettier too; skip t' m' Lou, my darlin' " (B 338). (J 26:54)

red up, redding up, rid up: [*v. phr.* to ready or to clean up.] We went to "redding up" [after a strong wind had lifted the roof, sending moss and dried chinking mud down on the floor] (B 83). [Listed under "archaic":] red up, also rid (J 2:597).

red pepper tea: [*n. phr.* herbal tea used as abortificant.] "Old Mis' Posey and Jim knocked it sky high with red-pepper tea" (J 4:841).

reel: [*v.t.* to twist.] [A bear called Old Reelfoot] "reeled" or twisted his hind feet in walking, as some horses do, leaving a peculiar track. This seems rather common among old bears, for I have known of several "reelfoots" in other, and widely separated, regions (B 108).

reg-lar: [*adj.*, variant of *regular.*] "Reg-lar old pop-skull it is too" (B 122).

rempshions: [*n. pl.* great quantities.] "There was rempshions of fish in the river" (C 3). [See also **rimpshions.**]

rench: [v.,] variant of *rinse.* Also La., Ill., S.Car., Kan., Ky., Mass., Cal. (A). rench or rinch (B 352). (C 2) [See also **rinch.**]

resk: [*v.t.*, variant of *risk.*] "Got to resk my mule's life as fur as he *can* go" (J 26:63).

resolute: *v.i.* to persevere. "To keep the hogs from *resolutin'* around" (A; J 2:642p). [Perhaps a comic metaphor; DAE has the term in the sense of "demonstrating."]

respec'ful: [*adj.*, variant of *respectful*] (J 2:642p).

restin' powder: [*n.* an opiate.] See **easin' powder** (A). (J 2:600, 642)

restin' spell: [*n. phr.* rest, nap.] When men want to "take a restin' spell" they lie down on the floor, regardless of spittle, and other filth (J 2:437).

resume: [*v.t.*] "to bring in, as 'Resume the breakfast into the dining room'" (C 2).

retch: [*v.t.* , variant of to *reach.*] "Retch me that whup" (J 2:641).

revenoo, revenue, revenuer: [*n.* a tax collector, from the revenue service.] "Up stepped two revenoo right to the door" (J 3:951.23). "He knows there'd be another revenue 'murdered'" (B 171). "You wunt find ary critter as has a good word to say for the revenue" (B 170). "They've heerd tell about the judges; and they've seed the revenuers in flesh and blood" (B 120). "When a revenuer comes sneakin' around, why, whut he gits, or whut we-uns gits, that's a 'fortune of war,' as the old sayin' is" (B 123). [DAE, DA suggest Midl. origin.]

rheumatiz: [*n.*, variant of *rheumatism.*] The old man complained only of "a touch o' rheumatiz" (B 105). "Mountaineers are not a notably healthy people. The man who exposes himself wantonly [to the elements] sooner or later "adopts a rheumatiz," [which] lasts till he dies (B 296).

rich weed: [*n.* horse balm.] (*Collinsonia* [*canadensis*]) (J 1:69). [VA, NC, DA, DAE]

rid: [*v.t.*, variant of *rode.*] "They jist rid saplin's gittin' out o' thar" (J 2:367). (B 358)

ridey-horse, ridey-hoss: [*n.* cock-horses.] The children have few toys other than rag dolls, . . . "play purties," and such "ridey-hosses" and so forth as they can make for themselves (B 333). **ridey-hoss** "Git you a stick for a r[idey]-h[oss] (J 2:600). (J 1) [Kurath claims that *ridy-horse* is App. term for a seesaw.]

ridin' critter: [*n.*] a saddle horse (J 2:361). The trail looks impossible for "ridin' critters," and is so for any that are not mountain bred. (Letter to Albert Britt, 23 Aug. 1919) (C 10). (J 2:592; B 360)

ridin' way: [*n.* probably a trail fit for horseback, rather than a foot trail] (J 2:600).

rifle: *v.t.*, [variant of] *raffle* (A; B 352). "Let's rifle off this watch." [Also:] **rifling off** (J 4:755).

rifle ball: [*n. phr.* the older form of projectile shot from rifles, not the same shape as a bullet.] "But saw the walls full o' holes an' set in glass winders, an' any feller that's got a mind to can pick ye off with a rifle ball as easy as not" (B 305).

rifle-gun: *n.* rifle (A). (J 2:401, 592; B 360) [S.Midl., DAE]

rift: [*v.t.*] rive, split [loggers' term] (Springer 68) (D 1). ["As used today, to rift saw is to 'quarter saw' lumber" (L. Monteith). "To rive at one time meant to split boards for a roof" (E. Monteith). Cf. riv.] [DAE provides quotation from MA in which "rift timber" is timber that could be split easily.]

right: [*adv.* very.] "Of course, I'm weak yit and right nervish" (J 2:475).

right at: *adv. ph.* nearly. Also Ill., Kan. (A).

rightly: [*adv.* exactly; correctly.] "I never could just rightly remember it" (Ralph) (J 2:641). "I don't rightly know" (B 80). (J 2:605)

right smart: [1. *adv.* considerably.] very (J 2:489). "Hit mocks gold right smart" (J 10:83). [2. adj. considerable.] "Yes, th'r's a right smart seenyuh around hyur" (J 1:7). [3. n. a considerable amount] "Likely to get up right smart o' hardness between 'em" (J 4:853). [DAE suggests S.Midl., S. usage; one quotation comes from Morley's *Carolina Mountains* (1913).]

rile: [*v.t.* to arouse, to roil.] "He was some considerably riled about it" (J 4:853). The idea that [a mountain man] speaks a dialect never enters his head unless some "furriner" puts it there. Then he is "riled" (J 2:491). (J 2:603) [Chiefly U.S., colloq. OED; DAE lists several examples.]

rimpshions, rimptions: *n. pl.* abundance. "There's *rimpshions* of squirrels in the Hickory Cove" (A). "Many, as 'Rimpshions of squirrels'" (C 2). If plenteous, then there are rimptions (B 367). [See also **rempshions.**].

rinch: [*v.t.*,] variant of *rinse* (A). "Rinch that out" (J 2:429). [See also **rench.**]

rippit: [*n.* quarrel.] If they quarrel, it is a ruction, a rippit (B 368). [Cf. **ruction.**]

rips: [n.; loggers' term] "'Rips' is a word used of a stretch of water, which is not long enough or rough enough to be called 'rapids'" (Hubbard vii) (D 1).

rise of, the: [1.] more than. "A leetle *the rise o'* six miles." Also Ill., Ky. (A). rising for exceeding (B 370). [2. *pres. part.,* becoming] rising. "He ain't but *risin'* sixteen" (A). [In contemporary usage the term appears in the expressions, *rising sophomore,* meaning one who is about to become a sophomore.] (C 2) [DAE suggests Midl., S.Midl. origin.]

risin': [1. *n.* a pimple, a boil;] risin' [means] inflammation (B 370). [Listed under "skin deseases" as "risins" in J 2:477 and as "Dialectal Words; Unknown to Standard."] "Dew pizen comes like a risin', and laws-a marcy how it does hurt!" (B 303). "I had a risin' on my side" (J 2:475) [2. conventionally, as pres. part. of rise] "My bread is risin'" (J 2:603).

Risin'-Sun quilt: [*n.* a pattern for a quilt; cf. **quilt patterns** and **kiver patterns**] (J 2:451).

riv: [1. *v. past tense;* variant of *rived* or *riven:* to split or cleave] "I riv some boards" (J 2:377). [Listed under "labor" in J 2:642.] (B 358) [Cf. **rift.**]

riz: [*v.i.*] [Although this appears to be a variant of vowel in *rose,* K erroneously suggests] a weak preterite supplants the proper strong one (B 358). Mrs. B. says: "In the morning, when they riz up, there lay all that filth yet" (J 2:439). "He riz right up" (J 2:641). [The bear] "riz an' knocked me down with his left paw, an' walked right over me, and lit up the ridge" (B 101). "She riz in the air" (B 91). [2. in the special sense of swelled:] "I bruised my ankle the other day and it riz" (J 2:476).

rock: [*n.* always preferred to stone.] A mountaineer does not throw a stone; he "flings a rock." He sharpens tools on a grindin'-rock or whet-rock (B 371).

rock clift: [*n.*, variant of *cliff.*] (J 2:592). A pleonasm (B 360). "Got to resk my mule's life as fur as he *can* go, then break my own back kerryin' meal through the blow-downs and laurel, and around rock-clifts, and over slidy shale, whar there ain't no trail atall" (J 26:63).

rock a hominy: [*n. phr.*] Indian corn parched without burning and reduced to powder. The fire drives out the watery parts of the corn, leaving the strength of it behind, and this being very dry, becomes much lighter for carriage and less liable to be spoilt by the moist air (J 4:521). [DAE includes two quotations from NC.]

rocking: [*vb. n.* throwing rocks.] A prime amusement of the small boys is "rocking" (throwing stones at marks or at each other), in which rather doubtful pastime they become singularly expert (B 333). throwing stones at adversaries (J 4:857). (J 2:605) [DAE suggests S.Midl., S.W. distribution.]

roke, ruck: [*v. pret.* of *rake*] (B 358; J 2:593).

Roll the Platter: [*n. phr.* a "play party" social game] (B 338).

rooster: [1.] *n.* captain, q.v. "He's a *rooster* of a feller" (A; J 2:642). [DAE defines the term as "a lascivious man" and provides a quotation from AL. We think it meant something more like "macho."] [2. v.t. a euphemism for "to cock" a gun; listed as an example of "vulgar squeamishness" in J 2:607.] "Then the dad-burned gun wouldn't stand roostered [cocked—K]; the feather-spring had jumped out o' place (B 101). (J 2:605) [DAE defines as "cock or hammer of a firearm."]

rough house: [*n.*] tavern (J 23:67).

roughness: [*n.*, variant of *roughage.*] Corn is topped for the blade-fodder, the ears gathered from the stalk, and the main stalks afterwards used as "roughness" (roughage) (B 381). "She's in the field, up yan, gittin' roughness.". . . "Roughness," in mountain lingo, is any kind of rough fodder, specifically corn fodder (B 112). (J 2:361) [DAE suggests NEng, Midl. usage.]

roust: [*v.t.* to awaken roughly, variant of *rouse.*] "Whar's that brekfust you're yellin' about?" "Hit's for you-uns to help *git!* I knowed I couldn't roust ye no other way" (B 84).

route: [*n.* variant of *rut.*] 'That road has such bad routes in it' " (C 1).

ruction: [*n.* riotous outburst or quarrel.] [If neighbors] quarrel, it is a ruction (B 368). "Them two preachers like to had a ruction" (J 4:855). "The older dog don't ginerally raise no ruction; hit's the younger one that's ill" (B 80). (J 2:603)

ruin: [*v.t.*] to injure (B 370). "I've about ruined my leg" (J 2:475).

ruinate: *v.t.* to ruin. (A; C 2)

ruint: [*v.t.*, variant of *ruined.*] "I'm bodaciously ruint" (seriously injured) (B 368). (C 3)

rumpus: [*n.* a violent disturbance or uproar.] "Their idea of a conversation is an argument; their idea of an argument is a rumpus" (B 233).

run: [1. *v.*, variant of *ran* (B 358).] "I run, an' she run" (B 91). [2. *n.* a trip, specifically "running" bootleg whiskey to market.] He and his party were on the way to some still-house, where they would stay until the "run" was made (B 220). [3. *v.* to go through a dance routine, probably derived from the popularity of the Kentucky Running Set, if not specifically referring to that.] "Runnin' their cotillion" (Louis) (J 4:761).

runnet: *n.*, variant of *rennet.* Also Ill. (A). [NEng, DAE]

runround: [*n.* a footloose youth, variant of *runaround.*] "You can't go for the cows 'thout a hearin some young runround poppin' at a squirrel or a jaybird or jist a fool spot on a tree" (J 4:74).

runt: [*n.*] tuberculous hogs (J 2:367).

rustle out: [*v.i.* to get moving, to be up and about.] "Rustle out, boys; we've got to get a soon start if you want bear brains an' liver for supper" (B 84).

ruther: [*adv.*, variant of *rather* (B 352).]

S

sacin-powder: [*n.* talcum powder] (J 2:601).

sad: [*adj.* sorry, poor.] Biscuits generally made with soda and buttermilk . . . The dough is not rolled out and cut with a cutter, but moulded in the hands, hence biscuits are tough and "sad" (J 2:419).

safety first: [probably intended as comic, perhaps merely an idiolectal form: M.H. suggests the phrase was] "used to apologize for first helping himself to butter when asked to pass it. Middle aged traveling man of this section" (C 11).

salat: *n.* greens (A). "Salat" never served with vinegar (J 2:421). never eaten raw (J 2:433). [S., DAE; chiefly MD, VA, NC, Kurath; cf. **wild salat.**]

salt: [*v.t.* to tame or keep tame by using salt; important in the mountains where both hogs and cattle were allowed to range freely during the summer but kept semi-dependent on man by occasional salting:] "He follers up his hogs, and salts them, and corn-feeds them a little and gentles them up" (J 2:367). [DAE suggests Midl., S.Midl. usage.]

salt of lemons: [*n.*] white wood sorrel (*Oxalis acetosella*) used to make "salt of lemons" (J 26:26).

(a) sample: [*n.*, variant of *example.*] "There's Jim Cody, for a sample" (B 170).

sang: [*n.*, variant of *ginseng* (*Panax quinquefolia*); used to designate both the plant and its root, the source of its value:] "Formerly, . . . digging 'sang,' as they call ginseng, was a general occupation . . . [but] mainly the occupation of the women and children, who went to work barefooted, amid briars and chestnut burrs, copperheads and rattlesnakes. Indeed, the women prefer to go barefooted, finding shoes a trouble and constraint" (Allen, "Cumberland") (J 2:642o). "I found a patch of sang in the hiddenest little place you ever seen" (J 1:81). Sang Hollow, Greenbrier Gulf (J 26:75). Sang Camp Fork (J 26:78). (J 2:603) [Midl., S., DAE]

santer: [*v.i.* variant of *to saunter.*] "Santerin' about" (J 4:734). "I'm santerin' about" (B 277). [Cf. **brogue.**]

sap: *v.t.* to outwit in trading (A). "I sapped him" (J 10:82). To green out or sap is to outwit in trade (B 368). (J 2:600)

sarcumstance: [*n.*, variant of *circumstance.*] "Hit is, under some sarcumstances" (B 120). "Reckon Pete was knowin' to the sarcumstance" (B 371).

sarmon: [*n.* variant of *sermon.*] "There was lots o' leetle boys of 'em that kem [to meeting] only in their shirt-tails. There was cracks between the logs that a dog could jump through, and them leetle fellers 'd git 'em a crack and grin in at us all through the sarmon" (B 312).

sartin: [1. *adj.*, variant of *certain*] "I didn't know fer sartin" (J 2:641). [Local name:] Hell fer Sartin (Lee, Leslie, Ky.) (J 26:82). [2. *adv.* certainly.] She's sartin shore to find out" (J 2:591).

sarvice: [*n.*, variant of *service.*] "We know whut [the revenuers] uster do afore they jined the sarvice, and why they did it. Most of them were blockaders their own selves, till they saw how they could make more money turncoatin'" (B 170).

sarvice, sarvis, or (infrequently) **sarviceberry:** [*n.*, shortened form or variant of *serviceberry* (*Amelanchier arborea*) and/or its fruit.] "As good a pie as ever I ate in my life is made of sarvice. It makes the best jelly and preserves. And it don't take much sugar. There's a bitter sarvice though: the berries turn such a deep red they're mighty near black; they're bitter, raw" (Mrs. Bob) (J 25:178). "Sarvices" greedily sought after. Berries generally procured by cutting down the trees; hence getting scarce in the vicinity of settlements. "Fruit sweet and with a very agreeable flavor; while in the northern States, so far as our experience goes, this fruit, even if it be said to be edible, is not worth eating" (Gray) (J 2:433). "That Thunder-head's a joyful place for sarvice-berries" (Louis) (J 2:433).

sarviceable: [*adj.*, variant of *serviceable*] "Thar's only one sarviceable wagon in this whole settlement, and you can't hire it without team and driver, which is two dollars and a half a day" (B 123).

sashiate: [*v.* to do a sashay in a square dance.] The third [word of clearly foreign origin] is sashiate (French *chassé*), used in calling figures at the country dances (B 364). "Partners sash-i-ate . . . gents and ladies swing in the center; own partners and half sash-i-ate" (B 337-38).

sass: [1. *n.* sauciness, pertness.] "Don't give me none o' yer sass" (J 4:853; 10:83) [2. *v.* to talk saucily.] "I sassed her back" (J 4:853). [3. *n.* apple sauce.] "Your hostess, proffering apple sauce, will ask, "Do you love sass?" (B 367; J 2:421). (J 2:603, 642u) [DAE attests to the first two of these uses and quotes Mark Twain for them; it does not narrow the definition for the third use to applesauce as K. would have it; rather it suggests "stewed fruit or preserves served at a meal as dessert. Colloq."]

sassafrack: [*n.*, variant of *sassafras* (*Sassafras albidum*)] (J 1:71; 2:642o). [*Sassifrax*, NEng, DAE]

sassaparilla: [*n.*, variant of *sarsaparilla;* in N. Amer. this usually designates plants resembling the true (tropical) sarsaparilla, especially wild sarsaparilla (*Aralia nudicaulis*); K lists this with these notes:] Flowers, May-June. Greenish. Root aromatic. (J 26:22); [but in the same list he notes,] The rope-like stems of the Dutchman's Pipe, called by woodsmen "sassaparilla," twining around the trees like tropical lianas (J 26:55). Dutchman's Pipe (*Aristolochia macrophylla*) [flowers] May-June. Greenish and purplish-brown (26:24). [Perhaps the "woodsmen" did make a nice distinction between "wild sassaparilla" and plain "sassaparilla."]

satify, satifaction: variants of *satisfy, satisfaction* (A). "He was n't sati'fied." / "Some sati'faction" (J 2:641).

saunt: *pret.*, variant of *sent* (A; B 358). "I saunt a boy to do it" (J 2:641). (C 2)

sawwhet: [1. *n.*, loggers' term; the hone used to sharpen saws, and metaphorically: 2. *n.* an owl whose call resembles the former.] "Sawwhets had been heard in the bush in the dead of night. This strange, weird mysterious sound, whether of bird, or animal, or tree, or demon no man knows, resembling somewhat the sharpening of a saw" (Fraser 276) (D 1).

scab: *v.t.* to scratch so as to remove scabs. "Just a-standin' and *scabbin'* yourself, and you bleedin' all over" (A).

scace: [*adj.*, variant of *scarce*] (C 3). **sca'ce** (J 2:642p).

scand'lous: [*adv.*, variant of *scandalously*, shamefully.] "We can't git a doctor up hyar less'n three days; and it costs scand'lous" (B 121).

scenery: *n.* curio. "He jes' wanted the skull fer a *scenery*" (A).

school: [*v.t.* to educate.] "So's t' he could be where he could school his children" (J 4:767).

scorpion: [*n.* a misnomer: lizard.] The mountaineers have an absurd notion that the little lizard so common in the hills is rank "pizen." Oddly enough, they call it a "scorpion" (B 70). (J 1:75; 2:642o) [S., Midl., DAE]

scour: [1.] *n.* scar (A). "He had a scour on his side about four inches long" (J 4:749). See also **scyar.** 2. *v., vb. adj.* to rub clean, to scrub.] "The woman's goin' to scour." "Damn these scour days and wash days; I don't like 'em" (Bob) (J 1:296).

scourge: [*n.* a portmanteau term ⟩ from *scour* and *purge:* a dose of strong medicine.] "I've got to take a scourge of something; my stummick's gone wrong" (J 2:476).

scout: [*v.t.*] scout [means] elude (B 370).

scrabble: [*v.i.* to work hard, to struggle.] So, as the years passed, a larger and larger proportion of the highlanders was forced back along the creek branches and up along the steep hillsides to "scrabble" for a living (B 444).

scrape: [*n.* (hunting term)] where a buck has pawed the earth, or has rubbed his antlers against a tree (D 2).

scrape-fire: *n.* flint-lock (A). "I was shootin' one o' them old scrape fires" (J 4:749). (J 2:401, 600)

scriffen: *n.*, [variant of *striffen*, as Bird spelled it in C 3; since K wrote to Mary Hunter (July 31, 1926) concerning his word list, "I had no chance to revise it, but just sent my rough notes"— most of which were copied from Cox and Bird. A change like this may well have been an error in transcription; *striffen* is the conventional spelling.] Membrane inclosing the visceral cavity or the brain. "The *scriffen* of the brain was cut.'" Also Kan. (A). (J 2:600)

scritch owl, scrootch owl: [*n.*, variants of *screech owl* (*Otus asio*); these are the most common forms found in the mountains, Kurath 136.] (C 3). [See also **squinch owl.**]

scrop: *n.*, variant of *scrap:* "Just put that little *scrop* (of trash) in the fire." (Mrs. K., aged 75, 6/27/26) (C 11).

scroudge or scrouge: [*v.i.* to squeeze together; pronounced with the same dipthong that occurs in *loud*] "crowd. 'Too many boys tried to scroudge in on one bench'" (C 3). "Git up, pup! you've scrouged right in hyur in front of the fire" (B 75). (J 2:603)

scrubby-headed: [*adj.* probably rough, bristly (OED)] (J 9:32).

scyar: *n.*, variant of *scar*. Also Ky. (A). "You can see the scyar yit" (J 2:475).

sech-like: [*adj.*, variant of *such.*] "But when yo're a-holdin' co't [courting] and sech-like maybe you'll want to shet the do' sometimes" (J 2:376).

sedge-grass broom: [*n.* a home-made broom.] "The broom was a bundle of sedge-grass about as long as one's arm, tied tightly at the stems with a string and wielded with one hand. The sweeper had to stoop with one-sided motion" (Jones) (J 2:415). [S., DA]

seed: [1. *v.*, nonstandard preterite of *see*, = *saw*] "I seed a man comin'" (J 2:641). [2. *v.*, variant of *seen.*] "I done seed him!" (B 24). "I've seed hit blow, here on top o' Smoky, till a hoss couldn't stand up agin it" (B 77).

seen: [*v.* in a specific context where *ever* is used with present perfect tense of *see*, *have* is dropped and *seen* = *have seen*:] "That was the beatenest snowstorm ever I seen" (B 72). "I'd believe he's a hant if 't wasn't for his tracks—they're the biggest I ever seen (B 91). (B 358)

seenyuh: *n.* scene or scenery. "Thar's a right smart *seenyuh* thar, too" (A; J 1:7). (J 2:642o)

sence: [*adv.*, from then until now; variant of *since.*] "Jim Cody ain't never showed his nose sence" (B 170-71). "He hasn't been thar sence" (J 2:641). [Given K's distaste for eye dialect spellings, we suspect that this is his way of noting the merger of /i/ and /ɛ/ before /n/ (since/sense, pin/pen) that is so common throughout the South.]

sensibly: [*adv.* perceptibly, palpably.] "Right sensibly atween the shoulders I've got a pain" (B 299; J 2:475)

sentiment: *n.* sensation. "I feel sick . . . No, my *sentiment's* gone" (A; J 2:475).

set: [*v.*, variant of *sit.*] "What would you do for a man if he broke his thigh and you couldn't get a surgeon?" / "We'd set around

and sing until he died" (B 300; J 2:642 reads "set up with him").
[Courtship:] "I'm goin' to set up with my feller to-night" (J
1:286). [See also **settin'-down.**]

set-along: *adj.* [toddler] "When my oldest was a little *set-along*
child (settin' along the flo')" (A); [the parenthetical explanation
is from J 1; B 359 plays variations on the same data.] (J 2:642p)

settin'-down work: [*n. phr.* a task that can be done while sitting.]
"Chair-bottoming is easy settin'-down work" (J 2:457; B 359).

settlements: [*n.* town; the stress is on the last syllable.] "Aren't
you afraid to live up here all alone?" / "No: the devil don't go
prowlin' around here in the mountains; he's kep too busy
down in the settle*ments*" (Walt Proctor) (J 4:717).

set to: [*v.* begin.] "Don't you set to cryin', honey" (J 4:856a).

several: "*adj.* many. 'We have several blackberries this year'" (C
1). I recalled that several, in the South, means many—"a good
many" (B 77). "How's the mast this year?" / "Better'n common." / "Plenty of chestnuts?" / "Yes, there's several" (J 2:361).

severe: [1.] *adj.* fierce. "A big *severe* dog" (A; J 2:371). "No hound'll
raelly fight a bear—hit takes a big severe dog to do that" (B 81).
[2. *adj.*, variant of *several*.] "I've cl'ared me a patch . . . now I
can raise me two or three severe craps!" (B 36). (J 2:642) [MO,
KY, DAE]

shackle: *v.i.* to shuffle, as if shackled. "Jist *shacklin'* along" (A).
"Me? I'm jes' shacklin' around." And "shacklin' around" pic-
tures a shackly, loose-jointed way of walking, expressive of the
idle vagabond" (B 277; J 1:256). [Cf. **brogue.**]

shackly: [*adj.* ramshackled.] Here is a land of lumber wagons,
and saddle-bags, and shackly little sleds that are dragged over
the bare ground by harnessed steers (B 29). A shackly, loose-
jointed way of walking (B 277).

shame-briar: *n.* sensitive plant [*Mimosa pudica;* the Latin means
modest, bashful] (A). (J 1:71; 2:600, 642o)

shammick: *v.i.* to lounge about idly. Also **shummick** (A). (J 2:642p)

shamp: *v.t.* to trim (hair) (A). To shamp means to shingle or trim
one's hair (B 368). "I must get somebody to shamp my hair" (C
1:274).

she-balsam: *n.* Frazer's balsam (A). Spruce is he-balsam, balsam
itself is she-balsam (B 369). (J 1:59, 71) [NC and TN mts, DAE]

she-bear: [*n*. a female bear.] "You'll git some o' that meanness shuck outen you if you tackle an old she-bear tomorrow!" (B 80).

sheep-sorrel: [*n*. a low growing dock (*Rumex acetosella;*) K lists this plant three times under "wild greens," the first with the tag, "mixed in," and the last two to illustrate what greens were used in "mixed greens": 2.) Wild Sage (Amer. Germander?) + Dock + sheep sorrel + wild mustard (May 23, 1911). 3.) We had a mess of greens consisting of 1) lamb's quarters 2) poke shoots 3) sheep sorrel 4) dock 5) plantain 6) young potato tops 7) wild mustard 8) cow pepper (May 21, 1910) (J 2:433). [Cf. **cow pepper.**]

sheriff: *v.i.* to serve as sheriff (A).

shet: [*v.t.* variant of *shut.*] (B 352, 358) "Lyin' John (whose mouth ain't no praar-book, if it *does* open and shet)" (C 3). "Ef somebody comes that ye don't want in, you can shet it [the window] and put up a bar" (B 305).

(to play) shet-mouth: [*v. phr.* to be quiet.] "Them roosters take a round o' crowin' and then play shet-mouth for a while" (J 2:371). (J 6, 2:600)

(be) shet of: [*v.* to be or get rid of someone or something.] "He's biggety and up headed and I'm glad to be shet o' him" (J 23:77). (J 2:603, 642)

shet up: [*v. phr.* to become silent.] "Hit shore shet up" (J 2:641).

shickle: *n.* shuttle (of a loom) (A). (J 2:603)

shimmick: [*v.* to be lazy] (J 6). [See also **shummick;** cf. **brogue.**]

shirt-tail: [1. *n.* the lower rear portion of a shirt; normally, it would be tucked into one's pants, so if exposed, it suggests partial nakedness or just slovenliness—either works for comedy.] "I'd as lief jump into a pant'er den in my shirt-tail" [i.e., half-naked, unprotected] (J 4:855). [At times the comedy may not be intended:] "When Matt Crisp (now preacher) was goin' to see his gal, . . . [he said,] "Lisbeth, I'll bet you cain't tell what I got tied up fer you in my shirt-tail.' / 'Well, what is it?' / 'Sugar.'" (J 1:286). [2. *adj.*] "shirt-tail boys" (J 2:642p). It still is common in many districts of the mountain country for small boys to go about through the summer in a single abbreviated garment; . . . they are called "shirt-tail boys" (B 312).

shite poke: [*n.*] green heron [*Butorides virescens;* the name derives from the bird's call (Palmer)] (J 26:54).

shit slinger: [*n. phr.* the name for one of the members of the logging crew; listed without explanation in J 2:642y.]

shive: [*n.,* logger's term;] splinter (Springer 80) (D 1).

shiver: [*n.* a combination of *shive* and *sliver,* both of which mean a splinter or fragment.] "A little shiver of bone come out" (J 2:475). (J 2:642)

shoe-mouth: *adv.* [probably also *n.*; if a shoe has a tongue, its opening or top would be its mouth.] "The fog is friz *shoe-mouth* deep on the mountains" [shoe-top deep] (A; J 1:38). shoe mouth deep (J 2:642o). (J 2:600)

shoo: [*v.t.* to drive away.] Bare-legged girl "shooin'" flies off the table (J 2:435). [Most likely K's use of quotation marks here indicates only his recognition of informal usage rather than as a token of uniquely App. speech.]

shoo-fly: [*adj.* used in square dancing call.] "Swing and circle four, ladies change and gents the same; right and left; the shoo-fly swing (and so on for each couple)" (B 338).

shoot: *n.* shot (A). "archaic" (J 2:597).

shootin'-arn: [*n.* shooting iron, gun.] "He drawed out his shootin'-arn" (J 2:401). [DAE suggests W. usage.]

shore and **shorely:** [*adv.,* variants of *sure, surely*] (B 352). "Hit shore shet up" (J 2:641). "Fellers, you want to mark whut you dream about, tonight: hit'll shore come true to-morrow" (B 83). [A dream about a woman:] "Hit means a she-bear, shore as a cap-shootin' gun; but you've done spiled it all by tellin'" (B 85). "Not the children, shorely: them that's young and innocent" (J 3:909). "That buck, shorely to God, has wings!" (B 91).

shore enough: [*adj.* real, variant of *surely enough.*] "We'll know by to-morrow whether he's a shore-enough bear dog" (B 94).

shortened bread: [*n.* bread made with cooking fats.] "My baby's sick; I believe it's [from] eatin' that shortened bread" (J 2:591).

short sweetening: [*n.* brown sugar.] "sorghum molasses, which they call 'long sweetening,' . . . sugar, which by contrast is known as 'short sweetening.'" (Allen, "Cumberland") (J 2:423). "a cheap grade of brown sugar" (Vincent, "Frontier") (J 2:425). [DAE suggests S.Midl., S. usage.]

shot-gun wad: [*n. phr.*, comic metaphor for "light bread," i.e. white bread] (J 2:429).

shoul over: [*v.*, variant of *shoulder over*, i.e. to wear over.] Man's boots very much "shouled over" at the sides so that the heels scarcely touched the ground (J 4:839).

shuck: [1. *v.t.*, variant of *shook, shaken* (B 358).] "He shuck him awake" (J 2:641). "You'll git some o' that meanness shuck outen you" (B 80). [2. *v.t.* to remove the husk from grain.] "I gather the corn, and shuck hit and grind hit my own self" (B 122). [3. *v.t.* to remove as in shucking.] I "shucked off my clothes," tumbled [into bed]. (B 320). [4.*vbl. n.*] "I'd trade it all and make a clean shuckin' of it" (J 10:84). [AR, GA, DAE; also in names:] Shuckstack Mt. (J 26:72).

shuck-beans: *n. pl.* beans in the pod (A). [This appears to be the only thing in A that K later corrected in B, as follows:] Green beans in the pod are called snaps; when shelled they are shuck-beans (B 366). [See also **snaps.**]

shucks: [*interj.*, expresses mild disappointment.] "Shucks! Why, man, whut could they gain by hurtin' you?" (B 118).

shummick or **shammick:** [*v.i.*] To "shummick" (also "shammick") is to shuffle about, idly nosing into things, as a bear does when there is nothing serious in view (B 277). "sorter shummickin' around" (J 1:256; 4:734). [Cf. **brogue**]

shun: [*pret.*, variant of *shone*] (B 358).

shut-in: *n.* a gorge or canyon. "That place is a *shut-in*" (A). The shut-in is a gorge (B 374). Marshall, the county seat of Madison Co., N.C., is "shut-in" by steep mountains. They say that pegged shoes were invented there, of necessity, because the cobbler had no room to draw his thread (J 1:212). "On each side it's the master place you ever seen—a shut-in shore enough" (J 1:81). "That Nantahala is a master shut-in, jest a plumb gorge" (B 357). (J 2:642o)

sich: [1. *adj.*, variant of *such.*] "No sich talk" (J 4:763). "No bear'll cross the mountain sich a night as this" (B 79). "Sich a stew over nothin'" (J 10:83). "W'y, you know there's three nights in the month when there ain't no moon at all. If anything comes on sich a night, it'll never grow up" (Mrs. Cooper) (J 2:683). [2. *pron.* such] "Hit's agin natur to put up with sich as that" (J 10:83)

sich like: [*adj.*, a pleonasm, such.] Lamp chimneys are hard to carry safely over the mountain roads, [but] "man can do without sich like, anyhow" (B 319).

side-trouble: [*n.* pleurisy.] "There's been a sight o' side-trouble (pleurisy) in the settlements" (J 2:462, 475). (J 2:600)

sifflicated: *p.a.* suffocated (A). "I was that nigh sifflicated" (J 2:475). "Sometimes I'm nigh sifflicated. Whut you reckon ails me?" (B 299). (J 2:603)

sight: [1. *adv.*] a sight [means] much (B 370). "I'm a sight better" / "There's been a sight o' side trouble" (J 2:475). [2. *n.* large amount.] "My woman she gives me a wonderful sight o' trouble" (J 10:83) "a sight of side trouble" (J 2:469). [DAE furnishes citations from Twain and J.C. Harris.]

sight of the eye: [*n. phr.*] pupil. Also Ill., Kan. (A). "The match head popped off and burnt him right next to the sight of the eye" (J 2:475). (J 2:642p)

sightly: [*adj.* open to view.] "This is mighty sightly" (Mac-G[owan]) (J 1:7). (J 2:603) [DAE furnishes citations from Twain and Warner.]

sign: [1. *n.*] tracks, droppings [usually scat], and other signs of an animal's trail (D 2). But John and the hunchback had found "sign" in the opposite direction (B 97). "We'll know by tomorrow whether he's a shore-enough bear dog; for I've larned now whar they're crossin'—seed sign a-plenty and it's spang fraish" (B 94). [2. *n.* by metaphorical extension, to mean signs of illicit distilling.] It must be ticklish business for an officer to prowl about the headwaters of these mountain streams, looking for "sign" (B 171). (J 2:642) [DAE suggests widespread use; earliest recorded uses, VA, NEng.]

si-godlin': *adv. slantdicular.* [diagonally]. "You sawed that log off a little *si-godlin'*. "Also **antigodlin', antigadlin', si-antigodlin'** (A). Si-godlin or si-antigodlin is out of plumb or out of square (factitious words, of course—mere nonsense terms, like catawampus) (B 368-69). [Montgomery suggests that "K was wrong here; sigodlin/antigodlin are anagrams of diagonal."] (J 2:601)

simblin or **simlin** [*n.* a summer squash.] Cf. **cymblin.** [LA, GA, DAE]

simples: [*n.*] herbal remedies, often found "hanging from the rafters" [i.e. drying] (J 2:481).

single-bitt axe: [*n. phr.* an axe head with a single cutting edge.] Axes have straight handles, some of them 3½ feet long. Same for both single-bitt and double-bitt axes (J 2:401).

singlings: *n. pl.* the liquor of first distillation ("low wines" of the trade) which moonshiners redistill at a lower temperature to make whiskey. [Also] Ky. (A). The product of this first distillation (the "low wines" of the trade, the "singlings" of the blockader) is a weak and impure liquid, which must be redistilled at a lower temperature to rid it of water and rank oils (B 135). (J 2:600)

sink, sink-hole: [*n. phr.* a hollow depression where drainage collects.] "The bear div down into a sink-hole with the dogs atop o' him. . . . Then I jumped down into the sink and kicked him loose from the dogs" (B 101).

sissle: [*n.* thistles, nettles.] "washin' sissles in a piggin'" (Mac-Gowan) (J:763). [Joan Hall of DARE suggests that washing thistles might be a preparation for making fabric.]

size: [*n.* a fixed portion of food or drink, having "English Dialect Authority" according to Fox, J 2:489.]

skeered or **skeert:** [*past. part.* frightened; listed as:] skeered (J 2:603). "I was that skeert!" (J 2:635).

skid, skidding: [K's source suggests these words are synonyms and may be either *n.* or *v.:* 1. *n.* poles placed in the low portions of logging roads; 2. *v.* filling in such roads] "The tops of the highest knolls [on the roads] are scraped off, and small poles called skids are laid across the road in the hollows between" (Springer 84; see also 97) (D 1). [Apparently in general use among loggers, DA]

skift: 1. [*n.*,] variant of *skiff* (A). "There warn't no skift on the river to take us over" (J 1:322f). 2. [*n.*] trace. "A thin skift of snow." Also Kan., Ky. (A). "A skift o' clouds." "A thin skift o' clouds" (J 1:38). (J 2:600, 642o) [DAE includes the first meaning; the second is British dial.]

skillet: [*n.* a frying pan; still used to distinguish a cast iron "skillet" from various more modern versions; the word, strangely enough, figures frequently in place names:] Lick Skillet, Mitchell, N.C. (Bob) (J 26:85); Skillet C[ree]k. (Mingo, W.Va.) (J 26:84).

skippers: [*n. pl.* maggots infesting meat.] "Pork alive with skippers in Granville's store" (J 2:435). [DAE suggests Midl. usage.]

Skip t' m' Lou: [*n. phr.* a social game or "play party" used as a substitute for dancing] pronounced "Skip-tum a-loo" (B 338).

skoot: [v.i. slide or skate] "He skooted down the bank" (C 3).

skreak: [*v.i.* variant of *squeak.*] "I'm so poor I skreak when I walk" (J 4:729).

slam: [*v.i.* collapse.] "He slammed clar out on the floor" (J 2:164, 641).

slanchways, slaunchways: *adv.* slantingly. [diagonally]. Also Ill., Kan. (A). Slaunchways denotes slanting (B 368). "She didn't cut the cloth slaunchways" (C 3). [Also] "slanchways, aslant" (C 2). (J 2:601)

slantdicular: [*adj., adv.*] out of plumb. [This is the gloss that K provides for the term **sigodlin'.**]

slick, slyke: [1. *n.*] A "hell" or "slick" . . . is a thicket of laurel, or rhododendron, impassable save where the bears have bored out trails (B 375). About noon, while descending from a high ridge into a creek valley, to get some water, I became enmeshed in a rhododendron "slick;" and, to some extent, lost my bearings (B 110). [See **hell, woolly-head, yaller patch.** 2. adj. probably clever or deft, possibly glib] "He was slick on a joke" (J 2:637). [Listed among archaic English words from Fox, in the form: slyke (J 2:489).] (J 2:600, 642o, p)

slicker: [*n.* raingear.] Slickers are worn only on horseback (B 291). [DAE suggests W. usage.]

slick-faced: [*pred. adj.* beardless.] "a slick-faced dude from Knoxville" (B 137).

slide: [*n.* an incline more gradual than rapids, down which the rafts are taken in logging.] "Alongside [the rapids and cascades] in long 'slides' the timber has to pass" (Fraser 340). [Fraser also describes "shooting the slides" on the "cribs" of logs bound together, 340 ff.] (D 1). [DAE lists as lumbering term used in Canada, NEng.]

sloat: [*n.*, hunters' term.] track (Steele 91) (D 2).

slorate: *v.t.* to slaughter (A).

slosh: [*n.* state of muddiness.] "The road was jist in a slosh" (J 1:322). (J 2:642o)

slubbered: [*past part.* disorderly; the residence of a "witch" is referred to as "a slubbered hut"] (J 10:57).

slug or **slung:** [*n.*, hunters' term.] unborn foetus (D 2).

slut: [*n.* a makeshift lamp.] But kerosene, also, is hard to transport, and so one sometimes will find pine knots used for illumination; but oftener the woman will pour hog's grease into a tin or saucer, twist up a bit of rag for the wick and so make a "slut" that, believe me, deserves the name (B 319).

smart: [*v.i.* to burn, to sting.] [On applying jimson weed to an eye,] the man said "hit smarts a leetle—not much" (B 313).

smidge, at a: *prep. phr.* next or near to (A).

smidgin': [*n.* very small amount.] If the provender be scant the hostess may say, "That's right at a smidgen," meaning little more than a mite (B 367; J 2:641). [Also] **smidgen** (J 2:600); "**smidgeon** 'the least bit'" (C 2). [DAE suggests S.Midl. usage.]

smokables: [*n.* tobacco products; term used in an ad in the Elizabethton, Tennessee, Carter County *News*, 23 Aug. 1912] (J 2:436). [App., but possibly not Smoky Mt. term.]

snaggy: [*adj.* prickly.] "My face gits so snaggy, gin I go a week without shavin'" (J 1:274).

snake master: [*n. phr.* any herbal snake bite remedy.] Bob says sweet fern is a mountain "snake master" (J 2:473).

snakeroot: [*n.* any plants reputed to serve as remedies for snake bites] "snakeroot or wild ginger" [the root is used as a] "pleasant tonic for the stomach" (Asheville *Citizen* 22 Jan. 1928) (J 2:480).

snaps: [1.] *n. pl. shuck-beans,* q.v. (A). [Note that K corrects this early definition in his book:] Green beans in the pod are called snaps; when shelled they are shuck-beans (B 366). "snap beans" (C 2). (J 2:419, 600) [Midl., S.Midl., S., DAE; W.VA, W.NC, Kurath.]

sneed: *n.* the snath of a scythe. Also Ky. (A). (J 2:600)

snipe: [*v.t.* to ambush, as a sniper.] Therefore it is proper and military for him to *snipe* his foes by deliberate sharp-shooting from behind any lurking place that he can find (B 402).

snowbird: [*n*. Slate-colored junco (*Junco hyemalis*)] (J 26:54). Little Snowbird C[ree]k. (Graham [Co.], N.C.) (J 26:76).

snub: [*v.t.* tie off; logger's term.] "As soon as the raft is 'snubbed' within the booms. . ." (Fraser 340) (D 1). [DAE suggests a wide usage, particularly with canal boats."

snuff: [*n*. pulverized tobacco, inhaled or placed in the mouth; possibly used as metaphor for snuff-like phlegm] "Every morning I cough up jest gobs o' snuff" (J 4:745).

snuff stick: [*n. phr.* a small twig chewed until frayed and used to dip snuff and bring it to the mouth.] The narrow mantel-shelf holds pipes and snuff and various other articles of frequent use, among them a twig or two of sweet birch that has been chewed to shreds at one end and is queerly discolored with something brown (this is what the mountain woman calls her "tooth brush"—a snuff stick understand. (B 318) [A letter from Walter Ponchot (18 Jan. 1928) draws attention to the salutary effects of diet on mountaineers who moved to Kent, Ohio:] "Red meat and vegetables have certainly wrought wonders. Even the old women have quit the snuff stick or at least they hide it away" (C 7). [DAE contains citation from Morley's *Carolina Mountains* (1913).]

snurl: [1. *n*.] a knot, gnarl (C 3). [Specifically, a burl in a tree or wood] snurl for burl (J 14:30). [2. *adj.*] **snurly:** knotty, gnarly (C 3). "A snurly tree" (J 1:53). (J 2:600, 642o)

so be (it): [*idiom*, it is so.] "If so be he's thar" (J 2:611).

sob: *v.i.* To become soggy. "If you let a pine pole stay out and *sob*, the bark will rot off" (A).

sobby: [*adj.*, variant of **soggy**.] Sobby wood means soggy or sodden, and the verb is to sob (B 370).

somap'n nuther, somethin' nuther: [variants of *something or other*] (J 2:641, 642).

some'ers, somewheres: [variants of *somewhere*.] "Sam orter be cooterin' around some'ers" (J 4:722). "No, he's out somewheres" (B 112).

soon: [1.] *adj.* early. "Give me a *soon* start" (A). Soon [is used] for early ("a soon start in the mornin'") (B 370). Soon for early [listed as] "an Anglo-Saxon survival" (Frost 22) (J 23:77). "we've got to git a soon start" (B 84). [2. adv. variant of *sooner*] "They'd get you soon or late" (J 23:77). (J 2:642)

soon's: [*contraction* of *soon as*] "Soon's I got home I just et like a hog." (Lily Calhoun) (J 4:745). "Soon's I could shoot without hittin' a dog, I let him have it" (B 101). (J 2:642)

soothing-syrup: [*n. phr.*, possibly a term for patent medicines, which might easily be 60 percent alcohol (J 1:201), but here, apparently, a euphemism for liquor:] But somebody . . . produced a bottle of soothing-syrup that was too new to have paid tax (B 81).

sorry: [*adj.* vile, worthless.] "Them sorry fellers" denotes scabby knaves, good-for-nothings. Sorry has no etymological connection with sorrow, but literally means sore-y, covered with sores, and the highlander sticks to its original import (B 365). [Listed as] "a startling survival of Anglo-Saxon speech" (Frost 22) (J 2:489). "Some sorry fellers come in thar full o' moonshine an' shot their revolvers" (J 3:1025).

sorter: [*qualifier*, variant of *sort of.*] "I'm feelin' sorter peaked" (J 2:475). "Sorter shamed to tell" (J 4:745).

so'st, so's't: [*contraction* of "so as that"] "So 'st she'd stay" (J 2:642). "So's't I wouldn't bark my shins!" (B 102). so 'st (J 2:642).

sot: [*v.*, variant of *sat.*] "I sot right thar and heerd it" (J 2:642). Mrs. B says, "They sot awhile, and then Pruitt pinched the other feller and says, 'Let's go out'" (J 2:439). "Thar sot the old womern" (J 4:785).

so't: [*conj.*,variant of *so that.*] "The Tennessee side of the mountain is powerful steep and laurely, so't man nor dog cain't git over it in lots o' places" (B 79).

soup in, soupin' in: [*v. phr., part.* eating from a common pot.] There is not enough tableware to go around, and children eat out of their parents' plates, or all "soup in together" around one bowl of stew or porridge (B 323). "We was all settin' round the pot, soupin' in together" (J 3:1050).

souple: [*adj.*, variant of *supple;* not defined, just listed among archaic words from Fox on J 2:489.]

sour mash: [*n.* in distilling corn liquor, the product of fermentation.] When done [fermenting], the sugar of what is now "sour mash" has been converted into carbonic acid and alcohol. The resulting liquid is technically called the "wash," but blockaders call it "beer." It is intoxicating, of course, but "sour enough to make a pig squeal" (B 134).

souse: [*v.t.* to scald, to plunge into hot water.] "You cain't scald the bristles offen a live hog, [but can off a mule.] I soused hit; you never heered sich brayin'" (M.B.) (J 2:367).

sow belly: [*n.* salt pork, especially the parts from the back, side, or belly of the hog.] "sow belly" (salted side of bacon) unusually strong, and fried to a crackling (J 2:419). Hams of razorbacks too lean to amount to much. Not cured for winter, as they will not last. "Sow belly" [apparently alluding to what was cured] (J 2:443). [In salting cattle on mountaintops] they find it burden enough to carry salt for their cattle, with a frying-pan, cup, corn pone, coffee, and "sow belly," all in a grain sack strapped to the man's back (B 293). (J 2:367, 603).

sow folks: [*n. pl.* sows] (slang) (J 2:603).

spang: *adv.* exactly; directly. "He was right *spang* on the spot." "*Spang* fraish." Also Ky. In Ill., *bang spang* (A). (Colloq.) (J 2:603). "The sign was spang fraish" (J 4:749). "I've larned now whar they're [the bear] crossin'—seed sign a-plenty and it's spang fraish" (B 94). [Describing a wind (a "blow") so great it "lifted the ground," "Doc" Jones says:] "I went up in the sky, my coat ripped off, and I went a-sailin' end-over-end. . . . About half an hour later, I lit *spang* in the mud" (B 78). "at once" (C 2). [Colloquial and rare, DA; AR, GA, DAE.]

sparrow bird: [*n.* used generically, any small bird.] "a bird in general" (C 1).

speciment: [*n.*, variant of *specimen.*] "Heap o' folks thinks he stole that speciment" (J 10:83).

speech: [*n.* in the phrase "to have speech," i.e. to talk.] "I want to have speech with you" (J 10:83).

spell: *n.* [an indefinite] "period of time. 'This is a rainy spell'" (C 1). Spell is used in the sense of while ("a good spell atterward") (B 370). "Hit was a good spell atter Christmas" (J 2:629). [marked:] (Colloq.) (J 2:603). (J 2:642o) [DA furnishes an instance of this usage from NC.]

sperrity: [*n.*, variant of *asperity*, contentiousness.] (J 2:603). [This aphetic form represents yet another instance of a learned word in the general vocabulary.]

spert: *n.* aphetic form of *expert* (A). "I'll have to have some 'spert come an' fix my sewin' machine" (J 2:403). "Wisht you'd 'zamine this rock fer me—I heern tell you was one o' them 'sperts" (B 351).

spew: [1. *v.i.* to form or grow out of; specifically with reference to frost, which in the mountains often emerges from the ground in crystalline spears, especially in spring and fall when the ground is very moist and thaws during the day but freezes again at night; this phenomenon is quite different from the way in which hoar frost or frozen dew seems to *settle* on objects and deserves a special verb like that which K records.] "Hit was along late in November, the grain only two, three inches high, and the ground all spewed up with frost" (J 1:38). "La! many's the night I've been out when the frost was spewed up so high [measuring three or four inches with the hand—K], and that was around the fire too" (B 293). [2. *v.* to vomit.] "I got so homesick I couldn't eat, and I spewed like a buzzard" (Lilly Calhoun) (J 4:745). (J 2:642)

spider: [*n.*] a cast iron skillet (J 2:403). [corn pone is] "baked in a Dutch oven, or in a cast iron spider" (J 2:419). [Chiefly NEng, Kurath; more common in E.NC, K may have heard this from some visitor or may be using his own vocabulary to describe an App. phenomenon.]

spignet: *n.* wild spikenard [*Aralia racemosa*]. Also Ky. (A; J 1:67). (Corrup.) [i.e. spignet from spikenard] (J 2:603). Shrub; clusters of small, elder-like berries. On hillsides around (J 1:69). (*Vagnera racemosa*) [Flowers] May-July. White. Berries aromatic. (J 26:23). [DAE includes an 1891 citation without providing any locale.]

spile: [1. to go bad; variant of *spoil*. K clipped out and saved an advertisement which began,] "Food Stuffs Absorb Stinks" [and continued with refreshing tactlessness,] "Some people don't know this; some don't care. They stink themselves and when they find something that don't they think it is 'spiled' and won't trade in a house that does not 'smell familiar.' " (Carter County *News*, Elizabethton, Tenn., 23 Aug. 1912) "You can talk as you please about a streak o' the cur spilin' a dog, but I know hit ain't so" (B 80). [On a dream:] "You've done spiled it all by tellin' " (B 85).

spit (snow): [*v.*a metaphor suggesting a very light snowfall, less than a flurry.] "Hit was spitten' snow" (J 2:629).

splutter: [*v.i.* to fuss, to bustle?] "She kep' splutterin' around" (J 1:256; 2:642; 10:83).

spoon: [*v.t.* to serve or pick up with a spoon.] "Spoon me some o' that gravy, Sal" (J 2:429). "Eddie made a deposit on the floor and then took the cover of a baking-powder can and went to 'spooning up' the filth" (J 2:435).

spot (trees): [*v. phr.*, loggers' term.] [Locating a road] "is done by an experienced hand, who 'spots' the trees where he wishes the road to be 'swamped' " (Springer 84) (D 1). [DAE suggests NEng distribution.]

spraint: [*n.*, hunters' term;] droppings (D 2).

sprangle: [1.] *v.i.* to spread out tortuously. "Little branches all *sprangle* out from Eagle Creek" (A; J 1:49). The streams sprangle in every direction like branches of mountain laurel (B 21). "sprangle—as— 'starry campions sprangling all around the upright stem' " (C 2). "Worm-eaten cabbages, tobacco, and sprangling tomato vines, here and there creeping out from among the rank grasses & tall weeds that overrun the place" (J 1:49). (J 2:603, 642o) [2. **sprangly:** adj.] "Sprangly bushes, like laurel." Also Kan. (A). (J 2:603) [DAE cites in NY, MO, and the *adj.* example from K.]

spread: [1. *n.* an expanse of land] (Colloq.) (J 2:603). "The spread o' the valley!" (J 1:23).

spring-box: [*n.* small covered reservoir located at a spring head which serves as a cistern and as a refrigerator.] "butter and milk [are stored] in spring-boxes" (J 2:373). [DA cites K as the source for its illustrative quotation for this term.]

spruce-pine: *n.* hemlock [*Tsuga canadensis*] (A; C 2). The hemlock tree is named spruce-pine, while spruce is he-balsam (B 369). Hemlock and Carolina Hemlock (both locally "spruce pine") (J 1:59). (J 1:71; 2:600)

spud (around): [*v.i.*] "Spuddin' around" means toddling or jolting along. "No, I ain't workin' none—jest spuddin' around" (B 277; J 1:256, 4:734).

spunk: [*n.* original form of *punk*; "any substance, as decayed wood, that smolders when ignited, used as tinder" (Webster's Third).] spunk for punk (D 2). (C 2; J 14:80)

spurtle: [*n.*, "a wooden stick for stirring porridge" chiefly Scot. (Webster NW).] spurtle for stirring porridge (J 2:403).

spy: [*v.t.* to see.] "I happened to spy him" (J 2:42, 10:83). "You'll spy, to-morrow, whar several trees has been wind-throwed and busted to kindlin' " (B 77).

squar: [1. *adj.* just, variant of *square.*] "Nobody refuses to pay his taxes, for taxes is fair and squar' " (B 120). [2. *adv.* honestly, straightforwardly.] "Say it squar' out" (J 3:983, 10:83). [3. *v.t.* to determine the area of an object in square feet. One bear,] dressed, without the hide, weighed 434 pounds, and the hide "squared eight feet" when stretched for drying (B 95-96). [DA, DAE suggest wide usage for first two uses; neither records third.]

squatters: [*n. pl.* people who settle on unoccupied land.] "There is among them a mobile element—squatters—who make a hillside clearing and live on it as long as it remains productive" (Allen, "Cumberland") (J 2:336). [K takes issue with Allen in his book:] The white freedmen generally became squatters on such land as was unfit for tobacco, cotton, and other crops profitable to slave-owners. . . . these poor whites had nothing to do with settling the mountains (B 432-43).

squidged: *p*[*red*].*a*[*dj*]. subsided. "His hand was all swoll up, but now it's all *squidged* down" (A).

squinch owl: *n.* screech owl [*Otus asio*] (A). "She had a baby no bigger 'n a squinch-owl" (J 1:272). (J 1:73) [See also **scritch owl;** *Squinch* is not the expected form in the mountains, Kurath; DA citations from J.C. Harris suggest term is familiar in S.]

(a)-squirrelin': [*v.* squirrel hunt.] "He's gone a-squirrelin' " (J 4:749). "Are ye fixin' to go squirrelin'?" (B 356).

staddle: [*n.*, hunters' term;] "a sapling bent to assist in hanging a deer's carcass" (D 2). ["Sapling" or a platform upon which to cure hay, DAE; citations appear to be N.Eng origin.]

stand: [*v.t.* to tolerate.] "He's very religious, but as long as he treats me nice, I'll try to stand it" (J 2:639). [K may have recorded this sentence because he found the use of *stand* to be peculiar, but we suspect that a more likely reason is the irony of the remark.]

standing cypress: [*n.* a flower grown with those on the list in which it appears.] Touchmenots, pansies, marigolds, nasturtiums, "standing cypress," phlox, xenias (J 2:359). [Handsome perennial herb, *Gilia rubra*, of S., S.W., DA]

stay-place: *n.* [temporary hut.] "That shack was put up fer a *stay-place* for them herders to pass the night in" (A; J 4:749). hunting term (J 4:749). (J 2:600)

a-steppin': [*v.* to step out, to leave.] "Well, I better be a-steppin'" (J 10:83).

stew: [1. *n.*] The resulting liquor [in the distilling process] is "backings," which is either used in the next run or is drunk as "stew" (J 3:951.23). [Cf. **beer, singlings, doublings.**] [2. *n.* a fuss, a mess.] "Sich a stew over nothin'" (J 10:83).

stick: [*n.*, log; logger's term.] ". . . the 'rafting up' process, that is, the binding together of the single pieces of square timber into 'cribs,' each containing about twenty-five sticks . . . up to this point the timber has been floating in the streams in loose single sticks" (Fraser 334-35). "The timber 'sticks' are bound together . . . into cribs" (Fraser 340) (D 1).

the sticks: [*n. pl.* the backwoods.] Backwoodsman is another term they deem opprobrious. Among themselves the backwoods are called "the sticks" (B 281). [Colloq., DAE, DA]

stiff-necked: [*adj.* proud, stubborn.] "They're too hard-hearted and stiff-necked" (J 2:637). (J 2:642p) [Biblical diction, cf. Exodus 32:9, 33:3,5]

still-house: [*n.* the hut in which corn liquor is distilled.] This house is sometimes inclosed with logs, but oftener it is no more than a shed, built low, so as to be well screened by the undergrowth (B 131). [DAE references range from 1687 through 1891, all apparently refer to reputable establishments—unlike the one K describes here.]

stillin': [*vbl. n.* distilling.] "The big fellers that makes lots of money out o' stillin', and lives in luxury, ought to pay handsome for it" (B 121).

still slop: [*n.* waste from the distillery.] Moreover, cattle, and especially hogs, are passionately fond of still slop, and can scent it a great distance, so that no still can long remain unknown to them. . . . horses despise the stuff. A celebrated revenue officer . . . rode a horse which was in the habit of drinking a mouthful from every stream that he forded; but if there was the least taint of still-slop in the water, he would whisk his nose about and refuse to drink. The officer then had only to follow up the stream, and he would infallibly find a still (B 129).

stingy vine: [*n. phr.*, listed under "vegetation"] (J 2:642o).

stob: [1.] *n.* stub. "I knocked her [a hen turkey] over with a birch stob" (B 91). "a stake" (C 2). "He was horse-throwed, and lit on a stob, and hurt his shoulder" (J 2:475). [2.] *v.*[*t.*,] variant of *stab.* Also Ky. (A). "Amos stobbed him" (J 4:863). "I'll bet he's stobbed somebody and is runnin' from the sheriff" (B 130). (J 2:642o)

stoke: [*v.t.* to share.] The mountaineers have an odd way of sharing the spoils of the chase. They call it "stoking the meat," a use of the word *stoke* that I have never heard elsewhere. The hide is sold, and the proceeds divided equally among the hunters, but the meat is cut up into as many pieces as there are partners in the chase; then one man goes indoors or behind a tree, and somebody at the carcass, laying his hand on a portion, calls out: "Whose piece is this?" [The "blind" man calls out the names of the partners in response to this repeated query.] And so on down the line. Everybody gets what chance determines for him, and there can be no charge of unfairness (B 102-103). "Boy's le's stoke this meat" (J 4:749). (J 2:603)

stone-dead: [*adj. phr.* dead.] "Pringle's a-been horse-throwed down the clift, and he's in a manner stone dead." (B 299).

store: [*n.* treasure.] "He sets a heap of store by you" (Mac-G[owan]) (J 2:611, 1:286).

store clothes: [*n. phr.* anything that is not homespun.] Shoddy "store clothes" are cheaper and easier to get (B 308).

store-house: [*n. phr.*, term listed under "stores;" it usually is a synonym for a separate storage house, a cellar, or some other place where food is stored (Mrs. Carrie Witherbee).] (J 2:461).

store-tea: [*n. phr.* imported tea.] I introduced "store-tea." Little John Cable had never seen any. Few liked it (J 2:419). It was the first time that Little John ever saw "store tea" (B 98). "store tea" (J 2:428). [Cf. **table tea, dittany.**]

stove: [*v.t. pret.* of to stave, to break in, or to jab:] stove [is used] for jabbed (B 370). "I stove a brier in my heel wunst" (B 303; J 2:471). (J 2:642)

straddle: *n.* crotch. "Wet up to the straddle." Also W. Mass., Ill.,

Ky. (A). [Currently used specifically for the seam in pants where the two legs meet (Weaver Taylor).] [2. *adv.*, in the idiom "ride straddle" it means with the legs apart, as opposed to riding sidesaddle; in the example K records, the a- prefix does not occur, though it is retained in other dialects: "ride a-straddle."] "Yes, the women-folks mainly rides straddle" (J 1:322).

stren'th: [*n.*, variant of *strength;* the spelling probably signals articulation with an alveolar rather than a velar nasal.] "He don't 'pear to have no stren'th left" (J 2:476).

striffin: [*n.*] "membrane. 'He cut away the striffin from the man's insides so as to be able to see what was wrong with him'" (C 3). [Cf. *scriffin.*]

strong: [*v.t* to have a strong effect on.] A verb will be coined from an . . . adjective: [e.g.] "Baby, that onion'll strong ye!" (B 357).

strut: [*n.*] hurry. "I'm in a powerful strut this morning" (J 2:642k). "You 'pear to be in a powerful strut this morning" (J 10:83).

study: [1. *v.t.* to] think (J 2:489). [2. *adj.*] "steady. 'He's a study boy'" (C 3).

studyment: [1.] *n.* [meditation, reflection, daydream.] "He sot thar in a *studyment.*" "Nancy, honey, what's your *studyments* tonight?" (A). [J 2:483 attributes the last quote to Becky Pilkey (Coot's wife), addressing Nance Laney, who was dying and, therefore, might have had some special wisdom.] "Dreaming" (C 2) (J 2:603)

stummick: [*n.* stomach; the spelling probably signals a high front vowel in the last syllable.] "Somethin' 's gone wrong with my stummick" (B 299; J 2:475). (J 2:642)

stump: [*v.i.* to remove stumps; logger's term] (Fraser 312) (D 1).

stump-shot: [*n. phr.*, loggers' term.] "A sawyer's term for the ridge left on the end of a board sawed by a single upright saw, where the board is split off from its neighbors" (D 1). [The Monteiths suggest that in current usage: "Stump shots are the large splinters left in a tree stump or in a log when a tree falls before it has been cut all the way through. These splinters can be very dangerous around a mill." E. Monteith has seen the mill machinery throw a stump shot through the roof.]

stump-water: [1. *n. phr.*] (rainwater standing in old hollow stumps) is supposed to be good for ivy-poisoning ("pizen vine"). "I'd as soon drink stump-water as that lager beer." [Bob's wry comment about K's "experiment" making beer] with Bob and John Walker at Knoxville (J 2:471). (J 2:600) [2. *n. phr.*, by metaphoric extension:] alcohol (J 6).

stuk: [*past and past part.* of *stick*; listed as English Dialect in Fox (J 2:489);]Montgomery thinks this may be eye dialect; we are uncertain what pronunciation is being suggested, although the spelling here, when contrasted with that of the following entry, does suggest a higher back vowel as in *took*.]

suck: [*n.*] a whirlpool (B 374). [Listed under "water":] The Suck (J 26:74) Suck C[ree]k. (Summers, W. Va.) South Suck C[ree]k. (Marion, Tenn.) (J 26:82). [VA, PA, MD, NC, DAE]

suddent and **suddenty:** [1. *adv.* suddenly.] "Down he come suddent" (B 106). [2. *n.* sudden;] all of a suddent (J 2:642). Hillsmen . . . sometimes [add] a syllable: loaferer, musicianer, suddenty (B 351).

suee: [a hog call] Suee C[ree]k. (Meigs, Tenn.) (J 26:85).

sugar tree, sugar: [*n.* sugar maple (*Acer saccharum*).] Sugar Tree Gap, Sugar Camp, Sugarland Mt. (J 26:75). No attempt at making maple sugar, although large groves of the finest sugar trees nearby. Rather buy white sugar at 12¢, or do without (J 2:421). [Citations from Ohio to Arkansas, DAE; W.PA, W.VA, WV, W.NC, Kurath.]

suggin: [*n.*] "Suggin" or "sujjit" (the *u* pronounced like the *oo* in *look*) is true mountain dialect for a pouch, valise, or carryall, its etymology being something to puzzle over (B 75). "Shut your face and go to bed. And be sure," he added wittingly, "you pull the soogans over your head, and you won't hear the dying shriek of our victims" (Bower, Ch. ix) (J 2:603). "Better put a ration in your suggin, Bob" (J 4:749). "Bill, hand me some Old Ned [salt pork] from that suggin o' mine" (B 75).

sulk around: [*v. phr.* to act resentfully, showing ill humor.] "And John Cable's sulkin' around with his nose out o' jint" (B 94). [Another expression, still in use, may be derived from this: "to sull up"; the *k* is lost and *up* replaces around, but the meaning seems the same: "If somebody gets mad, they go off and sull up" (George Frizzell). [Latter usage, MO, AR, DAE]

sulter: *v.i.* to swelter. "I went down to the valley, one time, an', I declar, I nigh *sultered* (A; B 386 reads the same except *wunst* for one time; J 2:475). verb from adj. (J 2:601). summer heat—sulter (J 2:642o). (J 2:603)

sumpshiously: [*adv.,* variant of *sumptuously.*] "We fared sumpshiously." [We ate well.] (J 2:429). [Another instance of a learned or bookish word in general use.]

supper: [*n.* suppertime.] "It'll be supper soon" (J 10:84).

a-surgin': [*part.* straining.] "The dog was a-surgin', tryin' to git loose" (J 4:749).

surround: *v.t.* to pass by going around. "I couldn't git through the laurel; so I jist *surrounded* it" (A; J 1). surround [is used] for go around (B 370).

survig'rous: *adj.* 1. In N.C., ambitious, enterprising: in the form *so vigrous.* 2. In Tenn. and Ky., able-bodied, active. "Toler'ble *survigrous* baby." "A most *survigrous* cusser" (A). [Note that in his book K drops this distinction:] Survigrous (ser-*vi*-grus) is a superlative of vigorous (here pronounced *vi*-grus, with long *i*): as "a survigrous baby," "a most survigrous cusser" (B 368). (J 2:601) [DA, DAE both mention *savagerous,* dating from 1832, as a blend of *savage* and *dangerous.* The term seems to have enjoyed much currency on the frontier; it also seems to have undergone both phonological and semantic transformation in the App. area.]

sut: [*n.* soot; the spelling probably signals a mid-central vowel.] "What do you do for a wound like that [a cut foot]?" / "Tie it up in sut and a rag and go to hoein' corn" (J 2:469; B 300). (J 6)

swaller: [*v.t.,* variant of *swallow.*] He had "'lowed to swaller it and see if it wouldn't ease his headache" (B 299).

swallerer: *n.* throat. *Slang* (A). "I've got a bone in my swallerer. Cain't you extrasize it?" (J 2:475). (J 2:600)

swampers: [*n.* the loggers who clear the trails and work on underbrush so sawyers can get at trees and the logs be removed; still current—L. Monteith] "Swampers . . . cut and clear the roads through the forest to the fallen trees" (Springer 92) (D 1). [DAE includes this usage.]

swamp roads: [*v. phr.* to clear away bushes and undergrowth and skid them out of the woods so that horses can get through

(L. Monteith) Locating a road] "is done by an experienced hand, who 'spots' the trees where he wishes the road to be 'swamped'" (Springer 84) (D 1).

swap: [*v.t.* to trade.] "I swapped hosses, and I'll tell you fer why" (B 371). [Widespread.]

swar: [*v.i.*, variant of *swear*] (Nancy Gunter) "Now, Columbus, will you swar before God that you never had nothin' to do with them women?" ("Lum" Gunter) "Nancy, I'll swear before Abraham, Isaac, and Jacob; but I won't have no sich talk as that before *my* Maker" (J 4:763).

sweet fern: [*n. phr.* an aromatic shrub] (*Comtonia geregrina*) [Flowers] Apr.-May. Greenish. Leaves fragrant. (J 26:17). Bob says sweet fern is a mountain "snake master" (J 2:473).

sweet-heartin': [*vbl. n.* courting.] "Josh ain't much on sweet-heartin'" (B 356).

sweet mash: [*n. phr.* mush of corn meal made for distilling.] The sprouted corn is then dried and ground into meal. This sweet meal is then made into a mush with boiling water, and is let stand for two or three days. The "sweet mash" thus made is then broken up, and a little rye malt, similarly prepared in the meantime, is added to it, if rye is procurable (B 134).

swelled: [*v.i.*, variant of *swollen*.] Mrs. C. worried about os of uterus being "swelled shut." Thought coition required that the penis enter the uterus. I was told that "all mountain people think so" (J 2:471).

swim (in the haid): [*v.* to be disturbed, dizzy] "My haid's a swimmin' up here, dad!" / "Well, then you won't drown" (J 2:642, 10:83).

Swing the Cymblin: [*n. phr.*] a "play-party" game (B 338).

swipe: [*v.t.*, loggers' term; listed but not explained in Fraser (136); normally, a groom, one who cares for horses.] (D 1).

swivvit: *n.* hurry. "He's always in a *swivvit*. Also La. (A). When a man is . . . in a hurry, he is in a swivvet (B 368). (J 2:600)

T

table-glass: *n.* tumbler (A). "One of them table-glasses" (J 2:428). (J 2:592; 6)

table tea: [*n. phr.* herbal or home-made tea.] Dittany: "There's no tea you buy in the stores that's better than this table-tea." (Mrs. B.) (J 2:433). "table tea," "store tea" (J 2:428). (J 2:592) [See **store tea, dittany.**]

taddle: *n.* toddick q.v. (A). a small measure (B 366). "Ben didn't git a full turn o' meal, but jest a toddick." [Dargan from Nantahala explained:] When a farmer goes to one of our little tubmills, . . . he leaves a portion of the meal as toll. This he measures out in a toll-dish or toddick or taddle (the name varies with the locality) which the mill owner left for that purpose (B 366). (J 2:600)

tail down: [*v. phr.* to tie down. "A person hooks two 'grabs' onto a log and ties the log down so it will not slide away, out of control. A loose log coming down a mountainside is dangerous" (L. Monteith).] "Loads are eased down hillsides by the use of 'tackle and fall,' or by a strong 'warp' taking a 'bite' around a tree, and hitching to one yoke of the oxen. In this manner the load is 'tailed down' where it would be impossible for the 'tongue oxen' to resist the pressure of the load" (Springer 104) (D 1).

tail-first: [*adv.* backwards.] Sins of the flesh are rarely punished, being regarded as amiable frailties of mankind. It should be understood that the mountaineer's morals are all "tail-first," like those of Alan Breck in Stevenson's *Kidnapped* (B 346).

'tain't: [variant of *it isn't*] "'Tain't so!" (B 80). "'T ain't no manner o' use to ax me what the tex' was that day!" (B 312).

take off: [*v. phr.*] Many common English words are used in peculiar senses . . . take off for help yourself (B 370).

take on: [1. *v. phr.* "crying and flailing around; having a hissy-fit" (Carrie Witherbee).] "moan. 'His father died last spring and he took on awful'" (C 2). [2. v.] "exult. 'The child just kept takin' on about its new dress'" (C 3). [3. v.] "express wonder. 'He

never did see an elephant till he went to that circus, and he ain't
never quit takin' on about how big it was' " (C 3). (J 2:642p)

take to the bushes: [*v.*, euphemism: to relieve oneself.] Not one
house in ten has a privy anywhere on the place. They "take to
the bushes" (J 2:407).

take up locality: *v. phr.* "Well, I reckon we've *tuk up locality* (said
after standing at the siding several minutes) (A).

take up with: [*v. phr.*] to befriend (J 2:605).

take a big through: [**through** = *n.* a spasm, fit.] In these backwoods revival meetings we can witness to-day the weird phe-
nomena of ungovernable shouting, ecstasy, bodily contortions, trance, catalepsy, and other results of hypnotic sugges-
tion and the contagious one-mindedness of an overwrought
crowd. This is called "taking a big through," and is regarded as
the madness of supernatural joy (B 344). "Nance tuk the biggest through at meetin'!" (shouting spell) (B 357; J 4:773). [See
also **through**]

ta-la-lah: [*n.*] red-headed woodpecker [*Melanerpes erythrocepha-
lus*] (Indian term) (J 3:1052).

tale [*n.*] Tale always means idle or malicious report (B 370).

tale-bearin': [*vbl. n.* possibly just gossiping; more likely bearing
false witness, since the sins it is listed among also breach the
Ten Commandments:] Sometimes a man is "churched" for
breaking the Sabbath, "cussin'," "tale-bearin' "; but sins of the
flesh are rarely punished, being regarded as amiable frailties of
mankind (B 346). "They churched Pitt for tale-bearin' " (B 356).

tar'd: [*past part*, variant of *tired*.] "Air ye much tar'd?" / "I was that
tar'd and het up!" (J 2:631).

'tarnal: [*adj.*, variant of *eternal*.] "Hit's all 'tarnal foolishness, the
notions some folks has!" (B 119). [Slang and dialectal from 1821,
DAE]

tasty: [*adj.*, listed as colloq.] (J 2:603).

'tater: [*n.*, variant of *potato*.] There was not a bite in her house
beyond potatoes, and "'taters don't go good 'thout salt" (B 33).
"If a man run out of meal, why, he was *out*, and he had to live
on 'taters or somethin' else. Nowadays we dress better, and
live better, but some other feller allers has his hands in our
pockets" (B 457). "Them 'taters ain't hurt a-bein' done." (M.B.,
returning sweet potatoes to oven) (J 2:642).

'tater holes: [*n. phr.* cold-cellar for potato storage.] "Their potatoes sometimes being kept during winter in a hole dug under the hearth-stone. More frequently a trap-door is made through the plank flooring in the middle of the room, and in a hole beneath are put potatoes, and, in case of some wealth, jellies and preserves" (Allen, "Blue Grass") (J 2:407).

tater patch: [*n. phr.* potato field.] " 'As for the 'tater patch: it was the nearest one to my cabin.' (letter to G.T. McCroskey, NYC, 30 Dec. 1912" (C 5).

tear up the patch: [*v. phr.* to break up housekeeping.] He would lose his wife, too, without even a bye-bye kiss; for . . . she would "tear up the patch" and forsake him, if he had to part with those five hundred dollars (B 210).

tejus: [*adj.*, variant of *tedious;* in the phrase "take it so tejus," it means "take the trouble."] "You needn't take it so tejus as to axe ary man you meet on Stecoah what his name is. Jist say, 'Hello, Mr. Crisp' " (J 2:642). tejus, take it so (J 2:642w). (B 352)

tek: [*v.t.*, variant of *take.*] "I tell yeou hit teks a moughty resol*ute* gal ter do what that thar gal has done" (B 468).

(I'd) tell a man!: [Yes!, Definitely!] [An] intensifying expression . . . with the stress [on "tell"; it] is simply a strong affirmative (B 360).

temper: [*n.* the property of hardness and resiliency in steel.] "I wish t' we *hed* roasted the temper outen them trap-springs, like we talked o' doin' " (B 93).

Tennessee: [*n.* usually pronounced with the accent on the first syllable.] (tənəsî) (A) "If a louse was over in Gray-ham County, it'd swim the Tennessy River to git on my head, or your'n either, Sairy" (Mollie Davis) (J 2:435).

ter: [*prep.*, variant of *to.*] "If you-uns can stand what we-uns has ter, w'y come right in and set you a cheer" (B 271).

terbacker: [*n.*, variant of *tobacco.*] "Gimme a chaw o' terbacker" (Bob Henry) (J 4:731).

territory: [*n.* expanse.] "Quite a territory of country" (J 1:7). (J 2:642o)

tetch: [*v.t.*, variant of *touch.*] "Don't tetch that gun, hit's loaded" (J 2:642). "Tetch me gin ye dar!" (B 328).

tetchious: *adj.* tetchy, [variant of *touchy*] (A). A choleric or fretful

person is tetchious (B 368). "He was right tetchious: easy to fly
up about anything" (J 2:637). (J 2:600, 642p; J 6)

thar: [*adv.*, variant of *there.*] "Stop thar!" (B 12). "I'll be thar in just
a breath" (J 2:641). In some cases an unconscious sense of
euphony seems to govern, as "There is a house over thar" (J
2:490). [Cf. **hit**]

thataway: [*adv.*, variant of *that way.*] "Hit was thataway in my
Pa's time, and in Gran'sir's, too" (B 160). (J 2:603)

their own selves: [*pron.*, intensifier; variant of *themselves*, having
greater emphasis than the conventional variant: *theirselves.*]
"Most of them were blockaders their own selves" (B 170). [Cf.
my own self, your own self]

them: [*pron.*, variant of *those.*] "Now, look at them dogs o' mine"
(B 81). [Asked what he would call a true foreigner, a mountaineer said:] "Them's the outlandish" (B 17). "Boys, them
dogs' eyes shined like new money" (B 101).

they: [*adv.*, variant of existential *there* but never of locative *there.*]
"They was a-plenty thar to do us" (about food) (J 2:428). "They
is a street in Asheville called Buzzard's Roost" (J 2:642w).

think: *v.t.* to remind. "You *think* me of it in the morning" (A; B
371; J 10:83).

think out: *v.t.* to recall. "I just cain't happen to think out his
name" (Ralph) (J 2:641).

this air: [*adj. phr.*, variant of *this here.*] "What brung ye up this air
way-off branch?" (J 4:739). [See also **air.**]

thisaway: [*n. phr.* used adverbially, variant of *this way.*] "I put the
case thisaway" (J 3:951.24). "Jest thisaway: . . ." (B 122).

thoughted: *p*[red.] *a*[dj.] thoughtful. "If I'd a-been thoughted
enough" (A; B 359; J 10:83). (J 2:642p)

'thout: [*prep.*, contraction for (actually a clipped form of) *without.*]
"'Taters don't go good 'thout salt" (B 33). "Yerbs . . . ain't no
good 'thout a leetle grain o' whiskey" (B 121).

th'owed, throwed: [*v. pret.* variant of *threw*] th'owed (slang) (J
2:603). throwed (B 358).

through: [1.] *n.* spasm. "I take a big *through* o' sneezin' every day"
(A). "Takin' a big through" / "Ol' Nan tuk the biggest through
today I ever seen" (J 4:773). [2. *n.* applied to religious ecstasy, a
shouting spell or spasm.] "Nance took the biggest through at
meetin'" (B 357). [See also **take a big through.**]

thumping-chist: *n.* a steam-chest through which "singlings" (q.v.) are run in order to make whiskey at one distillation (A). It is possible to make an inferior whiskey at one distillation, by running the singlings through a steam-chest, commonly known as a "thumpin'-chist." The advantage claimed is that "Hit allows you to make your whiskey afore the revenue gits it; that's all" (B 136). Two and a half gallons is all that can be got out of a bushel by blockaders' methods, even with the aid of a 'thumpin'-chist," unless lye be added (B 138-39). (J 2:600)

thundery weather: [*n. phr.* stormy weather] (J 14:80).

tide: [*n.* flash flood.] The only roads follow the beds of tortuous and rock-strewn water courses, which may be nearly dry when you start out in the morning, but within an hour may be raging torrents. . . . A spring "tide" will stop all travel, even from neighbor to neighbor, for a day or two at a time (B 21). "We caint go no furder." "There's a main big tide on the creek, an' we caint ford" (J 1:322).

tight houses: [*n. phr.* "air-tight" houses, either chinked or plastered to keep out the elements.] No mountain cabin needs a window to ventilate it: there are cracks and cat-holes everywhere, and, as I have said, the doors are always open except at night. "Tight houses," sheathed or plastered, are universally despised (B 304).

tinker: [*v.t.* to repair, as a tinker.] "Blacksmiths who can also tinker clocks, extract teeth, preach, and 'raise a crap'" (Frost 22) (J 2:457).

tip off: [*v. phr.* to inform, to give a tip.] Katch recently had been "tipped off" that the three Ruffs had fled together (B 210).

toad-frog: [*n.* a toad.] In the Smokies a toad is called a frog or a toad-frog, and a toadstool is a frog-stool (B 369). [See **frog.**]

toddick: *n.* a small amount. "I wouldn't take a full turn o'meal but jist a *toddick*" (A). Toddick, then, is a small measure (B 366). (J 2:600) [See also **taddle.**]

toe eetch: [*n.* glasswort (*Salicornia bigelovii.*)] Also called Glass Weed or Water Weed [and, apparently, eetch weed]—is used as an antidote for dew poison, also for poison ivy, the watery fluid in which the plant abounds being pressed out and applied to the part (J 2:481). [Cf. **eetch.**]

tol'able: [*adv.* somewhat, fairly; variant of *tolerably.*] "She's a tol'able big, large, fleshy woman" (J 4:722).

tole: *v.t.* to lure, entice [variant of *toll*]. "I could *tole* that pig around anywhere." Also Ill. (A; J 2:367). To lead by feeding, as pigs or wild turkeys (C 3). (J 2:642, J 6) [DAE furnishes several examples.]

toll-dish: [*n.* The toll-bucket was used in the mill to pay the miller with a portion (1/8) of the grain being milled; the term "toll dish" may also have been applied metaphorically to the collection plate in church] (J 2:453, 600).

tomato: [*n.*] Tomato, cabbage, molasses, and baking powder are always used as plural nouns (B 371). "Them tomatoes hits whar you hold 'em" (J 2:493). [K may be too rigid here; currently *tomatoes* is probably more frequently used than the singular: e.g. one sliced tomato will be treated as a plural: ("Pass the tomatoes"), but it is possible to buy "one tomato." *Maters* is also far more frequent than *mater*, but the latter is possible. Cf. **'taters.**]

tomtit: [*n.*] Carolina chickadee [*Parus carolinensis*] (J 26:55). [NC, GA, DAE]

tooth-brush: [*n.* a euphemism for a snuff-stick, q.v.] Pretty daughter of Jake Rose could not find her "tooth-brush" (snuff-stick); "Borry me yours, Aunt Vice" (J 2:437). [NC, DAE]

tooth brush hunt: [*v. phr.* to meddle, to pry after secrets, to be inquisitive] "Guess that's somebody a-tooth-brush huntin'" (M.B.) (J 4:739, 9:102).

tooth-dentist: *n.* dentist (A). "Is this whar the tooth-dentist is? I got a risin' on my jaw" (J 4:80). (J 2:600)

tooth-jumping: [*vbl. n.* the practice of extracting a tooth with hammer and nail.] "You take a cut nail (not one o' those round wire nails) and place its squar p'int agin the ridge of the tooth, jest under the edge of the gum. Then jump the tooth out with a hammer. A man who knows how can jump a tooth without it hurtin' half as bad as pullin'" (B 301). [K:] "I have told dentists and physicians in the North about 'tooth-jumping,' and they laughed at me." (Bob) "Well, they needn't to laugh; for it's so. Some men got to be as experienced at it as tooth-dentists are at pullin'. They'd cut around the gums, and then put the nail at jest sich an angle, slantin' downward for an upper tooth or upwards for a lower tooth, and hit one lick." [K:] "Would the tooth come out the first lick?" [Bob] "Ginerally. If it didn't, you might as well stick your head in a bee-gum & fergit about it." [K:] "Back teeth extracted that way?" [Bob:] "Yes, sir—any kind of a tooth" (J 2:470; cf. B 302-303).

tooth-pullers, pullers: [*n.*] He also owned the only "tooth-pullers" in the settlement: a pair of univeral forceps that he designed, forged, filed out, and wielded with barbaric grit (B 34). **pullers** (J 2:471).

toper: [*v.*] toper [variant of] *taper* (B 352). [Also] **topering:** p[red.] a[dj.] variant of *tapering* (A).

top out: [*v. phr.* surmount, come out on top of.] At a few minutes past 3 p.m. we "topped out" in the Gap (B 212). (J 1:322f)

tormentin': [*pres. part.* painful, difficult] "But I had one tormentin' time findin' my hat!" (B 78). [DAE lists two instances used in N.Eng.]

torn-down: *adj.* [*phr.* worthless, god-forsaken.] "The *torn-down* scoundrel (A; J 2:637, 642p). Peculiar adjectives are formed from verbs. . . . "That Thunderhead is the torn-downdest place!" [note superlative form] (B 359). "You torn-down scoundrel!" (J 10::82). "Torn-down scoundrels, every one" (B 169). (J 2:601)

tote: [*v.t.* to carry.] Our dictionaries mark this work as a Southern colloquialism. If so, it is a very old one (J 2:603). In Star Route days the mail was carried afoot, two bare-footed young men "toting the sacks on their own wethers" over this thirty-two mile round trip, for forty-eight cents a day; and they boarded themselves (B 31-32). "I paid the two Welches . . . 10¢ an hour each . . . They sawed, toted, and split an 18 in. yellow birch . . . in 3½ hours." (J 2:463) [S., DAE]

tote fair with: *v. phr.* to deal fairly with. Also S.Car., Ky. (A). [DAE contains two citations.]

t'other: [*adj.* the other.] "But, t'other way, no hound'll raelly fight a bear—hit takes a big severe dog to do that" (B 81). "Take your things in t'other house" (J 2:642).

tow sack: [*n. phr.* burlap bag.] In many districts the only means of transportation is with saddlebags on horseback, or with a "tow sack" afoot (B 21). "The best way to carry a pig is to put it in a tow sack with a hole cut for its nose, ensurin' it to breathe" (J 1:9). "Lord . . . bring a tow sack an' a hick'ry withe an' git me" (J 4:773).

traces: [*n. pl.* the straps of a harness; listed under "Make-shifts":] "Traces are made of hickory or paw paw" (Allen, "Cumberland") (J 2:455).

trade: [*v.i.* to do business; here applied comically:] "Them fellers ain't tradin' enough up there to break the Sabbath" (Jim Wallace) (J 2:461).

traffick, trafficking: [*v.i.* to loaf, to visit, to gossip.] "Jist trafficking around" (J 4:734; B 277). [Cf. **brogue.**]

trap-spring: [*n. phr.* the spring loading mechanism of an animal trap.] "Boys, I wish t' we *hed* roasted the temper outen them trap-springs, like we talked o' doin' " (B 93).

travellin'est: [*adj.* fastest] *adj.* from p[res.] p[art.] (J 2:601). "Them was the travellin'est horses you ever did see" (J 2:361; B 359 reads, "Them's the travellinest hosses ever I seed").

tree: [1. *v.t.* to chase up a tree.] "The dogs treed him in a minute" (B 101). [2. *v.i.* to climb a tree.] "Finally he gits so tired and het up that he trees to rest hisself" (B 81). [Both uses, S.Midl, DAE]

trembles: *n. pl.* tremor, palsy (A). "She had the weak trembles; drapped everything she tuk holt of" (J 2:475). trembles, weak (J 2:642s). Uncle Neddy Cyarter went to jump one of his own teeth out, one time, and missed the nail and mashed his nose with the hammer. He had the weak trembles" (Bob) (B 301-302).

triflin': [*pres. part.* lazy, shiftless.] "I allers did hold it was a mighty triflin' sort o' man'd let either his dog or his woman starve" (J 2:642). "He's a no-count triflin' feller" (J 1:256). "The triflin' scoundrel!" (J 2:637).

troft: *n.*, variant of *trough*. Also Ky. (A).

trollop: [*n.* a slattern or dirty woman; listed as a "distinct Scotticism"] (B 354). [Cf. **caigy.**]

tromp: [*v.i.* tramp.] "I tromped around all day" (J 2:642).

troughing: [*n*, variant of *trough*, listed as part of property seized in raid on an illicit distillery: "30 ft. troughing"] (C 4).

trousies: *n. pl.* trousers (A). old syllabic plural (B 359). [K's claim that this is an old syllabic plural like **beast/beasties** is attested in OED, trou, trousies. This is not merely a variant of *trousers*.]

trudle: [*n.*, variant of *trestle*.] "High tide washed the trudle (trestle) out" (J 2:639).

trustie: [*n.* a trusted and hence privileged convict.] "a trustie on a chain-gang" (J 2:639). [The more usual spelling is *trusty*, which appears in DAE]

tub-mill: [*n. phr.* a small mill for grinding corn.] "The grain is ground at their homes in a little hand tub-mill" (Allen, "Cumberland") (J 2:453). About every fourth or fifth farmer has a tiny tub-mill of his own (B 132). [DAE suggests App. origin; see also **tub-wheel**]

tub-wheel [mill]: [*n.* a type of mill used for grinding corn: small, water-powered.] "All the mills around Medlin are of tub-wheel construction" (J 2:453). [Wider distribution than preceding entry, DAE; see **tub-mill**.]

tuck: [*n.* a fit, or hang, as in "get the hang of" something or "get a handle" on something; listed as "archaic" in Webster's Third, "dialectal" in J 2:603.] "I don't seem to git the tuck on it, somehow." (J 2:642).

tuck up: [*v. phr.* to gather up, specifically a woman's skirts to ride a horse.] When traveling horseback they use a man's saddle and ride astride in their ordinary skirts with an ingenuity of "tucking up" that is beyond my understanding (B 311).

tuk: [1. *v.t.*, variant of *took, taken.*] "I tuk me a drink" (J 2:641). "I tuk my fut in my hand and lit out" (B 371). "I ain't never tuk money from company . . . and this ain't no time to begin" (B 274).

tump-line: [*n. phr.*, hunters' term;] pack-strap supported by the forehead (D 2). [DAE, citing Bartlett, places usage in ME.]

turkey corn: [*n. phr.* Dutchman's Breeches, q.v.; listed under "folk medicine" (J 2:480).] "In March, the feather-like leaves of the turkey corn are soon followed by the queer shaped white blossoms. The small tubers of the roots furnish the ingredients for mixtures known as "blood purifiers" (Asheville *Citizen*, 22 Jan. 1928) (J 2:480).

turkey-tail: *v.i.* to spread out like a turkey's tail. "The creek away up thar *turkey-tails* out into numerous little forks" (A; B 356).

twist 173

turn-about: [*n. phr.* turn.] "The four of us tuk turn-abouts crawlin' up out o' thar with the bear on our back" (B 107).

turncoatin': [*pres. part.* betraying: here used as a pejorative term for the act of joining the internal revenue service.] "Most of them were blockaders their own selves, till they saw how they could make more money turncoatin'" (B 170).

turn o' meal: [*n. phr.*] the quantity of meal taken at one load. Also Ky. (A). A turn o' meal is so called because "each man's corn is ground in turn—he waits his turn" (B 366). (J 2:453, 600) "a turn of corn taken to mill" (C 2) [TN, DAE; preferred to *grist* in W.NC, Kurath]

turrible: [*adv.*, variant of *terribly*.] "Thar come one turrible vyg'rous blow that jest nacherally lifted the ground" (B 78).

tushes: [*n. pl.*, variant of *tusks*.] "You'd orter heered his tushes pop" (J 4:749). [The bear] "gits so mad you can hear his tushes pop half a mile" (B 81).

tussle: [*v.t.* to carry.] "I tussled it [a sack of corn] acrost the mountain on my own wethers" (J 1:322f). "We haffter pack on mule-back or tussle it on our own wethers" (B 123).

tutor: [*v.t.* to prepare, to butcher.] "I b'lieve I can make a hundred pound o'pork out o' that pig—tutor it jist right"(J 2:366; B 361 reads: "I can make a hunderd pound o' pork outen that hog—tutor it jist right"). (J 2:642)

'twas a week ago: [as in "Thursday 'twas a week ago," i.e., a week ago Thursday; the opposite of "Thursday week," i.e. next Thursday] (B 370).

'twa'n't or **'twasn't:** [contraction of *it was not*] "'Twa'n't (so and so), for he hain't got no squar'-headed hobnails" (B 130). "'Twasn't no use" (J 2:642).

twicet or twiste: [*adv.*, variants of *twice*.] "Wunst or twicet" (J 2:642). "I had to fire twiste afore he tumbled" (B 107).

twinkles: *n. pl.* pine needles. "I'll go git a load o' *twinkles* to bed the cow" (A). In some places pine needles are called twinkles (B 369). (J 2:600)

twist: [*n.* tobacco leaves dried and twisted into the shape of a roll or tube for storage.] Generally some tobacco is grown for family consumption, the strong "twist" being smoked or chewed indifferently (B 39). [Earliest citations in DAE are from the S.Midl.].

twistification: [*n.*, pejorative term for dancing used by churchmen.] (J 4:757). Wherever the church has not put its ban on "twistifications" the country dance is the chief amusement of young and old (B 337).

two-in-a-hill: [*n. phr.* corn bread.] (corn bread, from dropping two kernels in a hill) (J 2:429).

U

Umbrell' (John Walker): [*n.* contraction of *umbrella.*] A man who was so eccentric as to carry an umbrella is known to this day as "Umbrell' " John Walker (B 291).

ummern: [*n.*, variant of *woman.*] In Mitchell County, North Carolina, we hear the extraordinary forms ummern and dummern (B 352-3). (J 2:603) [See also **dummern, wimmern.**]

unbeknownst: [*adj.* unknown] (J 2:600).

uncoupled: [*past part.* dislocated; under the heading: "Ignorance of mountain doctors," K noted:] Dr. Clark pressing woman's hip bone "back into place" for half an hour after confinement: "Push the bones back into place; don't you know they allers comes uncoupled in the socket?" (J 4:763; the quote appears alone in B 301).

unless'n: [*conj.*, variant of unless.] (J 2:603).

unthoughtless: [*adj.*, *n.* mindless or, unthinking; listed under "Habits, Manners" (J 2:642p).] Double negatives are the rule, and sometimes they are crowded into a single word, as "unthoughtless" (J:591). "I run into those turkeys *the unthoughtless of* anything I ever done" (A; J 4:749).

up: [1. *v.i.* to get up.] up and done it . . .these everyday expressions of the backwoods were contemporary with the *Canterbury Tales* (B 362). [2. *adv.*, abbrev. for "up river," the slang for "in jail":] "In jail . . . We was up fer blockadin' " (J 4:725).

upheaded: *adj.* carrying the head erect. "A fine lookin' *upheaded* gal" (A). "He's biggity and *upheaded,* and I'm glad to be shet o'him" (J 23:77). (J 2:603) [DAE suggests originally used with cattle and swine and later extended to humans.]

upright farms: [*n. phr.* farms located on a hillside, as distinct from those in a valley or in a cove.] "called upright farms in Kentucky" (Frost). Also called perpendicular farms (J 2: 338).

upscuddle: *n.* quarrel. "an *upscuddle* among the women generally gits their men into hit" (A). If they quarrel, it is . . . an upscuddle (B 368). [See also **jower**]

upsot: [*adv., v.*(?), variant of *upset*] (B 352).

up-tore: [*past part.* distressed; another instance of inverted syllables like *peckerwood.*] "I wouldn't be so up-tore about no gal" (J 1:286, 24:3rnff). (J 2:600)

up yan: [*prep. phr.* up there.] What was goin' on "up yan?" (B 115).

usen: [*v.,* variant of *used;* listed as Chaucer word in J 2:489 and B 362.] (J 2:642)

useter, uster: [*v. phr.,* variants of *used to.*] "He useter go" (J 2:642). "He useter get up agin a post forty times a day to scratch his back, and if anybody ast him what he was a-doin', he'd say, 'I'm a-hoggin'' " (M.B.) (J 2:441). "We know whut they uster do afore they jined the sarvice" (B 170).

using: [*pres. part.,* leaving sign through feeding.] Bears were crossing from Little River in the neighborhood of Thunderhead and Briar Knob, coming up just west of the Devil's Court House and "using" around Block House, Woolly Ridge, Bear Pen, and thereabouts (B 97-98). Calf-killer Run is "whar a meat-eatin' bear was usin'" (B 374). "The bears are using on the south side of the mountain now" (J 4:749).

V

varminous: [*adj.* infested with vermin, miserable.] "A varminous ole bear" (J 4:749). (J 2:603)

varmint: [*n.* vermin, hence any opprobrious creature.] A wild animal. "There's lots a varmints in these here mountains" (C 3). "My dogs can foller ary trail, same's a hound; but they'll run right in on the varmint" (B 81). " 'Any Episcopalians around here?' asked a clergyman at a mountain cabin. 'I don't know,' said the old woman. 'Jim's got the skins of a lot o' varmints up in the loft. Mebbe you can find one up thar' " (Fox) (B 342). [Many examples, including extension to humans, DAE.]

vascinator: *n.*, from *fascinator:* the sole instance noted of *v* for *f*. [Despite K's claim, we note that current usage includes *vertilize* for *fertilizer*.] A woman's head-wrap (A). fascinator—a woman's scarf (B 352). "A tall, peart sort of a gal, wearin' a vascinator" (J 2:637). (J 6)

vengeance: [*n.* great force or vehemence.] "That machinery has the vengeance" (J 2:642).

vennyline: [*n.*, variant of *vanilla;* listed under "foods"—"delicacies":] "Pete's 'cinnyment and vennyline' " (J 2:421, 10:82).

victuals: [*n.* food.] "Lo-o-ord, *bless* us in our victuals!" (J 4:737). [This fourteenth-century word represents a genuine archaism or linguistic relic in Appalachian speech. Lost from mainstream dialects in both Great Britain and America, except as a bookish or learned word, it remained current in K's Appalachia; indeed, its use has become a stock item in caricatures of Appalachian speech.]

vig'rous: [*adj.*, variant of *vigorous*, full of energy.] "He was so vi'grous to git at it" (J 1:256). [See also **vygorous.**]

vim: [*n.* energy, vigor.] "That soap smells as if it had the vim about it" (J 2:642, 417). [Several instances, DAE]

vomic: *v.i.* to vomit. Also Kan. (esp. a child's word), N.Y. (A). "It made me vomic" (J 2:475).

vygorous, vyg'rous: [1. *adv.*] vigorously. "The pig squealed *vygorous*" (A; J 2:366). [2. *adj.*] "Thar come one turrible vyg'rous blow that jest nacherally lifted the ground" (B 78). [See also **vig'grous**]

W

waal, wal: [*interj.*, variants of *well.*] "Waal, hit's like this" (B 80). "Waal, who dreamt him a good dream" (B 85). "Wal, sir, I was a-herdin'" (B 78).

wahoo: [*n.*] Fraser's magnolia [*Magnolia fraseri*] (J 1:59).

waiter: [*n.*] the best man and the bridesmaid. "Accompanied by the 'waiters,' the young couple immediately set out for the home of the groom" (Haney 54-55) (J 1:288). (J 24:3rn ff). [Chiefly NC, VA, WV, MD, Kurath]

walk-log: [*n.* a log bridge.] "There wasn't no walk-log acrost the creek" (J 1:322f). (J 2:642q; J 6)

wangun: [*n.*] provision boat; an Indian word meaning provision boat for the logging camp (Springer 170) (D 1). [NEng, DAE]

wa'n't: [elliptical form of *was not*] "There wa'n't none" (B 93). "He wa'n't hurt a bit" (B 101).

war: [1. *v.i.*] variant of *was, were*. Also Ill., Ky. (A). war (was or were—the *a* [pronounced] as in far) (B 358). "I hearn nobuddy knew er death war expected" (Poole 258-61) (J 2:485). "Him and me war pardners" (J 2:641)."My grandfather and his grandfather war half-brothers, anyhow" (J 1:304). [Cf. **'twa'n't** as in] "Twa'n't (so and so)" (B 130). [2. *v.t.* variant of *wear.*] "I'll war ye out with a hick'ry" (J 1:298).

warnut, warnet: *n.* walnut. Also Ky., Ill. (A). (J 1:71) [spelled:] warnet (J 2:642o).

was a week, was a year: [idiom for : a week ago.] "Thursday 'twas a week ago" (B 370). "Last Sunday 't was a week ago." (Sunday before last.) "This summer 't was a year ago." (last summer) (J 2:629). [Note that K consistently adds *ago*, which is not always done in current practice.]

washin' trough: [*n. phr.* wash tub.] Washing was done outside in a washin' trough, a hollowed log—which might also serve as water trough for stock (J 2:417).

washtub-soap: [*n.*soap used for washing clothes, probably lye] (J 2:417, 600).

water weed: [*n.* glasswort (*Salicornia bigelovii*), a salt-marsh plant.] Toe eetch . . . also called glass weed or water weed (J 2:481). [cf. **toe eetch.**]

way-off: [*adj.* remote.] "What brung ye up this air way-off branch?" (J 4:739, 2:603). [Several instances, DAE]

weakly: [*adj.* (despite -*ly* form) weak] "He was a weakly, sickly child" (J 2:745).

weak trembles: [*n. phr.* the shakes, probably not as severe as medical "shock."] "Uncle Neddy Cyarter went to jump one of his own teeth out, one time, and missed the nail and mashed his nose with the hammer. He had the weak trembles" (B 301-302). "She had the weak trembles and dropped everything she tuk holt of" (J 2:475).

weather: [*v.i.* to storm.] "Yes, hit's goin' to weather" (J 1:38; 10:83).

Weavilly Wheat: [*n. phr.* social game] ". . . 'play parties' are held, at which social games are practiced with childlike abandon, [including] Weavilly Wheat . . ." (B 338).

wed: *pret., past part.* Weeded. W. R[es.]. (rare) (A). "Did you-uns git them weeds wed out yit?" (J 2:359). There are many corrupt forms . . . wed (weeded) (B 358).

Wedgewood: [*n.* generic term for any china; listed as "coinage" on J 2:600.]

We Fish Who Bite: [*n. phr.* social game played at "play parties"] (B 338). [Cf. **Weavilly Wheat.**]

(go)/went by: [*v. phr.* to follow or believe, specifically in the phrase, "went by" someone.] " 'If we went by him' " (= If we took his advice.)" (MacG[owan]) (J 2:611).

(go)/went to: [1. *v. phr.* to begin/began.] "[She] tied [her gashed foot] up in sut and a rag, and went to hoein' corn" (B 300).

wethers: [*n.* shoulders; variant of *withers.*] In Star Route days the mail was carried afoot, two barefooted young men "toting the sacks on their own wethers" over this thirty-two mile round trip, for forty-eight cents a day, and they boarded themselves! (B 31-32). "We haffter pack on mule-back or tussle it on our own wethers" (B 123).

we-uns: [*pron.* we.] "Mister, we-uns hain't no call to be ashamed of ourselves, nor of ary thing we do" (B 119). "Then we-uns ketches up and finishes him" (B 81).

whar: [*adv.*, variant of *where.*] "Whar's you-uns a-goin' ter?" (B 12). "Hah! boys, that coffee hits whar ye hold it!" (B 92). "You'll spy, to-morrow, whar several trees has been wind-throwed" (B 77).

wheedle, whinnle: [*v.* to whine] (C 1). [See also **whinnle**]

whet off: [*v. phr.* to sharpen?] (J 2:642).

whetrock: *n.* whetstone. Also Ill., Ky. (A). grindin' rock (whet rock) (J 2:401). A mountaineer . . . sharpens tools on a grindin' rock or whetrock (B 371). (J 2:600; J 6)

which nor whether: [*n. phr.* anything.] "I ain't carin' which nor whether about it" (B 371; the quote is attributed to MacG[owan] in J 2:611).

while: [*n.* time.] during the while (J 2:611).

whilst: [*conj.*, variant of *while.*] "Any feller that's got a mind to can pick ye off with a rifle ball as easy as not whilst ye set by the fire of an evening" (B 305).

whinnle: *v.i.* to whine. "I never did cry but wunst; I *whinnled* a little endurin' the war" Also Ky. (A). (J 2:603) [Cf. **wheedle**]

whipsaw: [*n.* a crosscut saw, with two handles used by two men (Webster's Third).] "Two men with a whipsaw will get out 300 or 400 feet of boards from the logs in a day" (J 2:467). [DAE suggests widespread usage.]

whistle-pig: *n.* groundhog [or woodchuck (*Marmota monax*); the local name is derived from the alarm call that the animal makes] (A). (J 1:73; 2:600, 642o; 26:56)

white lightnin': [*n.* moonshine liquor; the name suggests the effect of its high percentage of alcohol.] "This white lightning'd make a rabbit spit in a bulldog's face" (J 3:951.23).

white snakeroot: [*n. Eupatorium rugosum (urticaefolium)*; the plant which caused milk-sickness in cattle and men; also called:] Indian sanicle, deerwort, richweed (J 2:473).

who-ee, who-ee, who-ee: "call to scattered dogs through the hills after hunt, at nightfall. Native huntsman." (C 11).

whoop: [exclamation] "Whoop! hear 'em a-comin'!" (B 79).

whope: *v.t.* to whip. "I *whoped* him." Also S.Car., Ky. (A). whoped (long *o*). Whope is sometimes used in the present tense, but whup is more common. By some the vowel of whup is sounded like *oo* in book (Mr. Fox writes "whoop," which, I

presume, he intends for that sound) (B 358). "She made off on
her legs like the devil whoppin' out fire" (B 91). "The devil's a-
whoppin' his wife—see the big tears a-fallin' " (J 1:38). (C 2; J 6)
[See **whup.**]

whup: *n.*, *v.* [, variant of] *whip.* Also Ill., Ky. (A). The variant
whupped is a Scotticism (B 358). "Retch me that whup" (J 2:641).
"I'll whup the hound out o' you!" (J 10:83).

whur: *"adv.*, [variant of] *where.* 'Whur's yer milk?' Mrs. Brown,
8/29/26" (C 11).

whyn't: [elliptical form of why don't, why didn't] (J 2:603).

widder-man: *n.* widow. Also Ky. (A).

(come) widdy, widdy: call for ducks and geese (J 2:371). (J 6)

wiggle and wingle, wiggling and wingling: [*v., part.* to twist and
turn; running brokenly, dodging along] All roads and trails
"wiggled and wingled around" so that some families were
several miles from a neighbor (B 30). I girded myself and ran,
"wiggling and wingling" along the main divide (B 100).

a wild Bill: [1. *n.* a rustic bed] "A 'Wild Bill' is a bed made by
boring auger holes into a log, driving sticks into these, and
overlaying them with hickory bark and sedgegrass—a favorite
couch" (Allen, "Cumberland") (J 2:399). [2. *n.*] bed cords of
hickory splints (J 2:455). [Listed as a "coinage" on J 2:600.] [KY,
DAE]

wild canary: [*n.* Eastern] goldfinch [*Spinus tristis tristis*] (J 26:54).

wild indigo: [*n.*] blue cohosh [*Caulophyllum thalictroides*] for female troubles (J 2:481).

wild lettuce: [*n.*] lettuce saxifrage (*Saxifraga micranthidifolia*)
[Flowers] May-June. White. Eaten as "wild lettuce" by mountaineers (J 26:24). [K earlier suggests that it is *S. erosa* (J 2:433)
and adds, "milky juice," "various species" in J 1:69.]

wild mire: [*n.*] "Hit's a bug or a sorter insect ginerally found on
pine trees. 'Bout as long as a jint o'yer thumb and thick as a
quill. Got legs somethin' like a spider's. When you come nigh
one, it squirts out a streak o' pizen that hits you in the eye and
burns like fire" (J 23:85). [Listed under "coinages" on J 2:600.]

wild mustard: [*n.* any of several wild mustards used as greens;
most commonly *Brassica kaber*] (J 2:433).

wild pea vine: [*n.*] (*Amphicarpae*) "In the large woods the surface of the soil is covered with a species of wild peas, which rise three feet above the earth, and of which the cattle are very greedy. They prefer this pasture to every other (Michaux 316) (J 1:67). [K lists it under "August" as: (*Flacata comosa*). [Flowers] Aug.-Sep. (J 26:39).

wild salat: [*n.* any native plants used as greens.] "This here wild salat'll he'p out" (J 2:433, 633). Keerless Knob is "a joyful place for wild salat" (*Amaranthus*) [probably *A. retroflexus*, pigweed] (B 375).

wild yam root: [*n.*] stone root (*Dioscorea villosa*). Pods developed [in late Sept.] (J 1:69).

wimmern: [*n.*, variant of *women*; see also **dummern, 'oman, ooman, ummern, womern.**] (B 352-53).

winder: [*n.*, variant of *window.*] "All these here glass winders is blame foolishness to me . . . you could be picked off with a rifle ball while you set by the fire" (J 2:377; B 305 expands on the journal quotation even more colloquially).

windin': [*pres. part.* blowing.] "Looks like to me we'll have a rainin', windin' spell" (B 372).

windstorm: [*n.* probably a frontal storm rather than a thunderstorm.] "Whut do you-uns know about wind-storms? . . . You remember the big storm three year ago, come grass, when the cattle all huddled up a-top o' each other and friz in one pile, solid" (B 78).

wind-throwed: [*part. phr.* blown down.] "Several trees has been wind-throwed and busted to kindlin'" (B 77).

winegar: "*n.*, [variant of] *vinegar*. 7/22/26" (C 11).

wingle: *v.i.* to wind in and out. "Kinder *wingle* around" (A). All roads and trails "wiggled and wingled around" (B 30). (J 2:603)

withe: [*n.* a twig or slender branch, a switch.] "Lord . . . bring a tow sack and hick'ry withe and git me" (J 4:773). [DAE furnishes several examples of this usage.]

withe rod: [*n.*] Appalachian tea (*Viburnum cassinoides*) [Flowers] June-July. Whitish. (J 26:29)

withey: *adj.* sinewy. "He's a *withey* little devil in a bear fight." Also Ill. (A; J 2:637). But the stamina of these "withey" little men was even more remarkable than their endurance of cold (B 92). (B 287)

wolf: *n.* the warble that appears in summer in the backs of rabbits and squirrels. Also. Ky. (A). "Summer rabbits all has wolfs in 'em" (J 4:749). (J 2:642o)

(the) woman: [*n.* wife.] Most mountaineers pronounce it correctly, but some drop the *w* ('oman) (B 352). "The woman," as every wife is called, has her kingdom within the house, and her man seldom meddles with its administration (B 331). If the man of the house has misgivings as to the state of the larder, he will say: "I'll ax the woman gin she can git ye a bite" (B 271-2). "Well, I'll ask the woman" (J 4:723). (J 2:642p) "Well, I guess I'd better git the woman some wood" (J 1:296).

women-folks: [*n. phr.* women; K listed as a common pleonasm] (B 360).

womern: [*n.* women;] other [speakers] add an *r* (womern and wimmern) (B 352-53). [See **dummern, 'oman, ooman, wimmern.**]

woodcock, woodhen: [*n.* Southern pileated woodpecker (*Hylatomus pileatus pileatus;* the model for Woody Woodpecker.] The giant woodpecker (A; J 1:73; 26:54). The giant woodpecker (here still a common bird) is known as a woodcock or woodhen (B 369). [*Woodhen* was sometimes used without reference to gender, but apparently as a euphemism for *woodcock;* it is listed as a substitute under "vulgar squeamishness" (J 2:607); obviously *cock* had the same slang meaning (penis) that is common today. Cf. **rooster.**] (J 2:600, 642)

wood-gitten, been: [*v.* gathering, carrying in wood.] "You been a wood-gitten?" (M.B. to me with armful) (J 2:417).

wood's chap: [*n.*] "bastard" (C 1). [A chap is a child, q.v.]

woodscolt: *n.* bastard (A). A bastard is a woods-colt or an outsider (B 368). (J 2:603; 4:843) [Chiefly NC, W.VA, WV, Kurath]

woolly-head: [*n.*] a thicket of laurel or rhododendron (B 375). [Listed under] "country landscapes" (J 2:642o). [See also **hell, slick, yaller patch**]

word: [*n.*] word [is used for] phrase (B 370).

work-brickle: [*n. phr.* a lazy person, one who would break into pieces if he were obliged to work—Carl Lambert] (J 2:603). [Cf. **brickle.**]

workinest: [*part.,* note unusual superlative.] "She's the workinest woman!" (B 359).

worry: [*v.* to suffer physically, not just mentally.] "She's might' nigh worried to death" (physical suffering) (J 2:475). When a man is tired he likely will call it worried (B 368).

wrastle: [*v.*, variant of *wrestle.*] (C 1) (J 6)

wrinkliest: [*adj.*, superl., most wrinkled.] "He's the wrinkliest young man I ever seen in my life" (J 2:637).

writ: *pret.* wrote. Also Ill., S, Car. (A). "I ain't writ to mammy" (J 2:642). (B 358)

wrop, wropped: [*v.*, variants of *wrap, wrapped.*] (B 352) [K records the following conversation about deadening nerves in teeth with hot wires:] "Didn't it hurt?" / "Hurt like hell for an instant. I held the wire once for _____ _____, who couldn't reach the spot hisself. I *told* him to hold his tongue back; but when I touched the holler he jumped and wropped his tongue agin the wire" (Bob) (J 2:470). [The story appears in B with this addition:] "The words that man used ain't fitty to tell" (B 303). "He went around with his thumb wropped up" (J 2:475).

wunst: [*adv.*, variant of *once.*] "I've . . . been to Asheville wunst, and to Waynesville a heap o' times" (B 120). "I stove a brier in my heel wunst" (B 303). "Wunst over on Lufty, I was eatin' with some Indians" (J 3:1050).

wunt: [*v.*, variant of *won't.*] "The law wunt let us have liquor shipped to us from anywhars in the state" (B 122).

wusser, wust: [comp. and superl. variants of *worse, worst.*] "She's wusser to-night" (J 2:475). "Hit's gittin' wusser" (B 77). "At the wust, s'posin' they was convicted by your own evidence, they'd only git a month or two in the pen" (B 118-19).

wuthless: [*adj.*, variant of *worthless.*] "Well, this stuff Johnny has is jist as wuthless" (J 10:83).

Y

yaller: [*adj.*, variant of *yellow.*] "yaller fever" (J 2:367). "Doc" Jones opined that it "looked yaller," and he even affirmed that it "tasted yaller" (B 98). (J 10:83)

yaller patch: [*n.*] a thicket of laurel or rhododendron, impassable save where the bears have bored out trails (B 375). [See also **hell, slick, woolly-head,**]

yan, yander: [*adv.* thither,] variants of *yon, yonder.* Also Ill., Kan., Ky. (A). The *o* sounds are more stable, but we have crap (crop), yan . . . (B 352). "Way over yan" (J 1). "Now, yan's my field o' corn" (B 122). "She's in the field, up yan, gittin' roughness" (B 112). "Looky yander comin'" (J 2:613, 18:62). "About half an hour later, I lit *spang* in the mud, way down yander in Tuckaleechee Cove—yes sir: ten mile as the crow flies, and a mile deeper 'n trout-fish swim" (B 78). [Note also that *yon* may be used:] "The main heft is on yon side" (J 2:641).

yarb: [*v.* to treat with medicinal herbs (yarbs.)] "I'm pretty well now, yarbin'" (having taken medicinal herbs) (J 2:639).

ye: [*pron.* Montgomery suggests this is a phonological variant of *you* (sing. and plural) brought over primarily by the Scotch-Irish] "I'll ax the woman gin she can git ye a bite" [*Ye* refers to one person.] (B 271-72). "I knowed I couldn't roust ye no other way" (B 84) [Here *ye* refers to a group]. (B 78)

year: [*n.*, variant of *ear*] "She cotched him by the ye'r (J 1:298). (J 2:642n) [2. *n.* year; singular in expressions of time where the plural would be standard:] "He's about twenty-five-year old, and has a seventy-five-year face; he's the wrinkliest young man I ever seen in my life" (J 2:637).

the year nineteen and eight: [idiom; the manner in which dates are normally given] (B 370).

yearn: [*v.*, variant of *earn*] (C 3).

yearth: [*n.*, variant of *earth.*] "Do you believe the yearth is round?" (B 346).

yellowhammer: [*n.* flicker] *Colaptes auratus.*] Yellowhammer C[ree]k. (Graham, N.C.) (J 26:76). [MA, CA, DAE]

yellowjacket: [*n.* wasp with a black body and bright yellow markings, *Sceliphron coementarium.*] Yellowjacket C[ree]k. (Troup, Ga.) (J 26:76). [Mostly So., DAE]

yer: [1. *pron.*, variant of *your;* from the list of Chaucer words in Fox (J 2:489).] "Hang on to yer hat, Doc!" (B 79). [Under the heading "Man Disdains Housework" Bob refuses to "git some wood fer dinner."] "I'm not a-comin'. Go chop some yerself."

[His wife responds:] "There's no use keepin' a dog an' doin' yer own barkin.' You go 'long now!" (J 1:296). (C 1) [2. *pron.*, variant of *you*.] "He will grab yer by the seat of yer pants" (B 341). [See also **yerself**.]

yerb: [*n.*, variant of *herb*.] "The only medicines we-uns has is yerbs, which customarily ain't no good 'thout a leetle grain o' whiskey" (B 121). "He swallowed some of it as if it had been boneset, under the impression that it was some sort of "yerb" that would be good for his insides (B 98). (J 2:479, 642o) [Cf. **yarbin'**.]

yerba mate: [*n.* a tea-like beverage.] "National drink of So. America . . . [it contains] none of the injurious qualities of coffee and Asiatic tea. Lacks oils which act as irritants. Also called 'Paraguay Tea.' . . . 2 lb. tin = $1.00" (C 9).

yerself: [*pron.*, variant of *yourself*.] "Go chop some yerself" (J 1:296). [See also **yer**.]

yistiddy: [n., variant of *yesterday*.] "He won't git me, Mister Man; not if I know these woods since yistiddy" (B 396).

yit: [*adv.*, variant of *yet*] (J 2:642).

yon: [*det.* thither] "The main heft in on yon side" (J 2:641). [See **yan, yander**.]

young-uns: [*pron.* young ones, children.] "A whole lot of little young-uns" (J 2:642t). (J 1).

yourunses, youerunses: *pl. pron.* yours. "Le's go over to *yourunses* house" (A; J 2:642). I have even heard such locution as this: "Let's we-uns all go over to youerunses house" (B 360). "Have you-uns got on youerunses coats?" (J 2:642). (C 2; J 10:83)

you-uns: [*pron.* you.] Along with other phrases which involve repetition] belong the famous double-barreled pronouns . . . we-uns and you-uns in Carolina and Tennessee (B 360). "Suppose . . . I should stumble on a moonshine still . . . What would they do?" / "They'd fust-place ask you some questions about yourself, and whut you-uns was doin' in that thar neck o' the woods" (117-18). "Whut's you-unses name? Whar's you-uns a-goin' ter?" (B 12). "Cain't you-uns give her some easin' powder?" (B 298). [W.PA; this usage competes with *you all* in WV, W.VA, W.NC, Kurath.]

your own self: [*pron. intensifier* yourself] "Then they'd git you to do some triflin' work about the still . . . jest so's't they could prove that you took a hand in it your own self" (B 118).

Z

'zamine: [*v.*, variant of *to examine.*] "Wisht you'd 'zamine this rock fer me" (B 351).

Bibliographic Note

The biographical sketch of Kephart is drawn from the manuscript of George Ellison of Bryson City, a revised version of which serves as the introduction to the most recent edition of *Our Southern Highlanders* (University of Tennessee Press, 1976). We are grateful to Mr. Ellison for sharing this information with us.

Principal sources

We used five principal sources in compiling the word list. The first, Horace Kephart's "A Word List from the Mountains of Western North Carolina," was published in *Dialect Notes* in 1917. Items from this list are labeled (A) in the text. A rich primary source was Kephart's *Our Southern Highlanders*, a collection of essays dealing with the mountaineers of the Smoky Mountain region. Our borrowings are taken from the enlarged edition published by Macmillan in 1922 and appear in this text bearing the label (B), with the appropriate page number.

We also made use of selected correspondence, lists of words and expressions, and letters sent to Kephart by correspondents who knew that he was interested in Appalachian dialect. Items taken from the correspondence are labeled (C 1) through (C 11). A brief description of each of these appears below, along with its location in the archives of Western Carolina University's Hunter Library.

(C 1) A list prepared by Mrs. Eddie Wilson of Cullowhee, North Carolina, dated 1926. MSS 80-24.2, folder 23.

(C 2) A list bearing the name "Mr. Tom Cox (Engineer) Cullowhee N.C. 1926." This list apparently pre-dates that of Bird (C 3), which is followed by a copy of (C 2) that appears to be in the same handwriting as (C 3). MSS 80-24.2, folder 23.

(C 3) A word list prepared by William E. Bird of Cullowhee, North Carolina, apparently designed as a supplement to Cox's list. MSS 80-24.2, folder 23.

(C 4) A carbon copy of a letter from Charles Beck dated 22 April 1921.

Beck was an internal revenue agent writing to his superior about the breakup of a still in Tuckaseegee, North Carolina. He lists many items confiscated from the site. MSS 80-24.1, folder 7.

(C 5) A copy of a letter to Mr. O.T. McCrosky dated 30 December 1912, discussing the habits of wild hogs. MSS 80-24.1, folder 1.

(C 6) A courtroom document sent to Kephart by Norman Harsell on 20 February 1922, concerning the murder of B.L. Harsell in Mitchell County, North Carolina. MSS 80-24.1, folder 8.

(C 7) A letter from Walter Ponchot discussing trout fishing practices in Western North Carolina, dated 18 January 1928. MSS 80-24.1, folder 11.

(C 8) A letter from the National Bakers' Egg Company of Sioux City, Iowa, dated 23 February 1916. MSS 80-24.1, folder 3.

(C 9) A letter from the Charles W. Jacob and Allison Company dated 19 April 1919. MSS 80-24.1, folder 5.

(C 10) A letter to Albert Britt, editor of *Outing*, dated 23 August 1919. MSS 80-24.1, folder 5.

(C 11) A word list compiled by M.H., probably Mary Hunter, which accompanies letters between her and Kephart and is marked "Cullowhee, 1926" and subtitled "Expressions heard by me." MSS 80-24.2, folder 23.

We also gleaned material from a list of logging terms, labeled (D 1), and another of hunters' terms (D 2). Both seem to be Kephart's work, and the former appeared in his own handwriting (MSS 80-24.2, folder 19).

Kephart's journals, twenty-seven canvas-bound, ledger-sized books, contain information collected by Kephart as well as his reflections on these pieces of information. Items taken from the journal bear the label (J :), with the journal number preceding the colon and the page number following. The journals are housed in the Hunter Library archives at Western Carolina University.

Kephart's sources

Following are the sources that Kephart quoted or alluded to. References to them appear parenthetically in the text. Several of Kephart's sources have eluded us. We do not know, for example, to what texts or articles "Hayward, *S & R*," or "Darling, *Sixty*," might refer, and modern technology in the form of electronic searches has not solved the problem. Hunter Library archivist George Frizzell recently discovered a list entitled "The Kephart Library," which apparently represents the items presented to Hunter Library but sheds no light on the unidentified sources. We thus include some partial entries below by way of self-reproach and as an enticement for future researchers.

Allen, James Lane. "Blue Grass Region of Kentucky." *Harper's Monthly* 72 (Feb. 1886): 365-82.

———. "Through Cumberland Gap on Horseback." *Harper's Monthly* 73 (June 1886): 30-66.

Bartram, William. *Travels through North and South Carolina*. Philadelphia: James & Johnson, 1791.

Bower, B.M. [pseud. Bertha Sinclair]. *The Flying-U Ranch*. New York: Grossett & Dunlap, 1914.

Byrd, William. *Writings of Colonel William Byrd*. Ed. John Spencer Bassett. New York: Doubleday, 1901.

Carrington, Henry Beebee. *U.S. Census Office 11th Census, 1890: Eastern Band of Cherokee of North Carolina*. Ed. Thomas Donaldson. Washington, D.C.: U.S. Census Printing Office, 1892.

Darling, [Jonathan?] *Sixty*. 8, 53. [?]

Day, Francis Holman. *King Spruce*. New York: Harper, 1908.

Forests, Rivers, Mountains of the Southern Appalachian Region. Various reports. Washington, D.C.: Government Printing Office, 1901.

Forest Service Bulletin 33 (1905): 15.

Ford.

Fox, John, Jr. *Blue-Grass and Rhododendron*. New York: Scribner's, 1901.

Fraser, Joshua. *Shanty: Forest and River Life in the Backwoods of Canada*. Montreal: Lovell, 1883.

Frost, William Goodell. "In the Land of Saddle-Bags." *Missionary Review* 24 (Jan. 1901): 21-31.

Gray, Asa. *Elements of Botany*. New York: American Book, 1887.

Haney, William Henry. *Mountain People of Kentucky*. Cincinnati: Roessler, 1906.

Harris, George W. *Sut Luvingood*. New York: Dick Fitzgerald, 1867.

Hayward, Dan. *S & R* 17:146.

Hubbard, Lucius L. *Hubbard's Guide to Moosehead Lake and Northern Maine*. 3rd ed. rev. Boston: Williams, 1882.

Jones, Louise Coffin. "In the Backwoods of Carolina." *Lippincott's Magazine* 23 (Dec. 1879): 747-56.

Lewis, Meriwether, and William Clark. *History of the Expedition Under the Command of Lewis and Clark*. Ed. Elliot Coues. New York: Francis P. Harper, 1893.

MacClintock, S.S. "Kentucky Mountains and Their Feuds, Part I." *American Journal of Sociology* 7 (July 1901): 1-28.

MacGowan, Alice. *Judith of the Cumberlands*. New York: Putnam, 1908. [References to this book by K may be variously identified as MG, MacG, or *Judith*.]

Mathews, F. Schuyler. *Fieldbook of American Trees and Shrubs*. New York: Putnam, 1915.

———. *Fieldbook of American Wildflowers*. New York: Putnam, 1903.

Michaux, F. Andre. *The North American Sylva*. Trans. J. Jay Smith, Philadelphia: Rice, Rutter, 1871.

Miles, Emma B. *Spirit of the Mountains*. New York: Pott, 1905.

Mooney, James. *Myths of the Cherokee*. U.S. Bureau of Ethnology: 19th Annual Report, 1897-98. Part I.

Murfree, Mary N. *The Ordeal*. Philadelphia: J. B. Lippincott Co., 1912.

Olmstead, Frederick L. *Journey in the Back County*. New York: Mason, 1860.

Peterson, Maude Gridley. *How to Know Wild Fruits*. New York: Macmillan, 1905.

Poole, Marie Louise. *In Buncombe County*.

Ralph, Julian. "Transformation in the Mountain White." *Harper's Magazine*. June 1903, 32, 269.

———. "Where Time Has Slumbered." *Dixie*. New York: Harper, 1896.

Springer, John S. *Forest Life and Forest Trees*. New York: Harper, 1851.

Steele, Thomas Sedgewick. *Paddle and Portage: From Moosehead Lake to the Aroostook River*. Boston: Lauriat, 1882.

Stevenson, Robert Louis. *The Black Arrow*. New York: Scribner's, 1925.

———. *The Master of Ballantrae*. New York: Scribner's, 1925.

Vincent, George E. "A Retarded Frontier." *American Journal of Sociology* 4 (July 1898): 1-20.

———. "Pawnshop in Petticoat Lane."

Warner, Charles Dudley. *On Horseback*. Boston: Houghton Mifflin, 1889.

Wilson's Report, 1901.

Wilson, Sam. *The Southern Mountaineers*. New York: Presbyterian Home Missions, 1906.

Ziegler, Wilbur B., and Ben S. Grosscup. *The Heart of the Alleghanies*. Raleigh [1883].

Reference Works

In preparing our definitions for words undefined in the journals, we consulted a number of sources—reference works of one sort or another. (A list of abbreviations precedes the word list.)

Bartlett, James R. *Dictionary of Americanisms: A Glossary of Words and Phrases Usually Regarded as Peculiar to the United States.* New York: Scholarly Press, 1976. Reprint of 1848 ed.

Dictionary of American Regional English. Vols. 1 and 2. Ed. Frederic G. Cassidy. Cambridge: Harvard Univ. Press, 1985, 1991.

Dictionary of American English on Historical Principles. Ed. William A. Cragie and James R. Hulbert. Chicago: Univ. of Chicago Press, 1938-1944.

A Dictionary of Americanisms. Ed. Mitford Mathews. Chicago: Univ. of Chicago Press, 1951.

Kurath, Hans. *A Word Geography of the Eastern United States.* Ann Arbor: Univ. of Michigan Press, 1949.

Oxford English Dictionary. Ed. James A.H. Murray, et al. Oxford: Clarendon, 1933.

Palmer, E. Laurence, and H. Seymour Fowler. *Fieldbook of Natural History.* 2d ed. New York: McGraw Hill, 1974.

Peterson, Roger. *A Field Guide to the Birds.* Boston: Houghton-Mifflin, 1947.

Webster's Third New International Dictionary of the English Language, Unabridged. Ed. Philip B. Gove and Staff. Springfield, Mass.: Merriam Webster, 1981.

Webster's New World Dictionary of the American Language. Second college edition. Ed. David B. Guralnik. New York: Simon and Schuster, 1982.